LⁿACS-1A (ARBN)

AⁿBN
Zub
Std

Zuberbühler / Hofmann / Oetiker / Rohner

IBA Rules of Evidence

Tobias Zuberbühler

Dieter Hofmann

Christian Oetiker

Thomas Rohner

IBA Rules of Evidence

Commentary on the IBA Rules
on the Taking of Evidence in
International Arbitration

sellier.

european law
publishers

Schulthess § 2012

Bibliographic information published by the Deutsche Nationalbibliothek
The Deutsche Nationalbibliothek lists this publication in the Deutsche Nationalbiblio-
grafie; detailed bibliographic data are available in the Internet at http://dnb.d-nb.de.

© Schulthess Juristische Medien AG, Zurich · Basel · Geneva 2012
   ISBN 978-3-7255-5654-0

www.schulthess.com

Introduction

This publication seeks to provide a comprehensive analysis and description of the "IBA Rules on the Taking of Evidence in International Arbitration", as adopted by the Council of the International Bar Association (IBA) in May 2010.

Neither arbitration laws nor institutional arbitration rules provide detailed and specific instructions for the taking of evidence in international arbitration. The "Supplementary Rules Governing the Presentation and Reception of Evidence in International Commercial Arbitration", as adopted by the IBA in 1983, represented a first attempt to both fill this perceived gap and to set forth specific rules for evidence-taking. The 1983 Rules were extensively revised in 1999 and renamed the "IBA Rules on the Taking of Evidence in International Commercial Arbitration". The 1999 Rules attempted to reflect best practice in international commercial arbitration, and were generally well received.

A decade later, the 1999 Rules were again taken under review and carefully revised. The revised rules were adopted on 29 May 2010 as the "IBA Rules on the Taking of Evidence in International Arbitration".

The 1999 Rules were developed by a Working Party of eminent international arbitration practitioners. Similarly, the 2010 Rules were drafted by distinguished arbitration specialists who formed the "2010 Review Subcommittee". The members of the 1999 Working Party and of the 2010 Review Subcommittee are listed in the 2010 Rules (see (i) and (iii) in Annex 1).

The effectiveness of the 2010 Rules in practice will only become clear over time. Hence, any comments on new developments or issues that should be dealt with in future editions of this Commentary are appreciated (by e-mail to the authors) and will assist the authors in continuing their work.

The authors are grateful to the IBA, the ICC and UNCITRAL for granting their permission to use the texts of the IBA Rules, the ICC "Techniques for Controlling Time and Costs in Arbitration" and the UNCITRAL Notes on Organizing Arbitral Proceedings.

Zurich, October 2011

Tobias Zuberbühler, Dieter Hofmann, Christian Oetiker & Thomas Rohner

Table of contents

Article 9   Admissibility and Assessment
of Evidence..   165

List of Authors

Tobias Zuberbühler, LL.M.
LUSTENBERGER RECHTSANWÄLTE
Wiesenstrasse 10
P.O. Box 1037
CH-8032 Zurich
zuberbuehler@lustenberger.pro

Dieter Hofmann
WALDER WYSS LTD.
Seefeldstrasse 123
P.O. Box 1236
CH 8034 Zurich
dieter.hofmann@walderwyss.com

Dr. Christian Oetiker, LL.M.
VISCHER LTD.
Aeschenvorstadt 4
CH-4010 Basel
coetiker@vischer.com

Dr. Thomas Rohner, LL.M.
PESTALOZZI
Löwenstrasse 1
CH-8001 Zurich
thomas.rohner@pestalozzilaw.com

List of Abbreviations

AAA	American Arbitration Association
ArbInt	Arbitration International, London
Arbitration	The Journal of the Chartered Institute of Arbitration, London
Am. Rev. Int'l Arb.	American Review of International Arbitration, New York
ASA	*Association Suisse de l'Arbitrage* (Swiss Arbitration Association)
ASA Bull	ASA Bulletin
BLI	Business Law International (IBA Legal Practice Division)
CIETAC	China International Economic and Trade Arbitration Commission
CO	Swiss Code of Obligations of 30 March 1911 (as amended; SR 220)
DFT	Decisions of the Federal Tribunal (= Swiss Federal Supreme Court)
DIS	*Deutsche Institution für Schiedsgerichtsbarkeit* (German Institution of Arbitration)
HKIAC	Hong Kong International Arbitration Centre
IBA	International Bar Association
ICC	International Chamber of Commerce
ICC Bull	The ICC International Court of Arbitration Bulletin, Paris
ICC Report	Techniques for Controlling Time and Costs in Arbitration, Report from the ICC Commission on Arbitration (ICC Publication No. 843)
ICC Rules	Rules of Arbitration of the International Chamber of Commerce (in force as from 1 January 2012)
ICCA	International Council for Commercial Arbitration

ICSID	International Centre for Settlement of Investment Disputes
IntALR	International Arbitration Law Review, London
JIDS	Journal of International Dispute Settlement, Oxford
JIntArb	Journal of International Arbitration, Geneva
LCIA	London Court of International Arbitration
LCIA Rules	LCIA Arbitration Rules in force as from 1 January 1998
Model Law	UNCITRAL Model Law on International Commercial Arbitration, adopted on 11 December 1985 (as amended on 7 July 2006)
NYC	United Nations Convention on the Recognition and Enforcement of Foreign Arbitral Awards (New York Convention; New York, 10 June 1958)
PILS	(Swiss Federal) Private International Law Statute of 18 December 1987 (as amended; SR 291)
Rev.arb.	*Revue de l'arbitrage*, Paris
Rules	IBA Rules on the Taking of Evidence in International Arbitration (as adopted by the IBA Council on 29 May 2010)
SchiedsVZ	*Zeitschrift für Schiedsverfahren* (German Arbitration Journal), Munich/Frankfurt/Basel
SIAC	Singapore International Arbitration Centre
SJZ	*Schweizerische Juristenzeitung*, Zurich
SR	*Systematische Sammlung des Bundesrechts/Recueil systématique du droit fédéral* (systematic digest of Swiss federal law; www.admin.ch/ch/d/sr/sr [German], www.admin.ch/ch/fr/rs/rs [French])
Swiss Rules	Swiss Rules of International Arbitration (in force as from 1 January 2012)
UNCITRAL	United Nations Commission on International Trade Law
UNCITRAL Notes	UNCITRAL Notes on Organizing Arbitral Proceedings (1996)

UNCITRAL Rules	UNCITRAL Arbitration Rules (in force as from 15 August 2010)
YB Comm. Arb.	Yearbook Commercial Arbitration (van den Berg ed.)
WIPO	World Intellectual Property Organization
WIPO Rules	WIPO Arbitration Rules (in force as from 1 October 2002)
ZCC	Zurich Chamber of Commerce
ZCC Rules	ZCC International Arbitration Rules (in force as from 1 January 1989)

Bibliography

Aden Menno, Internationale Handelsschiedsgerichtsbarkeit, 2nd ed., Munich 2003

Ashford Peter, Documentary Discovery and International Commercial Arbitration, Am. Rev. Int'l Arb. 1/2006, 89–141

Berger Klaus Peter, International Economic Arbitration, Deventer/Boston 1993 (cited Berger, Arbitration)

Berger Klaus Peter, Evidentiary Privileges: Best Practice Standards versus/ and Arbitral Discretion, ArbInt 4/2006, 501–520 (cited Berger, Evidentiary Privileges)

Berger Klaus Peter, Evidentiary Privileges Under the Revised IBA Rules on the Taking of Evidence in International Arbitration, IntALR 5/2010, 171–176 (cited Berger, IBA Rules)

Berger Klaus Peter, Internationale Wirtschaftsschiedsgerichtsbarkeit, Verfahrens- und materiellrechtliche Grundprobleme im Spiegel moderner Schiedsgesetze und Schiedspraxis, Recht des internationalen Wirtschaftsverkehrs (eds. Horn/Drobnig/Herber/Schütze), vol. 10, Berlin/New York 1992 (cited Berger, Wirtschaftsschiedsgerichtsbarkeit)

Berger Klaus Peter, The Settlement Privilege, A General Principle of International ADR Law, ArbInt 2/2008, 265–276 (cited Berger, Settlement Privilege)

Berger/Kellerhals, International and Domestic Arbitration in Switzerland, 2nd ed., Sweet & Maxwell/Stämpfli Publishers Ltd. 2010

Blessing Marc, Comparison of the Swiss Rules with the UNCITRAL Arbitration Rules and Others, ASA Special Series No. 22 (2004), 17–65

Böckstiegel Karl-Heinz, Taking Evidence in International Commercial Arbitration – Legal Framework and Trends in Practice, in: Böckstiegel/ Berger/Bredow (eds.), The Taking of Evidence in International Commercial Arbitration, Schriftenreihe der Deutschen Institution für Schiedsgerichtsbarkeit, vol. 26, Cologne 2010, 1–8

Boog Christopher, Die Durchsetzung einstweiliger Massnahmen in internationalen Schiedsverfahren, Zurich 2011

Born Gary B., International Commercial Arbitration, The Hague 2009

BOUCHENAKI Amal, The IBA Rules Lay the Ground for Solutions to Address Electronic-Document-Production Disputes, IntALR 5/2010, 180–185

BROWER/BRUESCHKE, The Iran-United States Claims Tribunal, The Hague 1998

BRUNETTI Maurizio, The Lex Mercatoria in Practice: The Experience of the Iran-United States Claims Tribunal, ArbInt 4/2002, 355–378

BÜHLER/DORGAN, Witness Testimony Pursuant to the 1999 IBA Rules of Evidence in International Commercial Arbitration – Novel or Tested Standards?, JIntArb 1/2000, 3–30

CARON/CAPLAN/PELLONPÄÄ, The UNCITRAL Arbitration Rules: A Commentary, New York 2006

CARTER James, Privilege Gets a New Framework, IntALR 5/2010, 177–179

COHEN KLÄSENER Amy, The Duty of Good Faith in the 2010 IBA Rules on the Taking of Evidence in International Arbitration, IntALR 5/2010, 160–164

COHEN KLÄSENER/DOLGORUKOW, Die Überarbeitung der IBA-Regeln zur Beweisaufnahme in der internationalen Schiedsgerichtsbarkeit, SchiedsVZ 6/2010, 302–310

COMMENTARY SWISS RULES, Zuberbühler/Müller/Habegger (eds.), Swiss Rules of International Arbitration, Commentary, Zurich 2005 (cited AUTHOR in COMMENTARY SWISS RULES)

CRAIG Nicholas, Arbitration Confidentiality and the IBA Rules on the Taking of Evidence in International Arbitration, IntALR 5/2010, 169–170

CRAIG/PARK/PAULSSON, International Chamber of Commerce Arbitration, 3rd ed., New York 2000

CREMADES Bernardo M., Powers of the Arbitrators to Decide on the Admissibility of Evidence and to Organise the Production of Evidence, ICC Bull 1/1999, 49–56

DALE Geoffrey, Rent Review and Property Valuation Arbitration, in: Tackaberry/Marriott (eds.), Bernstein's Handbook of Arbitration and Dispute Resolution Practice, vol. 1, London 2003, 839–875

DERAINS Yves, Towards Greater Efficiency in Document Production before Arbitral Tribunals – A Continental Viewpoint, ICC Bull 2006 Special Supplement, 83–91 (cited DERAINS, Document Production)

DERAINS Yves, La pratique de l'administration de la preuve dans l'arbitrage commercial international, Rev.arb. 2004, 781–802 (cited DERAINS, Preuve)

DERAINS Yves, Le témoin en matière d'arbitrage international, in: Bohnet/
Wessner (eds.), Mélanges François Knoepfler, Basel 2005, 227–233
(cited DERAINS, Témoin)

DERAINS/SCHWARTZ, A Guide to the ICC Rules of Arbitration, 2nd ed., The
Hague 2005

ELSING/TOWNSEND, Bridging the Common Law-Civil Law Divide in Arbitration,
ArbInt 1/2002, 59–65

FISCHER-ZERNIN/JUNKER, Between Scylla and Charybdis: Fact Gathering in German Arbitration, JIntArb 4/1987, 9–34

FOUCHARD/GAILLARD/GOLDMAN, On International Commercial Arbitration (eds.
Gaillard/Savage), The Hague/Boston/London 1999

GÉLINAS Paul-A., Evidence through witnesses, in: Lévy/Veeder (eds.), Arbitration and Oral Evidence, ICC Publication No. 689 (2005), 29–53

GILL/TAWIL/KREINDLER, The 2010 Revisions to the IBA Rules on the Taking
of Evidence in International Arbitration, Les Cahiers de L'Arbitrage
2011-1, 23–32

GIRSBERGER/VOSER, International Arbitration in Switzerland, Zurich 2008

GOTANDA John Yukio, Awarding Costs and Attorneys' Fees in International Commercial Arbitrations, Michigan Journal of International Law
1/1999, 1–49

GRIFFIN Peter R., Recent Trends in the Conduct of International Arbitration –
Discovery Procedures and Witness Hearings, JIntArb 2/2000, 19–30

HABEGGER Philipp, Document Production – An Overview of Swiss Court and
Arbitration Practice, ICC Bull 2006 Special Supplement, 21–32

HAFTER Peter, Strategie und Technik des Zivilprozesses, 2nd ed., Zurich
2011

HAMILTON Virginia, Document Production in ICC Arbitration, ICC Bull 2006
Special Supplement, 63–81

HANOTIAU Bernard, The Conduct of Hearings, in: Newman/Hill (eds.), The
Leading Arbitrators' Guide to International Arbitration, 2nd ed., New
York 2008, 359–379 (cited HANOTIAU, Conduct of Hearings)

HANOTIAU Bernard, Document Production in International Arbitration: A Ten-
tative Definition of "Best Practices", ICC Bull 2006 Special Supplement, 113–119 (cited HANOTIAU, Document Production)

HARRIS Christopher, Expert Evidence: The 2010 Revisions to the IBA Rules on the Taking of Evidence in International Arbitration, IntALR 5/2010, 212–215

HASCHER Dominique, Introduction, in: Decisions on ICC Arbitration Procedure, ICC Bull 2010 Special Supplement, 5–16

HEITZMANN Pierre, Confidentiality and Privileges in Cross-Border Legal Practice: the Need for a Global Standard?, ASA Bull 2/2008, 205–240

HILL Richard D., The New Reality of Electronic Document Production in International Arbitration: A Catalyst for Convergence?, ArbInt 1/2009, 87–102

IBA REVIEW SUBCOMMITTEE, Commentary on the Revised Text of the 2010 IBA Rules on the Taking of Evidence in International Arbitration (cited IBA REVIEW SUBCOMMITTEE 2010)

IBA WORKING PARTY, Commentary on the New IBA Rules of Evidence in International Commercial Arbitration, BLI 2000, 16–36 (cited IBA WORKING PARTY 1999)

JENKINS/STEBBINGS, International Construction Arbitration Law, The Hague 2006

JERMINI Cesare, Witnesses and the right to be heard in international arbitration: some remarks on recent decisions of the Swiss Federal Court, ASA Bull 3/2004, 605–609

JONES Doug, Party Appointed Expert Witnesses in International Arbitration: A Protocol at Last, ArbInt 1/2008, 137–155

KARRER Pierre, Beweislast und Beweiswürdigung, Podiumsdiskussion zur Praxis der Beweiserhebung in internationalen Schiedsverfahren, in: Böckstiegel (ed.), Beweiserhebung in internationalen Schiedsverfahren, Schriftenreihe der Deutschen Institution für Schiedsgerichtsbarkeit, vol. 14, Cologne/Berlin/Bonn/Munich 2001, 107–110

KAUFMANN-KOHLER/BÄRTSCH, Discovery in international arbitration: How much is too much?, SchiedsVZ 1/2004, 13–21

KNOBLACH Steffen, Sachverhaltsermittlung in der internationalen Wirtschaftsschiedsgerichtsbarkeit: eine rechtsvergleichende Untersuchung des deutschen und englischen Schiedsrechts und der IBA-Rules on the Taking of Evidence in International Commercial Arbitration, Berlin 2003

KNOF Manfred, Tatsachenfeststellung in Streitigkeiten des internationalen Wirtschaftsverkehrs, Cologne 1995

KREINDLER Richard H., The 2010 revision to the IBA Rules on the Taking of Evidence in International Commercial Arbitration: A study in both consistency and progress, IntALR 5/2010, 157–159 (cited KREINDLER, 2010 Revision)

KREINDLER Richard H., Benefiting from oral testimony of expert witnesses: Traditional and emerging techniques, in: Lévy/Veeder (eds.), Arbitration and Oral Evidence, ICC Publication No. 689 (2005), 87–104 (cited KREINDLER, Oral Testimony)

KÜHNER Detlev, The Revised IBA Rules on the Taking of Evidence in International Arbitration, IntALR 6/2010, 667–677

LACHMANN Jens-Peter, Handbuch für die Schiedsgerichtsbarkeit, 3rd ed., Cologne 2008

LÉVY Laurent, Les astreintes et l'arbitrage international en Suisse, ASA Bull 1/2001, 21–36 (cited LÉVY, Astreintes)

LÉVY Laurent, Witness Statements, in: Héritier Lachat/Hirsch (eds.), De Lege Ferenda: Etudes pour le professeur Alain Hirsch, Geneva 2004, 95–104 (cited LÉVY, Witness Statements)

LEW/MISTELIS/KRÖLL, Comparative International Commercial Arbitration, The Hague 2003

LÖRCHER Gino, Der vom Schiedsgericht bestellte Sachverständige im Verfahren, in: Briner et al. (eds.), Festschrift Karl-Heinz Böckstiegel, Law of International Business and Dispute Settlement in the 21st Century, Cologne/Berlin/Bonn/Munich 2001, 485–496

MADDEN John P., How to Present Witness Evidence in an Arbitration – American Style, ASA Bull 3/1993, 438–445

MARRIOTT Arthur L., Breaking the Deadlock, ArbInt 3/2006, 411–429 (cited MARRIOTT, Deadlock)

MARRIOTT Arthur L., Evidence in International Arbitration, ArbInt 1989, 280–290 (cited MARRIOTT, Evidence)

MCILWRATH/SAVAGE, International Arbitration and Mediation: A Practical Guide, The Hague 2010

MEIER Anke, The Production of Electronically Stored Information in International Commercial Arbitration, SchiedsVZ 4/2008, 179–189

MEYER Olaf, Time to Take a Closer Look: Privilege in International Arbitration, JIntArb 4/2007, 365–378

MEYER-HAUSER Bernhard, Anwaltsgeheimnis und Schiedsgericht, Schulthess 2004

MEYER-HAUSER/SIEBER, Attorney Secrecy v Attorney-Client Privilege in International Commercial Arbitration, Arbitration 2/2007, 148–188

MÜLLER Christoph, Swiss Case Law in International Arbitration, 2nd ed., Zurich/Basel/Geneva 2010 (cited MÜLLER, Case Law)

MÜLLER Thomas, IBA Rules of Evidence – ein Brückenschlag zwischen Common Law und Civil Law in internationalen Schiedsverfahren, in: Spühler (ed.), Internationales Zivilprozess- und Verfahrensrecht II, Zurich 2003, 51–71 (cited MÜLLER, IBA Rules)

NEWMARK Christopher, "Efficient, Economical and Fair": the Mantra of the New IBA Rules, IntALR 5/2010, 165–168

OETIKER Christian, Sense and Nonsense of Written Witness Statement, in: Müller/Rigozzi (eds.), New Developments in International Commercial Arbitration 2009, Zurich 2009, 29–41 (cited OETIKER, Sense and Nonsense)

OETIKER Christian, Witnesses before the International Arbitral Tribunal, ASA Bull 2/2007, 253–278 (cited OETIKER, Witnesses)

O'MALLEY Nathan D., An Annotated Commentary on the 2010 revised IBA Rules of Evidence for International Arbitration, International Construction Law Review 4/2010, 463–510 (cited O'MALLEY, Annotated Commentary)

O'MALLEY Nathan D., Document Production Under Art. 3 of the 2010 IBA Rules of Evidence, IntALR 5/2010, 186–194 (cited O'MALLEY, Document Production)

O'MALLEY Nathan D., The Procedural Rules Governing the Production of Documentary Evidence in International Arbitration As Applied in Practice, The Law and Practice of International Courts and Tribunals 1/2009, 27–90 (cited O'MALLEY, Procedural Rules)

O'MALLEY/CONWAY, Document Discovery in International Arbitration – Getting the Document You Need, The Transnational Lawyer 2/2005, 371–383

PARK William W., Arbitrators and Accuracy, JIDS 1/2010, 25–53 (cited PARK, Accuracy)

PARK William W., Arbitration's Discontents: Of Elephants and Pornography, ArbInt 3/2001, 263–274 (cited PARK, Elephants and Pornography)

PETER Wolfgang, Die neue Schweizerische Schiedsordnung – Anmerkungen für die Praxis, SchiedsVZ 2/2004, 57–65 (cited PETER, Schiedsordnung)

PETER Wolfgang, Witness "Conferencing", ArbInt 1/2002, 47–58 (cited PETER, Witness Conferencing)

PETROCHILOS Georgios, Procedural Law in International Arbitration, Oxford 2004

PIETROWSKI Robert, Evidence in International Arbitration, ArbInt 3/2006, 373–410

PILS (Basel), Honsell/Vogt/Schnyder/Berti (eds.), Basler Kommentar Internationales Privatrecht, 2nd ed., Basel 2007 (cit. PILS (Basel)-AUTHOR)

PILS (Zurich), Zürcher Kommentar zum IPRG, 2. ed., Zurich 2004 (cit. PILS (Zurich)-AUTHOR)

POUDRET Jean-François, Expertise et droit d'être entendu dans l'arbitrage international, in: Dominicé/Patry/Reymond (eds.), Liber amicorum Pierre Lalive, Basel 1993, 607–624

POUDRET/BESSON, Comparative Law of International Arbitration, 2nd ed., London/Zurich 2007

PRICE/STANS, Using Costs as a Case Management Tool in International Arbitration, ASA Bull 4/2007, 704–716

RAESCHKE-KESSLER Hilmar, Die IBA Rules über die Beweisaufnahme in Internationalen Schiedsverfahren, in: Böckstiegel (ed.), Beweiserhebung in Internationalen Schiedsverfahren, Schriftenreihe der Deutschen Institution für Schiedsgerichtsbarkeit, vol. 14, Cologne/Berlin/Bonn/Munich 2001, 41–75 (cited RAESCHKE-KESSLER, Beweisaufnahme)

RAESCHKE-KESSLER Hilmar, The Contribution of International Arbitration to Transnational Procedural Law, in: Aksen et al. (eds.), Global Reflections on International Law, Commerce and Dispute Resolution, Liber Amicorum Robert Briner, Paris 2005, 647–663 (cited RAESCHKE-KESSLER, Festschrift Briner)

RAESCHKE-KESSLER Hilmar, Die Präambel der IBA-Rules of Evidence – ein Programm für eine moderne Verfahrensgestaltung in internationalen Schiedsverfahren, in: Schütze (ed.), Einheit und Vielfalt des Rechts,

Festschrift für Reinhold Geimer zum 65. Geburtstag, Munich 2002, 855–871 (cited RAESCHKE-KESSLER, Festschrift Geimer)

RAESCHKE-KESSLER Hilmar, The Production of Documents in International Arbitration – A Commentary on Article 3 of the New IBA Rules of Evidence, ArbInt 4/2002, 411–430 (cited RAESCHKE-KESSLER, Production)

RAESCHKE-KESSLER Hilmar, The Arbitrator as Settlement Facilitator, ArbInt 4/2005, 523–536 (cited RAESCHKE-KESSLER, Settlement Facilitator)

RAESCHKE-KESSLER Hilmar, Witness Conferencing, in: Newman/Hill (eds.), The Leading Arbitrators' Guide to International Arbitration, 2nd ed., New York 2008, 415–428 (cited RAESCHKE-KESSLER, Witness Conferencing)

REDFERN/HUNTER/BLACKABY/PARTASIDES, Law and Practice of International Commercial Arbitration, 4th ed., London 2004 (cited REDFERN/HUNTER/ BLACKABY/PARTASIDES, 4th ed.)

REDFERN/HUNTER/BLACKABY/PARTASIDES, Redfern and Hunter on International Arbitration, 5th ed., Oxford 2009

REED/HILL ROSENKRANZ, The UNCITRAL Rules as Applied in the Iran-US Claims Tribunal, ASA Special Series No. 22 (2004), 119–129

REES Peter J., The Revised IBA Rules of Evidence, Arbitration 3/2010, 514–523

REINER Andreas, Burden and General Standards of Proof, ArbInt 3/1994, 328–340

RONEY David P., Effective Witness Preparation for International Commercial Arbitration: A Practical Guide for Counsel, JIntArb 5/2003, 429–435

RONEY/MÜLLER, The Arbitral Procedure, in: Kaufmann-Kohler/Stucki (eds.), International Arbitration in Switzerland: A Handbook for Practitioners, The Hague 2004, 49–68

RÜEDE/HADENFELDT, Schweizerische Schiedsgerichtsbarkeit, Zurich 1993

SACHS Klaus, Use of documents and document discovery: "Fishing expeditions" versus transparency and burden of proof, SchiedsVZ 5/2003, 193–198

SCHERER Matthias, The Limits of the IBA Rules on the Taking of Evidence in International Arbitration: Document Production Based on Contractual or Statutory Rights, IntALR 5/2010, 195–200

SCHLAEPFER Anne Véronique, Witness statements, in: Lévy/Veeder (eds.), Arbitration and Oral Evidence, ICC Publication No. 689 (2005), 65–75

SCHLOSSER Peter, Das Recht der internationalen privaten Schiedsgerichtsbarkeit, 2nd ed., Tübingen 1989

SCHNEIDER Michael E., Technical experts in international arbitration, introductory comments to the materials from arbitration practice, ASA Bull 3/1993, 446–465 (cited SCHNEIDER, Experts)

SCHNEIDER Michael E., Lean Arbitration: Cost Control and Efficiency Through Progressive Identification of Issues and Separate Pricing of Arbitration Services, ArbInt 2/1994, 119–140 (cited SCHNEIDER, Lean Arbitration)

SCHNEIDER, Michael E., Witnesses in international arbitration, presentation of materials from arbitration practice, ASA Bull 2/1993, 302–312 (cited SCHNEIDER, Witnesses)

SCHÜRMANN Hans-Jürg, Plädieren durch die Hintertür – Pleading through the back door, ASA Bull 3/2006, 433–441

SHARPE Jeremy, Drawing Adverse Inferences from the Non-production of Evidence, ArbInt 4/2006, 549–571

SHENTON D.W., An Introduction to the IBA Rules of Evidence, ArbInt 1/1985, 118–123

SHORE Lawrence, Three Evidentiary Problems in International Arbitration: Producing the Adverse Document, Listening to the Document that does not Speak for Itself, and Seeing the Witness through her Written Statement, SchiedsVZ 2/2004, 76–80

SINDLER/WÜSTEMANN, Privilege across borders in arbitration: multi-jurisdictional nightmare or a storm in a teacup?, ASA Bull 4/2005, 610–639

SMIT Robert H., E-disclosure Under the Revised IBA Rules on the Taking of Evidence in International Arbitration, IntALR 5/2010, 201–206

SMIT/ROBINSON, E-Disclosure in International Arbitration, ArbInt 1/2008, 105–135

SPÜHLER/GEHRI, Die Zulassung von Experten zur Urteilsberatung: Neue Wege für Schiedsverfahren?, ASA Bull 1/2003, 16–26

SUTCLIFFE/WIRTH, Witness Evidence: Written or Oral, Who asks the Questions?, in: Böckstiegel/Berger/Bredow (eds.), The Taking of Evidence in International Commercial Arbitration, Schriftenreihe der Deutschen Institution für Schiedsgerichtsbarkeit, vol. 26, Cologne 2010, 33–43

TACKABERRY/MARRIOTT, Preparing for a Hearing/The Conduct of the Hearing, in: Tackaberry/Marriott (eds.), Bernstein's Handbook of Arbitration and Dispute Resolution Practice, vol. 1, 4th ed., London 2003, 285–305

TALLERICO/BEHRENDT, The Use of Bifurcation and Direct Testimony Witness Statements in International Commercial Arbitration Proceedings, JIntArb 3/2003, 295–305

VAN DEN BERG Albert Jan, Organizing an International Arbitration: Practice Pointers, in: Newman/Hill (eds.), The Leading Arbitrators' Guide to International Arbitration, 2nd ed., New York 2008, 149–170

VAN HOUTTE Hans, Counsel-witness relations and professional misconduct in civil law systems, in: Lévy/Veeder (eds.), Arbitration and Oral Evidence, ICC Publication No. 689 (2005), 105–113

VEEDER Johnny V.V., The 2001 Goff Lecture, The Lawyer's Duty to Arbitrate in Good Faith, ArbInt 4/2002, 431–451 (cited VEEDER, Lawyer's Duty)

VEEDER Johnny V.V., Document Production in England: Legislative Developments and Current Arbitral Practice, ICC Bull 2006 Special Supplement, 57–61 (cited VEEDER, Document Production)

VERMEILLE François, Le choix de l'expert et le déroulement de l'expertise, ASA Bull 2/1994, 192–203

VON MEHREN Robert B., Burden of Proof in International Arbitration, ICCA Congress Series No. 7 (1996), 123–130

VON MEHREN/SALOMON, Submitting Evidence in an International Arbitration: The Common Lawyer's Guide, JIntArb 3/2003, 285–294

VON SCHLABRENDORFF/SHEPPARD, Conflict of Legal Privileges in International Arbitration: An Attempt to Find a Holistic Solution, in: Aksen et al. (eds.), Global Reflections on International Law, Commerce and Dispute Resolution, Liber Amicorum Robert Briner, ICC Publishing 2005, 743–774

VON SEGESSER Georg, The IBA Rules on the Taking of Evidence in International Arbitration: Revised version, adopted by the International Bar Association on 29 May 2010, ASA Bull 4/2010, 735–752 (cited VON SEGESSER, IBA Rules)

VON SEGESSER Georg, Witness Preparation in International Commercial Arbitration, ASA Bull 2/2002, 222–228 (cited VON SEGESSER, Witness Preparation)

Voser Nathalie, Harmonization by Promulgating Rules of Best International Practice in International Arbitration, SchiedsVZ 3/2005, 113–118

Weber Pierre C., La responsabilité de l'expert à l'égard des parties et du Tribunal arbitral, ASA Bull 2/1993, 190–209

Webster Thomas H., Obtaining Documents from Adverse Parties in International Arbitration, ArbInt 1/2001, 41–58

Weigand Frank-Bernd, Practitioner's Handbook on International Arbitration, 2nd ed., Bern 2002 (cited Weigand-Author)

Weiss/Bürgi Locatelli, Der vom Schiedsgericht bestellte Experte – ein Überblick aus Sicht eines Internationalen Schiedsgerichts mit Sitz in der Schweiz, ASA Bull 3/2004, 479–504

Wirth Markus, Ihr Zeuge, Herr Rechtsanwalt! Weshalb Civil-Law-Schiedsrichter Common-Law-Verfahrensrecht anwenden, SchiedsVZ 1/2003, 9–15

Wyss Lukas F., Vorsorgliche Massnahmen und Beweisaufnahme – die Rolle des Staatlichen Richters bei Internationalen Schiedsverfahren aus Schweizer Sicht, SchiedsVZ 4/2011, 194–203

ZPO (Basel), Spühler/Tenchio/Infanger (eds.), Schweizerische Zivilprozessordnung, Basel 2010 (cited ZPO (Basel)-Author)

Zuberbühler/Müller/Habegger (eds.), Swiss Rules of International Arbitration, Commentary, Zurich 2005 (cited Author in Commentary Swiss Rules)

Preamble

1. These IBA Rules on the Taking of Evidence in International Arbitration are intended to provide an efficient, economical and fair process for the taking of evidence in international arbitrations, particularly those between Parties from different legal traditions. They are designed to supplement the legal provisions and the institutional, ad hoc or other rules that apply to the conduct of the arbitration.

2. Parties and Arbitral Tribunals may adopt the IBA Rules of Evidence, in whole or in part, to govern arbitration proceedings, or they may vary them or use them as guidelines in developing their own procedures. The Rules are not intended to limit the flexibility that is inherent in, and an advantage of, international arbitration, and Parties and Arbitral Tribunals are free to adapt them to the particular circumstances of each arbitration.

3. The taking of evidence shall be conducted on the principles that each Party shall act in good faith and be entitled to know, reasonably in advance of any Evidentiary Hearing or any facts or merits determination, the evidence on which the other Parties rely.

Contents Note

Other Rules

Art. 22(1) and 22(4) ICC; Art. 15(1) and 15(7) Swiss Rules; Art. 17(1) UNCITRAL; Art. 14(1–2) LCIA; Rule 34(3) ICSID; Art. 38(b–c) WIPO.

I.   2010 Revision

The word "commercial" was deleted from the title of the Rules and from par. 1 of the Preamble to acknowledge the fact that the Rules are meant to be used both in **commercial and investment arbitration.**[1]   1

Furthermore, the former par. 3 of the Preamble on early identification of the relevant and material issues has been moved to the separate and **new Art. 2(3)** in order to give it more weight as part of the Rules instead of a mere encouragement in a preamble.[2]   2

---

[1]   IBA Review Subcommittee 2010, Introduction.
[2]   Von Segesser, IBA Rules, 740–741.

3   Finally, the Review Subcommittee included a **new requirement of fairness** in par. 1 of the Preamble and added in par. 3 that each party shall act "in good faith" in the taking of evidence.

II.   Efficient, Economic and Fair Taking of Evidence (par. 1)

4   The principle of efficiency in arbitration is receiving **more and more attention** in today's fast-paced business world. Following some dissatisfaction expressed by arbitration users and in a constant effort to improve arbitration services, institutions and practitioners are striving to achieve more time and cost efficiency. For example, the ICC Task Force on Reducing Time and Costs in Arbitration published its brochure on "Techniques for Controlling Time and Costs in Arbitration" in 2007.[3]

5   While the implementation of **fast-track procedures** is becoming more frequent,[4] explicit provisions in institutional rules and arbitration laws regarding efficiency for *regular* arbitral proceedings are still quite rare. Sect. 33(1)(b) of the English Arbitration Act 1996 provides that the arbitral tribunal shall *"adopt procedures suitable to the circumstances of the particular case, avoiding unnecessary delay or expense, so as to provide a fair means for the resolution of the matters falling to be determined"*. Sect. 21 of the Swedish Arbitration Act provides that the proceedings must be conducted rapidly.

6   The widespread adoption of the Rules *per se* already leads to a more efficient taking of evidence by the fact that arbitrators and counsel can agree on a basic set of rules and do not have to "reinvent the wheel" every time a procedural question regarding evidence arises. Despite some criticism by eminent practitioners,[5] the increasing **harmonisation** of arbitral practice and procedure constitutes more than just an *"additional layer of procedural order, taking a bit from here and a bit from there"*.[6]

---

[3]   ICC Publication No. 843, 2007. Reprinted in Annex 2.

[4]   E.g. WIPO Expedited Arbitration Rules, Art. 42 Swiss Rules, Rules for Expedited Arbitrations of the Arbitration Institute of the Stockholm Chamber of Commerce, Rules for Expedited Arbitration of the Arbitration Institute of the Central Chamber of Commerce of Finland, Expedited Procedures of the AAA Commercial Arbitration Rules, Art. 50–58 CIETAC Arbitration Rules, Art. 38 HKIAC Administered Arbitration Rules (Hong Kong International Arbitration Centre), Rule 5 SIAC Rules (Singapore International Arbitration Centre), Commercial Rules of the Korean Commercial Arbitration Board (Chapter XIII), Commercial Arbitration Rules of the Japan Commercial Arbitration Association (Chapter V), Art. 39 CAMCA Arbitration Rules (Commercial Arbitration and Mediation Center for the Americas).

[5]   Marriott, Deadlock, 426–427.

[6]   Id., 426.

The true benefit of harmonised guidelines such as the Rules is to raise **pre-** 7
dictability and assist parties with less experience. In arbitrations where
the Rules apply, the parties will know from the outset e.g. that an arbitral
tribunal may draw adverse inferences if they do not adhere to production orders. This knowledge alone will lead to better compliance with such
orders. Of course, the same result could be achieved by announcing the
sanction of adverse inference in the production order, but what if an inexperienced arbitrator forgets to do so? Harmonised rules first benefit the
inexperienced counsel and arbitrators, who cannot resort to similar cases
they have dealt with earlier and immediately come up with a well-balanced
and tested proposal or solution. It is equally clear that an experienced arbitrator most likely does not need to consult the Rules when confronted with
an evidentiary issue, since he or she has already "internalised" the basic
rules for such matters and can call them up almost instinctively. In this connection, it is important to note that the Rules are not intended to limit the
flexibility in international arbitration in any way, as the drafters clarified in
par. 2 of the Preamble.

Another important aspect of harmonised rules is that of bringing together 8
the common law and civil law systems. Rather than simply adapting concepts from the other legal system as it is discussed in litigation (e.g. for the
introduction of class actions in the EU[7]), the Rules are a synthesis of both
legal systems' accepted features, the "best of two worlds", and thus a contribution towards the development of an international *lex evidentia*[8].

The taking of evidence in an efficient and economical manner should pre- 9
dominantly be accomplished by the arbitrators. They are the "masters of
the proceedings"[9] and should admonish and encourage the parties and
their representatives to act in an efficient and cost-saving way. The following **strategies** might be helpful in this task:

a) promotion of settlement by the arbitrators;

b) focussing on decisive issues at an early stage of the proceedings;[10]

c) limitation of the duration of hearings;

d) reduction of party-appointed expert reports by greater use of tribunal-
   appointed experts;[11]

---

[7] Cf. e.g. the EU's Consumer Strategy 2007–2013, COM (2007) 99, 13 March 2007.
[8] Cf. SHARPE, 551–552, with respect to the drawing of adverse inferences.
[9] The International Arbitration Rules of the Zurich Chamber of Commerce, which have
    been replaced by the Swiss Rules, stated matter-of-factly in Art. 21(1): *"The chair-
    man leads the arbitration."*
[10] See Art. 2 N 13–15 below.
[11] MARRIOTT, Deadlock, 427.

e) separate pricing and cost awards for procedural motions.[12]

10   The 2010 Revision has added the principle of **fairness** to the criteria of
efficient and economical evidence-taking. One application of the fairness
principle could be seen in the "most favourable privilege" rule.[13]

III. Supplementation of Institutional, Ad Hoc or Other Rules (par. 1)

11   The Rules only deal with issues relating to the taking of evidence and are
not intended to provide an entire mechanism for the conduct of an international arbitration. Therefore, parties must still select a set of institutional
or *ad hoc* rules, such as those of the ICC, the Swiss Chambers, WIPO, AAA,
LCIA, UNCITRAL or ICSID, or design their own rules,[14] to establish the
overall procedural framework for their arbitration.[15] The Rules are merely
intended to **fill in the gaps** left open in those rules with respect to the
taking of evidence.[16]

IV. Adaptation of the Rules in Arbitral Proceedings (par. 2)

12   Recognising that there is no single best formula to conduct all international
arbitrations and that **flexibility** in proceedings is an advantage, the drafters felt it important to clarify that the Rules are not intended to limit this
flexibility.[17]

13   The Rules should be used by parties and arbitral tribunals in the **manner
that best suits them,** by either:

a) adopting them as a whole;

b) adopting them in part, i.e. using only certain provisions;

c) adopting them, but varying certain provisions to fit the particular circumstances of their arbitration;

---

[12]   SCHNEIDER, Lean Arbitration, 135–137; PRICE/STANS, 713–714.
[13]   Art. 9 N 30 below.
[14]   The term "other rules" was added by the drafters of the 2010 Revision to clarify that,
for *ad hoc* proceedings, the parties may also design completely independent procedural rules "from scratch", as opposed to pre-existing rules such as the UNCITRAL
Rules.
[15]   For a discussion of the advantages and disadvantages of institutional versus *ad
hoc* arbitration, cf. POUDRET/BESSON, N 93–97, and REDFERN/HUNTER/BLACKABY/PARTASIDES,
N 1.152–1.168.
[16]   IBA REVIEW SUBCOMMITTEE 2010, Preamble sect. (i).
[17]   IBA REVIEW SUBCOMMITTEE 2010, Preamble sect. (iii).

d) using them simply as guidelines in developing their own procedures.[18]

V. Good Faith Principle (par. 3)

In conjunction with the principle of fairness, the Review Subcommittee   14
has expressly included a requirement in par. 3 of the Preamble that each
party shall act "in good faith" in the taking of evidence pursuant to the
Rules. While the **universal principle** of good faith already applied to any
evidence-taking before the revision, the express stipulation in the revised
Rules is welcome and provides a solid basis for arbitrators e.g. to draw an
adverse inference (Art. 9(5–6)) or to sanction abusive conduct by imposing
costs on the respective party (Art. 9(7)). On the other hand, it is submitted that the good faith principle does not include an obligation to produce
documents manifestly helpful to the opponent's case or even harmful to a
party's own case.[19]

Despite some **criticism** that the obligation of good faith raises more ques-   15
tions than it answers,[20] the Review Subcommittee felt that embedding this
principle in the Rules was particularly helpful for those parties that have no
or less experience with international arbitration and for providing the arbitral tribunal with a yardstick to conduct the evidentiary proceedings.[21]

The type of conduct that will amount to a breach of the good faith obliga-   16
tion will be for arbitral tribunals to consider on a case-by-case basis. Commentators have stated the following **fact patterns** which might breach the
principle:[22]

- excessive document requests;

- burying responsive documents under unimportant ones;

- failure to comply with a document production order;

- raising objections to document production requests without a reasonable and good-faith basis;

- holding back documents or witnesses on which a party relies with the
  intent to surprise parties or witnesses with such documents and witnesses;

---

[18] BORN (at 1794) suggests that arbitral tribunals ordinarily have the power (in the exercise of their discretion over evidence-taking) to adopt the Rules and direct that the
parties proceed in accordance with them, but also points out that arbitral tribunals
will prefer to use the Rules as guidelines if any party objects to a strict application.
[19] COHEN KLÄSENER, 161; *contra* VON SEGESSER, IBA Rules, 741.
[20] REES, 515.
[21] VON SEGESSER, IBA Rules, 741.
[22] COHEN KLÄSENER, passim; NEWMARK, 166; REES, 515.

- deliberate concealment or destruction of evidence;

- tampering with documents submitted or produced;

- submitting misleading translations;

- disclosing confidential materials with the intent of pressuring or harming another participant in the arbitration;

- unduly influencing the testimony of a witness (e.g. by paying inappropriately high compensation in exchange for testimony, inciting false testimony, or relying on witness testimony notwithstanding the fact that the testimony is known to be false);

- deliberately asking confusing questions during cross-examination;

- seeking to portray witnesses in a bad light.

17   Another question raised is whether the good faith obligation applies only to parties (in accordance with the wording of par. 3 of the Preamble) or to counsel as well. Since nearly everything counsel does during arbitral proceedings is performed as the representative of a party, it would appear that the good faith obligation **also applies to counsel.**[23]

VI.   Knowledge of Evidence Sufficiently in Advance of the Hearing (par. 3)

18   As noted by the drafters, the Rules are designed to avoid surprises about procedures, in order to assist parties that may be unfamiliar with international arbitration. Similarly, the Rules seek to **avoid any surprises** at the evidentiary hearing.[24] The principle that each party shall know sufficiently in advance of the hearing the evidence which the other parties are relying on, is a basic rule for all other provisions of the Rules. In this sense, the drafters of the 1999 Rules stated that *"the best results are obtained when each party knows the arguments made by the other and is able to provide as effective a rebuttal as possible".*[25]

19   The underlying principle of an **"adversarial procedure"** is reflected amongst others in French law (principle of *"contradiction"*). Art. 15 of the *Nouveau Code de Procédure Civile* stipulates a duty of the parties to inform each other about the factual and legal basis of their allegations sufficiently

---

[23]   COHEN KLÄSENER, 163.
[24]   IBA WORKING PARTY 1999, Preamble sect. (iv).
[25]   Id.

in advance for the other party to prepare a defence.[26] This principle is also recognised under Swiss arbitration law.[27]

Late submission of evidence, unless it consists of truly new facts, should only be accepted by arbitrators with a certain restraint. The confrontation of witnesses with new evidence at hearings should also be avoided as far as possible. Civil law arbitrators will generally be more inclined to accept late evidence than common law arbitrators, since they are less familiar with the strict conditions for the admission of evidence as they exist in common law jurisdictions.   20

Many discussions about the admissibility of late evidence can be avoided by including **clear procedural rules** to specify the general rule stated in the Preamble of the Rules. Similar to Art. 27(1) ICC Rules, which instructs arbitrators to declare the proceedings closed as soon as possible after the last hearing or the filing of the last authorized submissions, arbitral tribunals could fix a deadline of e.g. ten days before the hearing, after which date no further evidence (not even new facts) may be introduced into the proceedings until the witness hearing is concluded. This would allow the parties to prepare the witness hearing and their witnesses without constantly being bombarded by the other side with new allegations and facts.   21

After the hearing, the arbitrators shall declare the proceedings as closed and shall not accept any further evidence.[28] A **reopening** of the proceedings to evaluate new evidence should only be possible under the following exceptional circumstances:[29]   22

a) if during the deliberations of the arbitral tribunal it turns out that certain issues need further clarification;[30]

b) if during the deliberations of the arbitral tribunal an issue comes up which was not dealt with during the proceedings and requires additional evidence-taking;

c) if it is discovered that a party fraudulently held back evidence it was ordered to produce;

---

[26] *"Les parties doivent se faire connaître mutuellement en temps utile les moyens de fait sur lesquels elles fondent leurs prétentions, les éléments de preuve qu'elles produisent et les moyens de droit qu'elles invoquent, afin que chacune soit à même d'organiser sa défense."*

[27] DFT 116 II 643, 117 II 347–348; cf. also PILS (Basel)-Schneider, Art. 182 N 56–61, and Müller, Case Law, 168–169.

[28] Art. 27 ICC Rules, Art. 29 Swiss Rules.

[29] Oetiker in Commentary Swiss Rules, Art. 29 N 11.

[30] It being understood that this must not lead to an unjustified remedy of a party's failure to submit certain evidence in time.

d) if a party becomes aware of decisive facts supporting its case which were not and could not have been known previously.

Definitions

In the IBA Rules of Evidence:

'Arbitral Tribunal' means a sole arbitrator or a panel of arbitrators;

'Claimant' means the Party or Parties who commenced the arbitration and any Party who, through joinder or otherwise, becomes aligned with such Party or Parties;

'Document' means a writing, communication, picture, drawing, program or data of any kind, whether recorded or maintained on paper or by electronic, audio, visual or any other means;

'Evidentiary Hearing' means any hearing, whether or not held on consecutive days, at which the Arbitral Tribunal, whether in person, by teleconference, videoconference or other method, receives oral or other evidence;

'Expert Report' means a written statement by a Tribunal-Appointed Expert or a Party-Appointed Expert;

'General Rules' mean the institutional, ad hoc or other rules that apply to the conduct of the arbitration;

'IBA Rules of Evidence' or *'Rules'* means these IBA Rules on the Taking of Evidence in International Arbitration, as they may be revised or amended from time to time;

'Party' means a party to the arbitration;

'Party-Appointed Expert' means a person or organisation appointed by a Party in order to report on specific issues determined by the Party;

'Request to Produce' means a written request by a Party that another Party produce Documents;

'Respondent' means the Party or Parties against whom the Claimant made its claim, and any Party who, through joinder or otherwise, becomes aligned with such Party or Parties, and includes a Respondent making a counter-claim;

'Tribunal-Appointed Expert' means a person or organisation appointed by the Arbitral Tribunal in order to report to it on specific issues determined by the Arbitral Tribunal; and

'Witness Statement' means a written statement of testimony by a witness of fact.

1   The Definitions section (no longer a numbered Article) sets forth the basic
     definitions to be applied in the Rules. The definitions themselves **do not
     provide** any **substantive rules** of conduct or evidence.[31]

2   The definition of "Document" was slightly modified to clarify and ensure
     that all forms of evidence, including electronic evidence, are subject to the
     Rules.[32] Furthermore, **technological advance** was taken into account for
     the new definition of "Evidentiary Hearing", which includes witness testi-
     mony by telephone conference, video conference or any other methods. Fi-
     nally, the definition of "Party-Appointed Expert" was expanded to allow not
     only for the appointment of persons, but also of organisations as experts.

---

[31]   IBA Review Subcommittee 2010, Definitions par. 1.
[32]   Id., Definitions par. 3.

Article 1   Scope of Application

1. **Whenever the Parties have agreed or the Arbitral Tribunal has determined to apply the IBA Rules of Evidence, the Rules shall govern the taking of evidence, except to the extent that any specific provision of them may be found to be in conflict with any mandatory provision of law determined to be applicable to the case by the Parties or by the Arbitral Tribunal.**

2. **Where the Parties have agreed to apply the IBA Rules of Evidence, they shall be deemed to have agreed, in the absence of a contrary indication, to the version as current on the date of such agreement.**

3. **In case of conflict between any provision of the IBA Rules of Evidence and the General Rules, the Arbitral Tribunal shall apply the IBA Rules of Evidence in the manner that it determines best in order to accomplish the purposes of both the General Rules and the IBA Rules of Evidence, unless the Parties agree to the contrary.**

4. **In the event of any dispute regarding the meaning of the IBA Rules of Evidence, the Arbitral Tribunal shall interpret them according to their purpose and in the manner most appropriate for the particular arbitration.**

5. **Insofar as the IBA Rules of Evidence and the General Rules are silent on any matter concerning the taking of evidence and the Parties have not agreed otherwise, the Arbitral Tribunal shall conduct the taking of evidence as it deems appropriate, in accordance with the general principles of the IBA Rules of Evidence.**

Because the Rules only deal with issues relating to the taking of evidence, parties must select another set of institutional or *ad hoc* rules to govern their proceedings. In addition, international arbitrations are subject to mandatory law at the seat of arbitration. **Conflicts** may arise between the Rules and these other rules or any mandatory legal provisions. 1

Art. 1 provides several **basic principles** as to how arbitral tribunals should apply the Rules in the event of a conflict with any of these other provisions: 2

par. 1:   In a conflict between the Rules and mandatory legal provisions determined to be applicable to the case, the **mandatory law** shall govern the taking of evidence.[33]

---

[33] Regarding the scope and application of mandatory law, see Poudret/Besson, N 705–708, with further references.

par. 3:   In a conflict between the Rules and the General Rules (as speci-
           fied in the Definitions section, i.e. the institutional or *ad hoc*
           rules chosen by the parties), arbitral tribunals shall attempt to
           harmonise the two sets of rules to the greatest extent possible.
           However, because party autonomy is central to any international
           arbitration, the parties have a right to resolve any such conflict in
           the manner they choose, as long as both parties agree.[34]

par. 4:   If a dispute exists as to the meaning of the Rules, arbitral tribu-
           nals shall interpret them *"according to their purpose and in the
           manner most appropriate for the particular arbitration"*, i.e. in
           greatest possible **compliance with the general principles** set
           forth in the Preamble.[35]

par. 5:   An application of the general principles is equally prescribed if
           both the Rules and the General Rules are **silent** on a particular
           issue.

3   With regard to conflicts between the Rules and the General Rules, it has
     been suggested that the Rules should **override** any conflicting provisions
     in the General Rules if the parties agree on the application of the Rules *after*
     the determination of the General Rules.[36]

4   The new Art. 1(2) specifies that the version of the Rules as current on
     the date of an agreement between the parties to apply them shall be ap-
     plicable for any subsequent dispute, absent any contrary indication. As a
     consequence, the **1999 Rules** will still apply in cases where the parties
     have explicitly agreed on the application of the Rules in their arbitration
     agreement. On the other hand, parties wishing to apply the version of the
     Rules current at the time of the arbitration should consider including this in
     the arbitration clause.[37]

---

[34]   IBA REVIEW SUBCOMMITTEE 2010, Art. 1 par. 1 sect. 2.
[35]   Id., Art. 1 par. 1 sect. 3.
[36]   MÜLLER, IBA Rules, 56–57.
[37]   The following language is suggested in the Foreword to the Rules: *"[In addition to
       the institutional,* ad hoc *or other rules chosen by the parties,] [t]he parties agree
       that the arbitration shall be conducted according to the IBA Rules of Evidence as
       current on the date of [this agreement/the commencement of the arbitration]"*.

Article 2 Consultation on Evidentiary Issues

1. The Arbitral Tribunal shall consult the Parties at the earliest appropriate time in the proceedings and invite them to consult each other with a view to agreeing on an efficient, economical and fair process for the taking of evidence.

2. The consultation on evidentiary issues may address the scope, timing and manner of the taking of evidence, including:

   (a) the preparation and submission of Witness Statements and Expert Reports;

   (b) the taking of oral testimony at any Evidentiary Hearing;

   (c) the requirements, procedure and format applicable to the production of Documents;

   (d) the level of confidentiality protection to be afforded to evidence in the arbitration; and

   (e) the promotion of efficiency, economy and conservation of resources in connection with the taking of evidence.

3. The Arbitral Tribunal is encouraged to identify to the Parties, as soon as it considers it to be appropriate, any issues:

   (a) that the Arbitral Tribunal may regard as relevant to the case and material to its outcome; and/or

   (b) for which a preliminary determination may be appropriate.

Contents   Note

Other Rules

Art. 24 and Appendix IV ICC; Art. 17(1–2) UNCITRAL; Art. 14(1)(ii) and 19(3) LCIA; Rule 20 and 21 ICSID; Art. 16 AAA; Art. 38(c) and 47 WIPO.

I.   2010 Revision

The new Art. 2 promulgates in par. 1 the so-called **"meet and consult"**   1
method, requiring[38] the arbitral tribunal to consult with the parties at the earliest appropriate time to discuss the specific approach to evidence-taking. Some issues which may be appropriate for consultation are listed in

---

[38] The word used is "shall", not "may".

Art. 2(2). Art. 2(3) is a slightly expanded version of the former par. 3 of the Preamble and encourages arbitral tribunals to identify to the parties, as early as possible, the issues they may regard as relevant to the case and material to its outcome as well as those issues for which a preliminary determination may be appropriate.

II.   Early Consultation With the Parties (par. 1)

2   The arbitration community seems to have reached a consensus that an early discussion between the arbitral tribunal and the parties regarding the procedure to be adopted for the arbitration is a good idea.[39] With respect to evidence-taking, Art. 2(1) stipulates a corresponding duty for the arbitral tribunal to consult with the parties. Respective instructions by arbitral tribunals are best communicated at a so-called **pre-hearing conference** (also referred to as "organisational hearing", "preparatory conference" or "case-management conference"[40]), after exchange of the first briefs, i.e. when the parties' positions have been set forth in a sufficient manner.[41] Pre-hearing conferences are not only a good opportunity for the arbitral tribunal to meet party counsel and representatives in person and identify material issues, but can serve other purposes such as signing the terms of reference (or constitutional order as it is sometimes referred to), organising the time schedule of the proceedings, exploring the possibilities of a settlement, or debating production requests (if already filed). As REED/HILL ROSENKRANZ correctly note, bringing all the participants to the same table early in the proceedings should outweigh the related costs, and a face-to-face meeting among arbitrators, counsel and principals may narrow issues or even lead to settlement.[42]

3   In any case, a first meeting can often establish a **good atmosphere** and thus ensure a smooth progress of the arbitration. While the current trend is to hold pre-hearing conferences by telephone or video conference,[43] it seems doubtful whether this is a good development. During telephone conferences, concentration usually drops much faster than during a meeting, and participants are easily distracted by incoming emails. Video confer-

---

[39]   NEWMARK, 166.

[40]   One of the few express mentions of pre-hearing conferences can be found in Art. 24 of the revised ICC Rules, according to which *"the arbitral tribunal shall convene a case management conference to consult the parties on procedural measures that may be adopted [...]"*. See also Art. 16(2) of the ICDR International Arbitration Rules, the Tribunal Rules of the Iran-US Claims Tribunal (Art. 15 N 4), Rule 21 of the ICSID Arbitration Rules, and Art. 47 WIPO Rules.

[41]   PILS (Basel)-SCHNEIDER, Art. 182 N 92.

[42]   REED/HILL ROSENKRANZ, 123.

[43]   Cf. Appendix IV(f) to the ICC Rules and par. 28 of the ICC Report on Techniques for Controlling Time and Costs in Arbitration (Annex 2).

ences on the other hand do not offer the same opportunities for informal communication which are essential to establish a certain level of interpersonal relationship.[44]

In order to be efficient, the chairperson should distribute a comprehensive   4
agenda along with a draft of any procedural documents the arbitral tribunal intends to issue (terms of reference, procedural orders, supplemental procedural rules, timetables etc.) to the parties in advance of the pre-hearing conference.

The first procedural discussion may also be used by the arbitrators to find   5
an agreement with the parties on certain other **open or disputed matters** such as the applicable law (if it is unclear or if the contract stipulates an exotic law that counsel and arbitrators are not acquainted with).[45]

Pre-hearing conferences are also required by Art. 24 ICC Rules and dis-   6
cussed in Appendix IV(g) to the ICC Rules as well as in its report on "Techniques for Controlling Time and Costs in Arbitration" (the **"ICC Report"**).[46]
Contrary to the view expressed in par. 23 of the ICC Report, pro-active case management can also be particularly important and helpful for complex cases. A pre-hearing conference should not be deferred until the parties have set out their cases in detail.[47] It is also clear, however, that new evidentiary issues may arise during the proceedings which may have to be addressed at a later stage.[48]

III. Issues to Address (par. 2)

It may be useful at an early stage in the proceedings for the arbitrators and   7
parties to consult the UNCITRAL Notes on Organizing Arbitral Proceedings **("UNCITRAL Notes").**[49] The UNCITRAL Notes provide a list of matters arbitral tribunals may need to keep in mind when they organise the proceedings. The list is not intended to be exhaustive, but gives a useful indication of points the arbitrators may wish to consider. With respect to evidence proceedings, the following is proposed for consideration:[50]

---

[44]   On the other hand, it should be kept in mind that telephone or video conferences might be warranted to save costs and resources, particularly in cases with a lower amount in dispute; cf. BORN, 1809, and N 12 below.

[45]   RAESCHKE-KESSLER, Settlement Facilitator, 527 mentions the further example of contract interpretation methods.

[46]   Par. 21–23 and 31–34 of the ICC Report (Annex 2).

[47]   See the note by Philipp Capper (Construction Arbitration: Challenges from new trends) in Global Arbitration Review 4/2008, 27–28.

[48]   VON SEGESSER, IBA Rules, 743.

[49]   Adopted by UNCITRAL in 1996. The text of the UNCITRAL Notes is set out in Annex 3.

[50]   Summarised by REDFERN/HUNTER/BLACKABY/PARTASIDES, N 6.38.

- The adoption of a set of **procedural rules,** in the event that the parties have not already done so (par. 14–16).

- The **language** of the proceedings, the language that is to be used in the hearings, the need (if any) for translation of oral presentations and documents, and the costs involved (par. 17–20).

- **Confidentiality** of information: The arbitral tribunal may need to make arrangements to ensure confidentiality (par. 31–32).[51]

- Definition of points of issue: The arbitral tribunal may prepare a **list of issues** and the order in which they should be decided and determine precisely the relief that is sought (par. 43–46).

- Possibility of **settlement negotiations:** The arbitral tribunal should consider the extent (if at all) to which it should offer to facilitate settlement negotiations (par. 47).

- **Documentary evidence:** The arbitral tribunal may set time limits for the submission of documents and determine the consequences of late submission (par. 48–49). It should also determine whether the parties are going to be compelled to produce documents (par. 50–51).[52] One issue that was not yet of particular significance when the UNCITRAL Notes were drafted, but is becoming more important and should also be addressed during a preliminary hearing, is the production of electronically stored documents.[53]

- **Physical evidence:** The arbitral tribunal may make arrangements for any physical evidence to be presented as well as any site inspections it may wish to undertake (par. 55–58).[54]

- **Witnesses of fact:**[55] The arbitral tribunal may wish to determine

  a) the advance notice required concerning witnesses and the content of such notice and the nature of the statement of the witness (par. 60);

  b) the possibility of pre-hearing witness depositions (par. 61);

  c) the manner in which the hearing of witnesses will take place, and the degree of control the arbitral tribunal wishes to exercise (par. 62–68).

---

[51]   See Art. 3 N 254–266 and Art. 9 N 50–53 below.
[52]   See Art. 3 below.
[53]   See MEIER, 187, and Art. 3 N 49–59 below.
[54]   See Art. 7 below.
[55]   See Art. 4 below.

- **Experts** and expert witnesses: The arbitral tribunal may wish to consider appointing an expert to report to it and determine how such a person is to be chosen. It may also determine the terms of reference for the expert and decide how the parties are to comment on such terms of reference (par. 69–73).[56]

- **Hearings:**[57] The arbitral tribunal may wish to decide on some or all of the following matters as concerning hearings:

    a) Should hearings be held at all? And if they are to be held, how are they to be structured? (par. 74–77)

    b) Should there be a limit on the time that each of the parties has? And in what order will the parties present their arguments? (par. 78–80)

    c) The length of the hearings and whether a record should be kept of the proceedings and how they are to be kept (par. 81–83).

    d) Whether the parties should be allowed to submit a summary of their oral arguments (par. 84–85).

Some of the items listed in the UNCITRAL Notes are also reflected in   8
Art. 2(2). The evidentiary **issues recommended for discussion** at an early stage as to the scope, timing and manner of the taking of evidence are:

a) the preparation and submission of witness statements and expert reports;

b) the taking of oral testimony at any evidence hearing;

c) the requirements, procedure and format applicable to the production of documents;

d) the level of confidentiality protection to be afforded to evidence in the arbitration; and

e) the promotion of efficiency, economy and conservation of resources in connection with the taking of evidence.

While Art. 2 provides a **framework** for discussing evidentiary issues, it is   9
not intended to prescribe how evidence should be taken in any particular arbitration.[58] For example, the arbitral tribunal and the parties may decide not to require witness statements or the disclosure of electronic evidence or not to hold an evidentiary hearing. On the other hand, if they determine

---

[56]   See Art. 5 below.
[57]   See Art. 8 below.
[58]   IBA Review Subcommittee 2010, Art. 2 par. 3.

that certain forms of evidence-taking should be applied, Art. 2 encourages arbitral tribunals and parties to discuss the related details at an early stage.

10   Furthermore, the list of course does **not** constitute a **comprehensive** catalogue, and arbitral tribunals must consider additional issues where appropriate.[59]

11   An important issue is the level of **confidentiality** protection to be afforded to evidence in the arbitration (Art. 2(2)(d)). In order to create a level playing field for parties from jurisdictions with differing standards on confidentiality (e.g. with respect to the attorney-client privilege of in-house counsel), the specific extent of confidentiality in connection with document production should be discussed and agreed at the outset of any proceedings.[60]

12   While Art. 2(2)(e) repeats the requirement of Art. 2(1) to consult on the promotion of efficiency and economy and thus appears to be duplicative, it also specifically refers to the **conservation of resources** in connection with the taking of evidence. This could include discussing ways to reduce (i) the economic and environmental costs of travel (e.g. by increased use of telephone and video conferencing) or (ii) document reproduction costs (by submitting documents via web-based platforms such as the ICC's NetCase or by email).[61]

IV.   Identification of Relevant and Material Issues (par. 3(a))

13   Each arbitral tribunal is encouraged under Art. 2(3)(a) to identify the relevant and material issues to the parties *"as soon as it considers it to be appropriate"*.[62] The focus on decisive issues probably has the largest potential for **improving cost control and efficiency** in international arbitration.[63] The parties are able to focus their pleadings on the points considered essential by the arbitral tribunal and have a better chance to strengthen certain arguments the arbitral tribunal disagrees with.[64]

14   On the other hand, some arbitrators might feel uncomfortable telling the parties at the outset of the proceedings which issues they consider to be

---

[59]   VON SEGESSER, IBA Rules, 743.
[60]   Cf. VON SEGESSER, IBA Rules, 743; REES, 516; Art. 9 N 27 below.
[61]   Cf. IBA REVIEW SUBCOMMITTEE 2010, Art. 2 par. 4.
[62]   A similar provision can be found in Appendix IV(g) to the ICC Rules and par. 38 of the ICC Report: *"The arbitral tribunal may consider using the occasion of the pre-hearing conference to indicate to the parties the issues on which it would like the parties to focus at the forthcoming hearing".*
[63]   SCHNEIDER, Lean Arbitration, 132.
[64]   NEWMARK, 167.

important. They might be concerned that this is **premature** and improper and could even lead to accusations of partiality.[65]

The fact that the provision on identification of relevant and material issues   15
is positioned within an article focussed on early case management confer-ences gives the impression that such identification by the arbitral tribunal should happen very early in the case. In practice, however, it will often be better to identify the relevant and material issues **later in the proceedings,** at a time when the arbitrators know more about the case (e.g. before the hearing).[66]

V.   Preliminary Determination / Bifurcation (par. 3(b))

While the drafters of the Rules did not intend to encourage litigation-style   16
motion practice, they recognised that in some cases certain issues may re-solve all or part of a case. In such circumstances, arbitral tribunals should seek to resolve the respective matters first in order to **avoid** potentially **unnecessary work** on issues that will not determine the outcome.[67]

In deciding whether to bifurcate, arbitral tribunals must first evaluate   17
whether substantive issues in the arbitration are easily separable and/ or significantly complex to justify bifurcation. Other **factors** to consider include:[68]

a) the amount and type of evidence needed to support each issue;

b) whether the evidence necessary for a later phase of the proceedings will overlap or will be mutually exclusive;

c) whether the evidence necessary for a later phase will be detrimental or disruptive to the proceedings;

d) whether evidence necessary for a later phase of the proceedings is sensitive or if there is a strategic reason to withhold certain key evidence until a later phase;

e) whether a second phase of the arbitration will be voluminous;

f) the effect that bifurcation may have on discovery (if allowed);

g) whether bifurcation will somehow result in prejudice or unfair advantage;

---

[65]   NEWMARK, 167; cf. also BORN, 1816.
[66]   NEWMARK, 167. Cf. Art. 19(3) LCIA Rules: *"The Arbitral Tribunal may in advance of any hearing submit to the parties a list of questions which it wishes them to answer with special attention."*
[67]   IBA REVIEW SUBCOMMITTEE 2010, Art. 2 par. 5.
[68]   TALLERICO/BEHRENDT, 298.

h) whether bifurcation will result in greater convenience to witnesses, the parties or the arbitral tribunal;

i) whether bifurcation will act to expedite the proceedings and help to conserve resources.

18   It must be taken into account that bifurcation may ultimately result in **longer and more complex proceedings,** because (i) every step of an arbitral procedure (e.g. two exchanges of briefs, expert reports, witness hearing) may have to be repeated in the second phase, and (ii) the party which lost in the first phase is likely to defend its position more fiercely in the second phase, since it already knows e.g. that it will be ordered to pay damages. Such parties may tend to be recalcitrant and less cooperative, resulting in higher costs and a longer duration of the proceedings.

19   Furthermore, it is sometimes necessary to **enquire fully** into all the circumstances of a case in order to determine a preliminary issue. In these cases, it is preferable to deal with the preliminary issue in the final award.[69] There is also a danger that evidence presented during the second phase would have had a material impact on the decisions made in the first phase which however cannot be amended as they have become final.[70]

20   The possibility of a separate decision on **jurisdiction** is considered the rule under arbitration laws.[71] Another common example of preliminary determination is that of the law governing the arbitration or the law applicable to the merits[72] or a decision on interim measures.

21   Bifurcation is also frequent with respect to issues of **liability and quantum,** particularly where the quantification of claims is a major exercise.[73] The reverse is also conceivable: A respondent may prefer to have the arbitral tribunal hear evidence of a claimant's allegations on damages prior to a hearing on liability because the lack of proof of damages may be decisive and involve less analysis than the question of liability.[74] Such reverse bifurcation can also assist the parties in trying to shape settlement negotiations based upon the outcome of a hearing on damages.[75]

---

[69]   POUDRET/BESSON, N 474; REDFERN/HUNTER/BLACKABY/PARTASIDES, N 6–47.
[70]   VAN DEN BERG, 169–170.
[71]   Art. 186(3) PILS; § 1040(3) German ZPO. Cf. POUDRET/BESSON, N 474.
[72]   REDFERN/HUNTER/BLACKABY/PARTASIDES, N 6.42, mentioning the *Aminoil* arbitration as an example of such preliminary determination ([1982] 21 I.L.M. 976). Cf. also BORN, 1816.
[73]   BORN, 1816–1817; REDFERN/HUNTER/BLACKABY/PARTASIDES, N 6.43–6.48.
[74]   TALLERICO/BEHRENDT, 297.
[75]   Id., 298.

Because it might lead to a termination of the proceedings, the arbitral tri-   22
bunal's decision following a bifurcation should be rendered in the form of an
award and not by procedural order.[76]

---

[76]   Cf. Poudret/Besson, N 727–730.

Article 3   Documents

1. Within the time ordered by the Arbitral Tribunal, each Party shall submit to the Arbitral Tribunal and to the other Parties all Documents available to it on which it relies, including public Documents and those in the public domain, except for any Documents that have already been submitted by another Party.

2. Within the time ordered by the Arbitral Tribunal, any Party may submit to the Arbitral Tribunal and to the other Parties a Request to Produce.

3. A Request to Produce shall contain:

    (a) *(i)* a description of each requested Document sufficient to identify it, or

    (ii) a description in sufficient detail (including subject matter) of a narrow and specific requested category of Documents that are reasonably believed to exist; in the case of Documents maintained in electronic form, the requesting Party may, or the Arbitral Tribunal may order that it shall be required to, identify specific files, search terms, individuals or other means of searching for such Documents in an efficient and economical manner;

    (b) a statement as to how the Documents requested are relevant to the case and material to its outcome; and

    (c) *(i)* a statement that the Documents requested are not in the possession, custody or control of the requesting Party or a statement of the reasons why it would be unreasonably burdensome for the requesting Party to produce such Documents, and

    (ii) a statement of the reasons why the requesting Party assumes the Documents requested are in the possession, custody or control of another Party.

4. Within the time ordered by the Arbitral Tribunal, the Party to whom the Request to Produce is addressed shall produce to the other Parties and, if the Arbitral Tribunal so orders, to it, all the Documents requested in its possession, custody or control as to which it makes no objection.

5. If the Party to whom the Request to Produce is addressed has an objection to some or all of the Documents requested, it shall state the objection in writing to the Arbitral Tribunal and the other Parties within the time ordered by the Arbitral Tribunal. The reasons for such objection shall be any of those set forth in Article 9.2 or a failure to satisfy any of the requirements of Article 3.3.

6. Upon receipt of any such objection, The Arbitral Tribunal may invite the relevant Parties to consult with each other with a view to resolving the objection.

7. Either party may, within the time ordered by the Arbitral Tribunal, request the Arbitral Tribunal to rule on the objection. The Arbitral Tribunal shall then, in consultation with the Parties and in timely fashion, consider the Request to Produce and the objection. The Arbitral Tribunal may order the Party to whom such Request is addressed to produce any requested Document in its possession, custody or control as to which the Arbitral Tribunal determines that *(i)* the issues that the requesting Party wishes to prove are relevant to the case and material to its outcome; *(ii)* none of the reasons for objection set forth in Article 9.2 applies; and *(iii)* the requirements of Article 3.3 have been satisfied. Any such Document shall be produced to the other Parties and, if the Arbitral Tribunal so orders, to it.

8. In exceptional circumstances, if the propriety of an objection can be determined only by review of the Document, the Arbitral Tribunal may determine that it should not review the Document. In that event, the Arbitral Tribunal may, after consultation with the Parties, appoint an independent and impartial expert, bound to confidentiality, to review any such Document and to report on the objection. To the extent that the objection is upheld by the Arbitral Tribunal, the expert shall not disclose to the Arbitral Tribunal and to the other Parties the contents of the Document reviewed.

9. If a Party wishes to obtain the production of Documents from a person or organisation who is not a Party to the arbitration and from whom the Party cannot obtain the Documents on its own, the Party may, within the time ordered by the Arbitral Tribunal, ask it to take whatever steps are legally available to obtain the requested Documents, or seek leave from the Arbitral Tribunal to take such steps itself. The Party shall submit such request to the Arbitral Tribunal and to the other Parties in writing, and the request shall contain the particulars set forth in Article 3.3, as applicable. The Arbitral Tribunal shall decide on this request and shall take, authorize the requesting Party to take, or order any other Party to take, such steps as the Arbitral Tribunal considers appropriate if, in its discretion, it determines that *(i)* the Documents would be relevant to the case and material to its outcome, *(ii)* the requirements of Article 3.3, as applicable, have been satisfied and *(iii)* none of the reasons for objection set forth in Article 9.2 applies.

10. At any time before the arbitration is concluded, the Arbitral Tribunal may *(i)* request any Party to produce Documents, *(ii)* request any Party to use its best efforts to take or *(iii)* itself take, any step that it considers appropriate to obtain Documents from any person or organisation. A Party to whom such a request for Documents is

addressed may object to the request for any of the reasons set forth in Article 9.2. In such cases, Article 3.4 to Article 3.8 shall apply correspondingly.

11. Within the time ordered by the Arbitral Tribunal, the Parties may submit to the Arbitral Tribunal and to the other Parties any additional Documents on which they intend to rely or which they believe have become relevant to the case and material to its outcome as a consequence of the issues raised in Documents, Witness Statements or Expert Reports submitted or produced, or in other submissions of the Parties.

12. With respect to the form of submission or production of Documents:

(a) copies of Documents shall conform to the originals and, at the request of the Arbitral Tribunal, any original shall be presented for inspection;

(b) Documents that a Party maintains in electronic form shall be submitted or produced in the form most convenient or economical to it that is reasonably usable by the recipients, unless the Parties agree otherwise or, in the absence of such agreement, the Arbitral Tribunal decides otherwise;

(c) a Party is not obligated to produce multiple copies of Documents which are essentially identical unless the Arbitral Tribunal decides otherwise; and

(d) translations of Documents shall be submitted together with the originals and marked as translations with the original language identified.

13. Any Document submitted or produced by a Party or non-Party in the arbitration and not otherwise in the public domain shall be kept confidential by the Arbitral Tribunal and the other Parties, and shall be used only in connection with the arbitration. This requirement shall apply except and to the extent that disclosure may be required of a Party to fulfil a legal duty, protect or pursue a legal right, or enforce or challenge an award in bona fide legal proceedings before a state court or other judicial authority. The Arbitral Tribunal may issue orders to set forth the terms of this confidentiality. This requirement shall be without prejudice to all other obligations of confidentiality in the arbitration.

14. If the arbitration is organised into separate issues or phases (such as jurisdiction, preliminary determinations, liability or damages), the Arbitral Tribunal may, after consultation with the Parties, schedule the submission of Documents and Requests to Produce separately for each issue or phase.

Contents   Note

Other Rules

Art. 25(1) and 25(5) ICC; Art. 18(3), 19(2) and 24(3) Swiss Rules; Art. 20(4), 21(2) and 27(3) UNCITRAL; Art. 15(6) and 22(1)(e) LCIA; Rules 24 and 34(2)(a) ICSID; Art. 19(2-3) AAA; Art. 41(c), 42(b) and 48 WIPO.

I.   The 2010 Revision

Art. 3 primarily deals with the **production of documentary evidence** and   1
thus a core issue of the taking of evidence. Accordingly, **particular attention** was paid to this provision in the course of the review and revision of the 1999 Rules.[77]

The text of Art. 3 of the 1999 Rules was **preserved** by the 2010 Revision   2
to quite some extent,[78] but there were certain **important amendments** made. These changes are set out in detail in the commentary on the individual paragraphs of Art. 3 below.[79]

II.   Objective and Structure of Art. 3

Art. 3 provides rules as to the **submission** and the **production** (by the   3
other party)[80] of **documents**[81] that the parties wish to introduce as evidence in the arbitration.[82]

Art. 3 first contains the basic rule (and reflects the standard practice) that   4
the parties shall **submit,** to each other and to the arbitral tribunal, all documents **available** to them on which they rely (Art. 3(1)).[83] Art. 3(11) provides for a second round of submission of additional documents that have become relevant in light of earlier submissions.

Second, Art. 3 sets out the **requirements and limits** under which the   5
parties may **request** the **production** of documents and under which the arbitral tribunal may **order** document production (Art. 3(2-9)).

In addition, Art. 3 deals with certain other aspects of document submission   6
and production:

---

[77] KREINDLER, 2010 Revision, 158; O'MALLEY, Document Production, 186.
[78] In line with the overall approach taken by the 2010 Review Subcommittee, in the words of its Chair: *"It is fair to say that the work of the Subcommittee [...] resulted in a careful consideration of every single provision and every single word of the 1999 Rules, while at the same time being strictly guided and informed by the overarching maxim of: 'If it is not broken, do not fix it.'";* KREINDLER, 2010 Revision, 157.
[79] See N 70-272; Annex 1 (Art. 3).
[80] As to terminology with regard to submission and production, see below N 18-19.
[81] See below, N 9-12.
[82] IBA REVIEW SUBCOMMITTEE 2010, 6.
[83] Id., 6.

- Art. 3(10) provides that the **arbitral tribunal** may, **on its own motion** *(sua sponte)* and at any time, request the production of documents from a party or request that a document is sought from a third party.

- Art. 3(12) sets out the **form** in which documents are to be submitted or produced, in particular regarding electronic documents.

- Art. 3(13) provides for **confidentiality** in relation to documents submitted or produced.

- Art. 3(14) provides that in cases where the arbitration is organised into **separate issues or phases** (bifurcation), the submission and production of documents may be scheduled separately for each issue or phase.

7   Hence, Art. 3 primarily distinguishes between documents depending on who is in possession of a document:[84] Art. 3(1) relates to documents that are **available** to a party. In contrast, Art. 3(2–9) relate to documents that a party wishes to use as evidence but cannot introduce on its own since they are in the **control**[85] **of the other party** to the arbitration **or of a third party not participating** in the arbitration.

8   Art. 3 is drafted to generally apply the **same set of rules to all forms of documents** (whilst providing for some additional rules as to certain aspects of electronic documents).[86]

III.   What Is a "Document" Under the Rules?

9   The Rules define **"Document"** to mean *"a writing, communication, picture, drawing, program or data of any kind, whether recorded or maintained on paper or by electronic, audio, visual or any other means".*[87]

10   The **2010 Revision** amended the previous definition by adding *"communication, picture, drawing, program or data"* and *"maintained".*[88] It did, however, **not** bring a **substantive** change to the definition of "Document".[89]

11   The definition is **very broad** and includes, *inter alia,* letters, faxes, emails, deeds, instruments, contracts, minutes, notes of phone conversations, invoices, etc.

---

[84]   Id., 6.
[85]   In full language of the Rules (see Art. 3(3)(c), 3(4), 3(7)): "in the possession, custody or control", see also below, N 145–155.
[86]   See below, N 9–12 and 54.
[87]   See also above, Definitions N 2.
[88]   See also Annex 1 (Definitions).
[89]   IBA Review Subcommittee 2010, 4; Von Segesser, IBA Rules, 742.

The definition of "Document" in the 1999 Rules was already broad enough   12
to include any form of **electronic** evidence.[90] The minor amendments in
the definition contained in the 2010 Rules were intended to make even
clearer that all forms of electronic evidence fall within the scope of the
Rules.[91] In particular, the amendment to expressly include electronic data
also confirms that **metadata** (i.e. data about electronically stored data)
falls within the scope of Documents.[92]

IV. Documentary Evidence in International Arbitration in General

A. Importance of Documentary Evidence

The taking and presentation of documentary evidence is an important fea-   13
ture in any legal proceeding. Documentary evidence often plays a **major
role** compared to other means of evidence.[93] In international arbitration,
documentary evidence is generally seen as more credible and thus stronger
than other evidentiary means.[94] This view is generally shared among international arbitration practitioners – irrespective of which country they
received their legal training in. This can be illustrated, e.g., by the following
two comments:

- In the words of English practitioners: *"In international arbitrations, the
  best evidence that can be presented in relation to any issue of fact is
  almost invariably contained in the documents which came into existence
  at the time of the events giving rise to the dispute."*[95]

- Similarly, from a Swiss perspective: *"In many cases, documents may
  be considered as the most important pieces of evidence. They normally
  provide the most accurate form of 'contemporaneous evidence', i.e. they
  are able to provide a straight and objective record of what the parties
  undertook, omitted, agreed or thought before or at the time when their
  business relationship went sour."*[96]

The general preference for documentary evidence can also be explained by   14
the fact that it is usually easier, more efficient, less costly and less time-
consuming to present than evidence introduced by witnesses.[97]

---

[90]   REDFERN/HUNTER/BLACKABY/PARTASIDES, N 6.123.
[91]   IBA REVIEW SUBCOMMITTEE 2010, 4.
[92]   COHEN KLÄSENER/DOLGORUKOW, 305. As to electronic documents in particular, see also
       below, N 49–59.
[93]   O'MALLEY, Document Production, 186.
[94]   GIRSBERGER/VOSER, 734; PILS (Basel)-SCHNEIDER, Art. 184 N 15.
[95]   REDFERN/HUNTER/BLACKABY/PARTASIDES, N 6.97.
[96]   BERGER/KELLERHALS, N 1210.
[97]   REDFERN/HUNTER/BLACKABY/PARTASIDES, N 6.98.

B.   Terminology and Its Limits

15   In the context of document production, the terms **"discovery"** or **"disclosure"** are often used.

16   It has been suggested that the term "discovery" **should not be used** in connection with international arbitration and that terms such as "disclosure" or "evidence-taking" should be preferred. In the words of eminent arbitration practitioners: *"[...] it is better to avoid the use of the term 'discovery' because it is an ambiguous term. To a civil lawyer it means nothing; to a US lawyer it encompasses production of documents and depositions of potential witnesses and experts as well as inspection of the subject-matter of the dispute; to an English lawyer it refers only to production of documents."*[98]

17   Another approach recognises that the terms "discovery" and "disclosure" both refer to tribunal-ordered (or court-ordered) production of materials for use in substantiating the parties' claims in the arbitral proceedings, and that the actually relevant issue is not the terminology, but rather the **scope** of the documents that must be produced.[99]

18   Given that discovery and disclosure may mean quite different things, and since the prevailing view is that neither US-style court-litigation discovery nor English court-litigation disclosure (or similar features from other systems) should be practiced in international arbitration (at least under the Rules),[100] **this Commentary** (generally and in line with the language of the Rules) uses the term **"document production"**.

19   Similarly, this Commentary generally refers to "submitting" and "submission", respectively, where parties introduce documents voluntarily to support their case.

C.   Controversy as to Document Production Due to Differing Concepts

20   Whether, to what extent, under what conditions and requirements and how a party may request production of **documents from the other party** (in particular, **internal and potentially adverse documents**[101]), was and still is to some extent **controversial.**

---

[98]   REDFERN/HUNTER/BLACKABY/PARTASIDES, 4th ed., N 6–71.
[99]   BORN, 1878, also pointing out that disagreements over terminology in this context *"do not advance analysis materially"* and that the term "discovery" does not necessarily encompass a broader notion and range of materials than "disclosure".
[100] See in more detail below, N 29–37 and 83.
[101] In this context, one can generally distinguish between three categories of documents: (1) documents that are favourable to a party which has them in its possession; (2) documents that are unfavourable; and (3) documents that are neutral. The first and

The issue was already a main topic in the discussions of the IBA Working   21
Party 1999.[102] Consequently, in the course of the 2010 Revision, particular
attention was paid to Art. 3.[103]

The topic of document production in international arbitration has also gen-   22
erated quite some scholarly writing.[104]

The issue was lively debated and is still under discussion because the tra-   23
ditions, concepts and rules with regard to document production vary fundamentally between the **different legal systems,** in particular between
common law and civil law jurisdictions.[105]

There are important **differences between the legal traditions** in state   24
court litigation of civil law and common law jurisdictions regarding documentary evidence and the taking and presentation of such evidence.

In general, it seems fair to say that civil law countries tend to regard **docu-**   25
ments as the primary source of evidence, whilst common law countries
put more weight on **witnesses.**[106] In state courts in common law countries,
facts are mainly proved by direct oral testimony, and even documentary
evidence must in principle be introduced by a witness.[107]

Moreover, state court litigation in many common law countries usually in-   26
volves **automatic "discovery"** of documents. This means that each party
must disclose to the other party the existence of all relevant documents,
whether favourable or adverse to their case and, in particular, including
internal papers such as notes and memoranda. There is no such obligation
in civil law systems (to an extent similar to common law countries).[108]

---

the third category usually raise no peculiar difficulty as to submission or production
(whilst they may raise issues as to their authenticity and their evidentiary weight
with regard to the allegations they are submitted for), in contrast to the category of
unfavourable documents; REDFERN/HUNTER/BLACKABY/PARTASIDES, 4th ed., N 6–70.

[102] IBA WORKING PARTY 1999, 5; IBA REVIEW SUBCOMMITTEE 2010, 7.
[103] O'MALLEY, Document Production, 186.
[104] KAUFMANN-KOHLER/BÄRTSCH, 14. See, as an illustration, the publications listed above, for
       example by Ashford, O'Malley, Sachs, von Segesser, Raeschke-Kessler, and others.
[105] IBA REVIEW SUBCOMMITTEE, 7: *"The vigour with which this issue was debated demonst-*
       rated that the question of document production was the key area in which practiti-
       oners from common law countries and civil law countries differ." SACHS, 194: *"Civil*
       law practitioners generally have an allergic reaction to any attempt by their common
       law opponents to introduce pre-trial discovery proceedings or common law style
       document production in international arbitration proceedings. Any such attempt is
       immediately rejected as an inadmissible 'fishing expedition' or 'unzulässiger Aus-
       forschungsbeweis'. [...] By contrast, document discovery is seen by common law
       practitioners as an indispensable tool for determining the truth."
[106] SHENTON, 122.
[107] REDFERN/HUNTER/BLACKABY/PARTASIDES, N 6.97.
[108] KAUFMANN-KOHLER/BÄRTSCH, 14.

27   Yet, **generalisation is always risky,** and one should bear in mind that,
      whilst the distinction between common law and civil law countries as re-
      gards discovery or disclosure is obvious, there are also important differ-
      ences between countries of the same group.[109] For example, in the United
      States, discovery is much wider in its scope than in many other common
      law countries in that it is not limited to production of documents, but in-
      cludes depositions of potential fact and expert witnesses as well as inspec-
      tions of the subject-matter of the dispute.[110]

28   National legislation as to document production in state court litigation is
      developing over time. This development may bring the ancestral positions
      closer together. For example, Germany introduced legislation providing for
      document production which could be considered as broader than the IBA
      Rules, whilst England narrowed the scope of disclosure.[111]

D.   Harmonised Rules and Document Production in Arbitral Practice

29   The procedural systems differ from jurisdiction to jurisdiction, and there is
      no denying that arbitration practitioners – arbitrators and counsel alike –
      are generally influenced by their own **national procedural background,**
      in particular their legal training and experience.[112]

30   Nevertheless, international arbitration has over long years developed its
      own practice and established **harmonised "transnational" rules,** in the
      sense of a blend of different legal traditions and systems.[113]

31   This approach has become particularly manifest in the field of document
      production, where the usual practice in international arbitration today is a
      combination of the approaches taken by civil and common law jurisdic-
      tions.[114]

32   The issue of document production in international arbitration has led and
      may sometimes still lead to **heated discussions** (and even more so when
      dealt with under the term "discovery").[115] It is, however, worthwhile to note

---

[109] SHORE, 76.
[110] REDFERN/HUNTER/BLACKABY/PARTASIDES, 4th ed., N 6–71; KAUFMANN-KOHLER/BÄRTSCH, 15.
[111] SACHS, 198.
[112] HANOTIAU, Document Production, 113.
[113] The ICC Bulletin 2006 Special Supplement on Document Production in International
       Arbitration provides an overview as to document production practice in arbitration in
       different parts of the world.
[114] REDFERN/HUNTER/BLACKABY/PARTASIDES, 4th ed., N 6–74: *"The usual practice in internatio-
       nal commercial arbitration is for the parties, and for the tribunal, to follow a blend of
       common law and civil law procedures, with the latter being predominant."*
[115] See also above, N 20; SACHS, 193.

that *"the power on the part of the arbitral tribunal to require the parties to produce documentary or other materials, relevant and important to resolving the matters in dispute, is a venerable and highly important aspect of the arbitral process."*[116]

Today, it seems fair to say that document production is **standard in in-   33 ternational arbitration.**[117] It is also common knowledge that the number and scope of requests for document production in international arbitrations have increased over the years.[118] It has been suggested that the increase of document production was in part also a result of the 1999 Rules which introduced a comprehensive set of provisions on this question.[119] There is also a pattern that, as soon as one party starts to make requests for document production, the counterparty will usually do the same.[120]

Consequently, in international arbitral practice, the actual issue nowadays   34 is not whether there should be document production or not, but rather **to what extent.**

However, it is clear that *"there is **no** practice of **automatic discovery** in*   35 *international commercial arbitration."*[121] National laws or institutional rules do not grant parties to international arbitrations an automatic right to request documents to be produced by the counterparty. There is **no general obligation** on parties to disclose any or all documents that may be relevant to the dispute.[122]

Typically, arbitral tribunals will provide for document production with **rela-**   36 **tive restraint.** In particular, they will refuse to grant expansive "fishing-expedition" production requests. *"There is no tradition or practice of the wholesale (or 'warehouse') production of documents."*[123]

There are a number of reasons for the relative restraint of arbitral tribunals   37 in ordering document production. In part, this approach may stem from the legal background and traditions of the members of an arbitral tribunal.[124]

---

[116] BORN, 1876, with references.
[117] Id., 1896 *("it is fair to say that some measure of document disclosure occurs in a substantial proportion of contemporary international commercial arbitrations.");* KAUFMANN-KOHLER/BÄRTSCH, 14 *("there is hardly an arbitration nowadays without a request for document production").* The above is actually attested by the Rules themselves and the large space document production takes in the Rules.
[118] SACHS, 197: *"[...] and this independently of whether Anglo-American parties or counsel are involved in the proceedings."*
[119] HANOTIAU, Document Production, 114.
[120] SACHS, 197.
[121] REDFERN/HUNTER/BLACKABY/PARTASIDES, 4th ed., N 6–71.
[122] BORN, 1897.
[123] REDFERN/HUNTER/BLACKABY/PARTASIDES, 4th ed., N 6–71.
[124] See above, N 23–26 and 29.

In addition, arbitral tribunals will take into account that document production is normally **time-consuming and expensive,** two features that are inconsistent with the overall aspirations of arbitration. Furthermore, arbitral tribunals will take into account that most parties will have agreed to arbitration and the confidentiality that normally is connected with it in the expectation that the arbitral proceedings will not expose them to broad discovery.[125]

E.   The Arbitral Tribunal's Power to Order Document Production in General

38   All arbitration is ultimately based on the parties' agreement to arbitrate. Usually, **arbitration clauses or agreements** do not expressly deal with document production.[126] Occasionally, arbitration agreements refer to the Rules.[127] In order to avoid later discussions as to whether there should be document production or not and if there should be, to what extent, one may wish to consider providing for clear language on the issue in the arbitration agreement.[128]

39   International arbitrations are generally governed by the **national arbitration law** of the place or seat of the arbitration *(lex arbitri).*

40   Certain national arbitration laws **expressly** provide for the power of the arbitral tribunal to order document production. E.g., Sect. 7 of the United States Federal Arbitration Act and Sect. 34(2)(d) of the 1996 English Arbitration Act grant the power to order document production to the arbitral tribunal, as well as Art. 1467(3) of the French *Code de Procédure Civile.* However, most national arbitration laws are **silent** in this regard.[129]

41   The **UNCITRAL Model Law** is also silent on the issue of document production. Under the broad language of Art. 19 Model Law, however, and the broad discretion granted to the arbitral tribunal to determine the procedure, the power to order document production is generally deemed to be conferred to the arbitral tribunal.[130]

42   Since document production is seen as a **procedural** issue, the arbitral tribunal's power to order document production is governed by the rules on procedure. In accordance with the general principle of party autonomy, the procedural rules are determined by the parties' agreement. The parties

---

[125] BORN, 1907–1908.
[126] SACHS, 196.
[127] Id., 196.
[128] Cf. id., 196, 198.
[129] KAUFMANN-KOHLER/BÄRTSCH, 14; SACHS, 194.
[130] SACHS, 194; BORN, 1880–1881.

may agree on the procedure directly or indirectly by reference to a set of arbitration rules which is in practice the more frequent approach.[131]

In the absence of an agreement in this regard between the parties the **arbitrators have the power** to set the rules on procedure and therefore to determine if and under what requirements they may order document production.[132]   43

The majority of international arbitration rules provide that the arbitral tribunal has the **power to order the parties to produce documents.** In most cases, the rules state that production orders may be made on the arbitral tribunal's own motion. Some rules state that production orders may be rendered either at a party's request or on the arbitral tribunal's own motion. Certain rules contain more specific provisions, whilst others contain a more general rule pursuant to which the arbitral tribunal must establish the facts "by all appropriate means". Some rules state that the requests for document production must relate to specific documents. Normally, confidentiality issues are not addressed. Whilst most of the widely used institutional arbitration rules deal with the production of documents, they generally do not deal with the issue in great detail.[133]   44

This may be illustrated by the following **examples:**[134]   45

* Art. 25(5) ICC Rules 2012 (former Art. 20(5) ICC Rules 1998) provides that *"at any time during the proceedings, the arbitral tribunal may summon any party to provide additional evidence"*. Usually, this provision is invoked in connection with document production requests. A party has no right to the production of documents in an ICC arbitration. However, document production is not excluded either; it is for the arbitral tribunal to decide.[135]

* Pursuant to Art. 24(3) Swiss Rules, the arbitral tribunal may, at any time during the proceedings, require the parties to produce documents. The arbitral tribunal may do so at its own initiative or at the parties' request.[136]

The **arbitral tribunal's power** to order document production is well **established** today.[137]   46

---

[131] Kaufmann-Kohler/Bärtsch, 14.
[132] Id., 14.
[133] Id., 14–15; Sachs, 195; Born, 1886; O'Malley/Conway, 383.
[134] Under Art. 27(3) UNCITRAL Rules, the arbitral tribunal may require the parties to produce documents.
[135] Derains/Schwartz, 281; Sachs, 195.
[136] Nater-Bass in Commentary Swiss Rules, Art. 24 N 11.
[137] Kaufmann-Kohler/Bärtsch, 14–15.

47   Moreover, *"practice does confirm that arbitrators have no hesitation as-*
        suming the power to order document production",[138] and this regardless of
        whether such power is expressly granted by the relevant national legisla-
        tion, the parties' agreement or the applicable arbitration rules. In the ab-
        sence of an express granting of such power, arbitrators regard it as **inher-
        ent in their general authority** to determine the procedure.[139]

48   Generally, neither national arbitration laws nor institutional arbitration rules
        set out the requirements and standards for document production. Conse-
        quently, arbitral tribunals generally have **broad discretion** in this regard,
        and they decide on a case-by-case basis.[140]

F.   Production of Electronic Documents in Particular

49   Electronically stored documents, in particular emails, have become a **very
        important,** perhaps the most important, **source of information** in busi-
        ness life and hence in commercial disputes.[141] The importance of electronic
        information and data is likely to increase even more in time.

50   Consequently, discovery of electronic documents **("e-discovery")** is now-
        adays a big issue in particular in state court litigation in the United States,
        where detailed rules have been adopted.

51   It will remain for quite some time a controversial issue whether and if, to
        what extent, the production of electronically stored data and electronic
        documents (often labelled as **"e-discovery" or "e-disclosure"**[142]) should
        be permitted in international arbitration. In this context, it has been stated
        that *"if 'discovery' is a dirty word in international arbitration, 'e-discovery'
        promises to be downright obscene"*.[143] Not surprisingly, the issue of discov-
        ery or disclosure of electronic information was one of the main issues dis-
        cussed by the 1999 Working Party and the 2010 Review Subcommittee.[144]

52   A main reason for the scepticism towards e-discovery is the great concern
        that allowing e-discovery to a bigger extent would jeopardise arbitration
        as an efficient tool for dispute resolution. In particular, it would aggravate
        a growing concern that arbitration is in danger of becoming too expensive
        and taking too much time, which concern is to quite some extent based
        on the increasing volume of documents filed in arbitral proceedings. It is

---

[138] Id., 15.
[139] Id., 15.
[140] Id., 15.
[141] IBA Review Subcommittee 2010, 9.
[142] As with discovery and disclosure in general (see above, N 15–19), the terminology is
      not clear.
[143] Smit/Robinson, 105.
[144] Von Segesser, IBA Rules, 737; see also below, N 54.

generally felt that there were good reasons not to have US-style discovery in international arbitration, and that there are even **stronger reasons not to have US-style e-discovery,** since e-discovery is seen as multiplying the negative implications of traditional paper discovery.

On the other hand, obtaining access to electronic documents of the coun-   53
terparty may often seem **tempting.** A main reason for this is that experience shows that people are often less concerned with putting potentially adverse information in an email than they would on paper. The "smoking gun" is more often thought to be hiding in a sloppy email than in formal minutes of a board meeting. In addition, because of the more and more sophisticated electronic archiving and search tools, the search and production of electronic documents may in reality often be less time-consuming, more efficient and less costly than a search by traditional means.[145]

Although the issue was intensively discussed, the increase in the impor-   54
tance of electronic documents since 1999 has not resulted in radical chang es of the 2010 Rules. Rather than prescribing new rules for production of electronic documents, the 2010 Rules **maintain the basic approach** of the 1999 Rules. The 2010 Rules continue to define "documents" to include electronic documents,[146] and provide a **single set of rules to govern the production of all types of documents,** regardless whether in paper or in electronic form. However, the 2010 Rules include a few new specific provisions that are designed to address certain unique issues posed by the production of electronic documents.[147]

The **guiding principles** for the production of electronically stored evidence   55
introduced by the 2010 Rules are commented below.[148]

The 2010 **Rules** are intended to be **neutral** as to whether electronic docu-   56
ments should be produced in arbitral proceedings.[149] They simply provide a framework in case the parties agree to, or the arbitral tribunal orders, the production of electronic documents.[150] In particular, the amendments introduced by the 2010 Revision to regulate issues arising in connection with the production of electronic documents should not be misunderstood to

---

[145] HILL, 90.

[146] Above, N 12.

[147] The 2010 Revision of the Rules regarding disclosure and production of electronic documents expanded the definition of "document" to include *"data [...] maintained [...] by electronic [...] means"* and added language to the new Art. 3(3)(a)(ii) and Art. 3(12)(b) regarding the form of submission or production of electronic documents (Annex 1, Art. 3(3)(a)(ii) and Art. 3(12)(b)); SMIT, 202–205; BOUCHENAKI, 180; COHEN KLÄSENER/DOLGORUKOW, 304.

[148] See in particular N 119–123 and 244–248.

[149] IBA REVIEW SUBCOMMITTEE 2010, 9; GILL/TAWIL/KREINDLER, 29.

[150] IBA REVIEW SUBCOMMITTEE 2010, 9; GILL/TAWIL/KREINDLER, 29.

answer the question whether e-disclosure should generally be possible in an international arbitration.[151] The Rules leave flexibility to the parties and the arbitral tribunal to deal with the specific requirements of a case. In any event, the Rules clarify that there is no US-style e-discovery when they are applicable.[152] In line with their general approach, *"the Rules are concerned to ensure that if e-disclosure occurs it is done efficiently and without unnecessary cost".*[153]

57   The approach chosen[154] by the 2010 Revision is **appropriate.** The ongoing move from information that is (or rather was) predominantly on paper to information that is predominantly stored electronically requires no general or fundamental reconsideration of the principles of document production in international arbitration.[155]

58   Issuing an **entire set of new rules** for production of electronic documents as part of the 2010 Rules would have been likely to lead to unwanted and unfortunate results. In particular, new detailed rules may well have led to an increase of the production of electronic documents and hence document production in general. As mentioned above,[156] it is thought that the 1999 Rules contributed to an overall increase of document production in international arbitration practice, and the same might have happened if the 2010 Rules had been amended by detailed rules on e-disclosure. Accordingly, a well-intended "cure" may have eventually become a part of the "disease" itself. Moreover, a new set of rules as to production of electronic documents might, in effect, jeopardise the flexibility of the parties and the arbitrators to address such issues in view of the particular circumstances of the case.[157]

59   There will be **different views** on the issue among practitioners. Some will feel there is a lack of clear rules that would have been helpful. It has been suggested that the general reference to e-discovery in the 2010 Rules raises a fundamental difficulty of preparing for e-discovery in international arbitration.[158] It has been further suggested that, in light of this lack of specific guidance, the practice of United States courts might offer detailed insights into possible approaches regarding electronic evidence and that it may be possible to draw principles from the United States practice, of course limit-

---

[151] COHEN KLÄSENER/DOLGORUKOW, 304.
[152] BOUCHENAKI, 181.
[153] GILL/TAWIL/KREINDLER, 29.
[154] In line with the 2010 Review Subcommittee's overall approach; see above, fn. 78.
[155] IBA REVIEW SUBCOMMITTEE 2010, 9; SMIT, 203.
[156] N 33.
[157] Cf. also SMIT, 203.
[158] BOUCHENAKI, 181, also pointing out that a broad discretion of individual arbitrators means that decisions do not offer much predictive value and that there are only few published decisions regarding procedural and evidentiary matters.

ing the application of such principles to suit the particular nature of international arbitration.[159] It is submitted that the United States practice should be considered only with great caution and restraint. If, however, the parties to an arbitration require specific rules for a given case, detailed guidelines for production of electronically stored information in international arbitration have been suggested by some authors.[160]

G.   Statutory and Contractual Rights to Production

The IBA Rules are **procedural rules** only, not substantive rules. This follows clearly from the Foreword to the Rules and from their terms and content. The Rules govern the taking and presentation of evidence only in the framework of arbitral proceedings.[161]   60

Document production based on procedural rules, and in particular the IBA Rules, is to be clearly distinguished from the right to obtain documents from another party derived from other sources, in particular **statutory rules or contractual rights.** For example, depending on the applicable law and/or the contract, an agent or sales representative is entitled to obtain information about certain business activities, in particular to the extent that his or her remuneration depends on such figures.[162]   61

The Rules **do not limit substantive rights** to documents based on statutory rules or contractual rights. Accordingly, a party may not use the Rules to limit its statutory and/or contractual obligations to disclose certain documents.[163]   62

In practice, a party may nevertheless try to use the Rules as a **defence against contractual or statutory obligations** to disclose documents. Such attempts must fail. Form and substance of document production requests having their basis in statutory law and/or the contract are governed exclusively by, and have to be examined against, the applicable substantive rules.[164]   63

---

[159] Id., 181–182, recognising that this proposal is unlikely to win many friends, but that there is a difference between simply following an approach and drawing lessons from others, also with regard to the issues of an "arbitration hold" (similar to a "litigation hold", that is a prohibition to delete any documents pending the proceedings) and whether backup tapes are considered accessible (BOUCHENAKI, 182–185).

[160] SMIT/ROBINSON, 130–133.

[161] SCHERER, 195.

[162] Id., 195.

[163] Id., 195.

[164] SCHERER, 195, giving the example of a bank that is obliged under the applicable banking regulations and/or the contract to disclose to its customers information regarding the customer's account so that it may not object to the customer's disclosure request on the ground that the request would not comply with the Rules.

H.   General Remarks on the Provisions of Art. 3

64   It is generally held that Art. 3 constitutes a **well-balanced compromise**
      between civil and common law systems. Art. 3 is an emanation of the
      development of transnational procedural rules and of the standardisation
      of international arbitration, and reflects **best practice.** In essence, the
      standards that have emerged from international arbitration practice have
      been "codified" in the Rules.[165]

65   Yet, there is also **criticism.** It has, e.g., been suggested that the 1999
      Rules were *"a misguided combination of various aspects of different tradi-*
      tions", that it was doubtful whether the compromise was a significant ad-
      vance for arbitration, and that the Rules preferred documentary evidence
      far too strongly over evidence introduced by witnesses.[166] Moreover, it has
      been stated that the 1999 Rules led to an increase of document production
      in practice.[167] It has also been suggested that, in the first years after their
      introduction, the Rules were often not used appropriately.[168]

66   Art. 3 is **particularly useful in arbitrations involving parties from**
      civil and common law countries.[169] A civil law party may find the Rules
      helpful when seeking to limit an extensive request for document produc-
      tion by a common law party; and a common law party may be able to use
      the Rules to obtain at least some internal documents from a civil law party
      which this party would otherwise not provide.[170]

67   Art. 3 is a **core provision** of the Rules.[171] Within Art. 3, the great impor-
      tance of document production (compared to document submission) is re-
      flected in the structure of this provision: Whilst the voluntary submission of
      documents that are available to one party is basically dealt with by a single

---

[165] KAUFMANN-KOHLER/BÄRTSCH, 17–18; SACHS, 196; ELSING/TOWNSEND, 61; RAESCHKE-KESSLER,
      Production, 416, 429; MÜLLER, IBA Rules, 57; IBA REVIEW SUBCOMMITTEE 2010, 7. In
      view of the 1999 Working Party and the 2010 Review Subcommittee, the document
      production rules are *"a balanced compromise between the broader view generally*
      taken in common law countries and the more narrow view generally held in civil law
      countries". The 2010 Revision "preserves this balance" (IBA REVIEW SUBCOMMITTEE 2010,
      8).
[166] SHORE, 76, 78.
[167] HANOTIAU, Document Production, 114.
[168] Id., 114 *("It is now generally acknowledged that when the IBA Rules were first disco-*
      vered and applied by arbitral tribunals at the end of the last century, they were often
      misused").
[169] IBA REVIEW SUBCOMMITTEE 2010, 8.
[170] Id., 8.
[171] KREINDLER, 2010 Revision, 158, refers to Art. 3 as arguably being *"the mainstay of the*
      IBA Rules".

paragraph (Art. 3(1)),[172] the production of documents is dealt with by nine paragraphs (Art. 3(2–10)).

Like the Rules in general, Art. 3 may also be used (merely) as a source of **inspiration or guideline** for dealing with document production; in practice, this approach is more frequent than the adoption of the Rules.[173] Indeed, the Rules may not always present the best approach to a given case. The most adequate procedure for document production will differ from case to case, depending upon the dispute, the parties and their legal representatives.[174]

68

Irrespective of whether Art. 3 is directly applicable by reference or merely used as a source of inspiration, this should be set forth in the terms of reference or a procedural order, preferably in agreement with the parties and at the **outset of the proceedings.**[175]

69

V. Submission of Documents That Are Available to Each Party (par. 1)

Art. 3(1) provides that each party shall submit to the arbitral tribunal and to the other parties all documents **available** to it on which it **relies,** within the time ordered by the arbitral tribunal. Pursuant to Art. 3(1), the parties shall submit **public documents** and **documents in the public domain** as well, but they do not need to and should not submit documents that have already been submitted by another party.

70

The **2010 Revision** did not bring any changes to the text of Art. 3(1) with one minor exception.[176]

71

Art. 3(1) embodies the general rule that the parties shall introduce the documents available to them and which they wish to rely on as evidence.[177] This rule can be found expressly or implicitly in the major arbitration rules.[178] It is common practice in international arbitration for each party to submit to the arbitral tribunal and to the other party the documents on which it relies in support of its case.[179] This is also in line with the general principle that

72

---

[172] Art. 3(11) provides for a second round of submission of additional documents.

[173] The reason being that many arbitrators prefer to keep some flexibility when dealing with evidentiary issues; Sachs, 196.

[174] Hanotiau, Document Production, 114; Veeder, Document Production, 60.

[175] Sachs, 196.

[176] The 2010 Rules refer to "Documents" instead of "documents"; O'Malley, Document Production, 186.

[177] IBA Review Subcommittee 2010, 6.

[178] See, e.g., Art. 25(2) ICC Rules 2012 (former Art. 20(2) ICC Rules 1998), Art. 18(3) and 19(2) Swiss Rules, Art. 23(1) Model Law, Art. 15(6) LCIA Rules, Art. 20(4) and 21(2) UNCITRAL Rules.

[179] Redfern/Hunter/Blackaby/Partasides, N 6.101.

the parties have **a burden to introduce the evidence supporting their case,**[180] which principle is generally accepted both in civil and in common law countries.[181]

73   The wording of Art. 3(1) clarifies that a party is only required to submit the documents it relies on. Consequently, a party is *per se* **not required** to submit documents that are **adverse** to its case. Thus, failure to submit or disclose adverse documents (or adverse evidence in general) is – in the absence of an order of the arbitral tribunal to this extent – not an infringement of the Rules,[182] and in particular no violation of the good faith principle set out in par. 3 of the Preamble.[183]

74   It is for the arbitral tribunal to specify the **manner in which the parties shall present the documents** they submit. In general, it would be useful for the arbitral tribunal to indicate early in the proceedings how this should be done. In the interest of efficiency, the arbitral tribunal should also prevent any attempts by a party to over-complicate the arbitration by submitting an enormous amount of documents.

75   It is common practice for the parties to file all documents they regard as relevant **along with their written submissions.**[184] Art. 18(3) Swiss Rules provides, for example, that as a rule the claimant shall annex to its statement of claim all documents it deems relevant.[185]

76   There are, of course, different possibilities and practices for the presentation of documents. Apart from, or possibly also in addition to, the above mentioned practice of filing documents along with the parties' submissions, there is also a practice of preparing so-called **bundles** for the arbitral tribunal.[186]

77   The documents must be submitted **to the arbitral tribunal and to the other parties.** This ensures that the other parties are in a position to study the documents in due course and may comment on them and present their own evidence in order to defend their rights of due process and their right to be heard.

---

[180] IBA Review Subcommittee 2010, 6.
[181] Id., 6.
[182] O'Malley, Document Production, 186.
[183] Cf. also Rees, 515 (critical on the good faith duty); see also above, Preamble N 14.
[184] Berger/Kellerhals, N 1211 (recommending that the arbitral tribunal insist on compliance with a rule that any document shall be attached to the written submission first referring to it).
[185] The same rule applies as per Art. 19(2) last sentence Swiss Rules to the respondent's statement of defence.
[186] Redfern/Hunter/Blackaby/Partasides, N 6.131.

Under Art. 3(1), if a party wishes to rely on documents that are **public** or   78
in the public domain, it must also submit those documents.

There is no need to submit any documents that have **already** been **sub-**   79
mitted by another party (Art. 3(1)).

Art. 3(1) does not contain a specific time limit for the submission of docu-   80
ments (in contrast to an early draft of the Rules).[187] The Working Party of
the 1999 Rules (as well as the Review Subcommittee of the 2010 Rules)
were of the opinion that the best route to take was to provide for maximum
flexibility for the parties and the arbitral tribunal.[188] Consequently, the Rules
leave the time frames to be determined by the arbitral tribunal (**"within
the time ordered by the arbitral tribunal"**[189]), and after consulting with
the parties.[190] Time frames will generally vary depending on the complexity
and the concrete circumstances of the case, the parties' resources, etc.[191]

With regard to the submission of written pleadings, the arbitral tribunal will   81
usually set **time limits** for the submission of documents. Within the time
limit ordered by the arbitral tribunal, each party is required to submit all
documents that are available to it and on which it relies. This is to prevent
the other parties – and the arbitral tribunal – from being surprised by new
documents shortly before a hearing or even during a hearing.

Once an initial submission of documents has been completed, later sub-   82
missions in the arbitration of, e.g., witness statements or expert reports,
may make it necessary for the parties to submit **additional documents**
to rebut statements contained in these submissions.[192] Consequently, Art.
3(11) provides for a **second round** of submission of documents. It is again
for the arbitral tribunal to determine when such second round shall take
place.[193]

---

[187] IBA WORKING PARTY 1999, 4.
[188] IBA REVIEW SUBCOMMITTEE 2010, 6.
[189] Art. 3(1) contains, for the first time in the Rules, the wording "within the time ordered by the arbitral tribunal". The same wording is used throughout the Rules when a
submission is to be made or a step to be taken by the parties; IBA REVIEW SUBCOMMITTEE
2010, 6.
[190] IBA REVIEW SUBCOMMITTEE 2010, 6.
[191] Id., 7.
[192] Id., 7.
[193] Id., 7.

VI.   Production of Documents

A.   Principles Governing Document Production (par. 2–9)

83   The 1999 Working Party as well as the 2010 Review Subcommittee agreed
on and were guided by certain **principles** that resulted in Art. 3(2–9):[194]

a) **Extensive** US-style discovery or English-style disclosure is, in general, **inappropriate** in international arbitration.[195] In particular, so-
called **"fishing expeditions"** shall be **excluded** from the outset. In addition, a "general discovery procedure" was not desired. Consequently,
in international arbitration, a party is not required to submit any and all
documents and other documentary evidence, including internal documents such as internal memoranda, file notes, minutes, expert reports,
etc., regardless of whether they may be relevant and would support the
counterparty's case. Rather, requests for document production should
be carefully tailored to issues that are relevant and material to the determination of the merits of the case.[196]

b) There was a general consensus that **some level of document production** is **appropriate** in international arbitration, even among practitioners from civil law countries. It is a principle reflected in the rules of some
of the major international arbitration institutions that an arbitral tribunal
shall establish the facts of the case "by all appropriate means".[197] This
includes the competence of the arbitral tribunal to order a party to produce certain internal documents in the arbitration upon request of the
other party. This position is also based on the fact that some civil law
systems entitle state courts to order a party to produce internal documents.[198]

c) It is for the **arbitral tribunal** to **decide** whether a party must produce
internal documents against its will, and to decide on the scope of document production. Furthermore, only the arbitral tribunal has the competence to make a decision on the request if the opposing party refuses to
produce the requested documents.[199]

d) The **scope** of what is to be produced is **limited** by certain objections as
set out in Art. 9(2) and the requirements set forth in Art. 3(3). If the

---

[194] IBA Working Party 1999, 5–6; IBA Review Subcommittee 2010, 7–8; Raeschke-Kessler,
Production, 415–416; Sachs, 196.
[195] IBA Review Subcommittee 2010, 7; O'Malley, Document Production, 187.
[196] IBA Review Subcommittee 2010, 7; Sachs, 196.
[197] E.g., Art. 25(1) ICC Rules 2012 (former Art. 20(1) ICC Rules 1998).
[198] IBA Review Subcommittee 2010, 7; IBA Working Party 1999, 5–6; Sachs, 196.
[199] IBA Review Subcommittee 2010, 8; Sachs, 196.

other party does not wish to comply with the request for production, it may defend its position by raising any of the reasons for **objection.**[200]

e) If an objection is made, the arbitral tribunal may first invite the parties to consult (Art. 3(6)). If the objection is not resolved by way of such consultation, either party may request the arbitral tribunal to decide. The arbitral tribunal shall order the production if it is convinced, first, that the issues the requesting party wishes to prove are **relevant to the case and material to its outcome;** second, that none of the reasons for objection set forth in Art. 9(2) applies; and third, that the requirements of Art. 3(3) have been satisfied.[201]

The rules set out in Art. 3(2–9) are derived from these principles.[202]   84

B.   Production of Documents in the Control of the Opposing Party (par. 2–7)

1.   Introduction

Art. 3(2–7) provide for the production of documents that are in the con-   85
trol of an opposing party and set out the requirements and limits under which a party may **request** the **production** of such documents and under which the arbitral tribunal may **order** document production from **another party.**

2.   Request to Produce to the Arbitral Tribunal and to the Other Parties (par. 2)

Pursuant to Art. 3(2), a party may submit to the arbitral tribunal and to   86
the other parties a **request to produce,** within the time ordered by the arbitral tribunal.

The **2010 Revision** amended Art. 3(2) by providing that the request to   87
produce must be made to the arbitral tribunal *and* to the other parties.

This is in line with the revised definition of a request to produce. A **"Re-**   88
quest to Produce" is characterised in the Definitions section[203] to mean *"a written request by a Party that another Party produce Documents"*.[204] The amendments to the definition and to Art. 3(2) make clear that a request

---

[200] IBA Review Subcommittee 2010, 8; Sachs, 196.
[201] IBA Review Subcommittee 2010, 8.
[202] Id., 8; Sachs, 196.
[203] See above, Definitions, N 1–2.
[204] The 1999 Rules had defined the term as *"a written request by a Party for a proce-dural order by which the Arbitral Tribunal would direct another Party to produce documents";* von Segesser, IBA Rules, 742–743.

to produce may not be made *ex parte* and that a request to produce is, at the outset, **primarily a request to the other party rather than a request for an order** of the arbitral tribunal.[205] The arbitral tribunal, unless it decides otherwise, only becomes involved if there is an objection to the request and if the parties are not able to resolve the objection (Art. 3(5–7)). The 2010 Revision thus reflects general practice and the manner in which the Rules are usually applied. It would be unusual for a party to submit a request for production *ex parte*.[206] Moreover, it seems likely that an arbitral tribunal deciding on an *ex parte* production request, without hearing the other party, would violate the latter party's right to be heard and mandatory provisions of most *leges arbitri*.[207]

89   A request to produce must be made **within the time limit** set by the arbitral tribunal for such a request (Art. 3(2)).

90   It has been suggested that the parties should be free to request documents from each other at any time. However, it is important to provide time in the **procedural calendar** for the filing of a (formal) request for document production and objections to it, for the arbitral tribunal's decision and for the production of documents. *"Failure to do so will inevitably cause slippage in the calendar and may make it necessary to postpone the hearing."*[208]

91   **At what time** should (disputed) document production take place? The answer depends on the specific case: *"Neither too early nor too late, is the general answer which is necessarily subject to the specifications of a given case."*[209]

92   The general view is that disputed document production should take place **between the first and the second exchange of (full) written briefs** (i.e. after the submission of both the statement of claim and the statement of defence). This timing is seen as best practice, although it is clear that the specific circumstances of a case may require a different approach.[210]

93   There are a **number of reasons** for the above timing: At said stage of the arbitral proceedings, the parties will have exchanged their first (full) written briefs, usually along with the documents they intend to rely on

---

[205] VON SEGESSER, IBA Rules, 742–743.
[206] O'MALLEY, Document Production, 186.
[207] Id., 186.
[208] HANOTIAU, Document Production, 115–116.
[209] KAUFMANN-KOHLER/BÄRTSCH, 20.
[210] HANOTIAU, Document Production, 115. In a case where the claimant is not in a position to properly set out and substantiate its claim without having certain documents to be produced by the respondent, it may be appropriate to set the document production phase at an earlier stage of the proceedings. In any case, the arbitral tribunal should be flexible and consider the specific circumstances of a given case.

(Art. 3(1)). The parties will then also have seen what documents the other party submitted. It may well be that a party actually submits a document voluntarily so that there is no need for a production request. Or a party is confronted with the fact that the other party did not submit certain documents. Accordingly, at this stage, a party will have a better knowledge as to whether it should submit a production request. And at this stage, the arbitral tribunal will have sufficient knowledge of the case to be able to decide on the request, if necessary.[211]

This timing is also appropriate with regard to the **specificity required** in the request to produce (Art. 3(3)).[212] Requests to produce will normally be made once the issues of the arbitration have become sufficiently clear.[213] Before this stage, it will usually not make sense for a party to file such a request and for the arbitral tribunal to decide on it. Thus, normally, a request to produce cannot simply be included by the claimant in a request for arbitration pursuant to (e.g.) Art. 4(3) ICC Rules or by the respondent in a general answer to the request for arbitration in accordance with (e.g.) Art. 5(1) ICC Rules.[214]   94

Therefore, as a rule, the arbitral tribunal will not be able to make a decision on the request to produce unless and until the parties have **exchanged full factual and legal submissions in a first round** and the issues of the case are sufficiently clear.[215]   95

Thus, arbitral tribunals normally provide for document production at the **earliest time once the parties have set out their respective claims** and defences in their first full written briefs. In this manner, document production can take place on the basis of the parties' positions, but still at an early stage in the arbitral proceedings.[216]   96

There will **not always be agreement** about the appropriate timing of document production. Parties may be tempted to obtain document production soon after the arbitral proceedings have been instituted, i.e., after the request for arbitration and the answer to the request have been served.   97

---

[211] Sachs, 196–197; Hanotiau, Document Production, 115; O'Malley, Document Production, 186; O'Malley, Procedural Rules, 41.

[212] See below, N 104.

[213] IBA Review Subcommittee 2010, 10; in particular, regarding the required relevance and materiality. In fact, the level of likelihood of these requirements and the timing of production requests are connected; see also below, N 141.

[214] These documents that are necessary to institute arbitral proceedings often do not set out the issues of the dispute in detail. However, the request for arbitration may also take the form of a fully fledged brief setting out all relevant factual, legal and procedural issues in detail. In this case the claimant is in a position to include a request for production, and the arbitral tribunal has a basis to decide on it.

[215] O'Malley, Document Production, 186.

[216] Born, 1900; Hanotiau, Document Production, 115.

On the other hand, there may be parties that attempt to delay document production until shortly before the hearing.[217]

98   In any case, the precise timing of requests to produce will be **determined by the arbitral tribunal** and will depend on the specificity of the initial pleadings and the documents submitted along with them, the terms of reference or other documents that identify the issues.[218]

99   If the party filing a request does **not meet** the set **time limit** and cannot excuse this in a proper manner, the arbitral tribunal may reject the request on this formal ground.[219]

100   In the event of a request that appears to be **premature,** an arbitral tribunal may also request a party to re-submit the request at a later stage in the proceedings.[220]

101   In general, arbitral tribunals will allow the parties to make document production requests to **supplement a previous request.** However, arbitral tribunals will react warily if parties attempt to reargue issues that have already been decided by the arbitral tribunal. In principle, it may be appropriate to revert to a request that has previously been denied, in particular if the parties' legal or factual positions have changed or if an unforeseen issue is raised, e.g., in the course of witness testimony. However, arbitral tribunals will often be critical regarding such attempts.[221]

---

[217] BORN, 1899.

[218] IBA REVIEW SUBCOMMITTEE 2010, 10. See also an ICSID Award in which the Arbitral Tribunal found that *"[...] at a time when only the short Request for Arbitration Proceeding submitted by Claimant [...] and the submissions on the production request itself are available to identify the relief sought and the factual allegations and legal arguments on which Claimant intends to rely in this regard for the alleged breaches, [...] the Tribunal is not in a position to identify, within the many and broad requests submitted by Claimant, which documents must be considered relevant and material for the Tribunal to decide on the relief sought."* Award in *Noble Ventures Inc (US) v Romania* (ICSID ARB/01/11) October 2005 at 32, available at http://ita.law.uvic.ca/documents/Noble.pdf [last visited 23 September 2011]; see also O'MALLEY, Document Production, 186. Cf. regarding the stage of proceedings of a request with respect to confidentiality: *Giovanna a Beccara and Others v. The Argentine Republic*, ICSID Case No. ARB/07/5 (27 January 2010), procedural order No 3 (confidentiality order) at 81, available at http://ita.law.uvic.ca/documents/BeccaraConfidentiality-Order_000.pdf; see also O'MALLEY, Annotated Commentary, 476.

[219] See also below, N 168.

[220] HANOTIAU, Document Production, 117. See also an ICSID Award in which the Arbitral Tribunal found that *"[...] the Parties may, if they consider it necessary, submit new requests for the production of documents together with their first memorials presenting their factual allegations and legal arguments supporting their claims and counter-claims respectively [...]"*. Award in *Noble Ventures Inc (US) v Romania* (ICSID ARB/01/11) October 2005 at 33, available at http://ita.law.uvic.ca/documents/Noble.pdf [last visited 23 September 2011].

[221] BORN, 1900.

Often, the parties will present their document production requests and ob-   102
jections thereto on their own motion or upon an order by the arbitral tribunal, in the form of a table commonly referred to as a **"Redfern Schedule"**.
This schedule lists the documents requested and the objections made to the
production of such documents.[222] The schedule takes the form of a spreadsheet. In this spreadsheet, the first column sets out a list and description
of the documents requested; the second column sets out the requesting
party's justification for the request (including relevance and materiality);
the third column sets out the requested party's reasons for refusing the
request (for example, no such document exists, lack of relevance, proportionality, legal professional privilege, etc.). The fourth column is left blank,
for the tribunal to record its decision.[223]

3.   Requirements as to the Content of a Request to Produce (par. 3)

a)   2010 Revision

The **2010 Revision** expanded upon the wording of the 1999 Rules (which   103
in turn had expanded upon the wording of the 1983 Rules).[224] Art. 3(3) of
the 2010 Rules contains **two main new features:** It specifically deals with
the issue of **electronic documents,** and it provides an **exception** to the
general rule that a party may not seek a document from another party if
the document would be considered as being within its own control.[225]

b)   Overview

Art. 3(3) sets forth the requirements for a request and thus also determines   104
the general framework for document production.[226] The requirements of Art.
3(3) are generally designed to make the request **specifically describe** the
documents being sought.[227] The **degree** of specificity generally depends on
the specific case.[228]

Art. 3(3) as introduced by the 1999 Rules was a marked step from the 1983   105
Rules under which **internal documents** were effectively excluded from

---

[222] REDFERN/HUNTER/BLACKABY/PARTASIDES, N 6.113–6.114; HANOTIAU, Document Production, 116, 118; BORN, 1898.
[223] REDFERN/HUNTER/BLACKABY/PARTASIDES, N 6.115; HANOTIAU, Document Production, 116.
[224] O'MALLEY, Document Production, 186–187.
[225] Id., 187 (labelling the new wording of Art. 3(3) as "remarkable" for these two reasons).
[226] O'MALLEY, Document Production, 186.
[227] IBA REVIEW SUBCOMMITTEE 2010, 8.
[228] Cf. also HANOTIAU, Document Production, 117.

production. Similarly, production requests regarding **categories of documents** were excluded in the 1983 Rules.[229]

106   It is generally appropriate for the arbitral tribunal, when discussing document production with the parties at the first **organisational meeting,** to make clear that *"sweeping requests asking for 'all documents relating to' or 'all minutes of the board' over a long period of time will not usually satisfy the criterion of specificity"*.[230] Similarly, it generally seems advisable to raise the issue of production of documents in electronic form at the outset.

107   Pursuant to Art. 3(3), a request to produce shall contain

- a **description**

   o of each requested **document,** sufficient in detail to **identify** the document, **or**

   o of a **narrow and specific** requested **category,** sufficient in detail (including subject matter), of documents that are reasonably believed to exist; and

   o in the case of documents maintained in electronic form, the requesting party may – *sua sponte* or upon order by the arbitral tribunal – identify specific files, search terms, individuals or other means of searching in an efficient and economical manner;[231]

- a **statement**[232] as to how the requested documents are **relevant** to the case and **material** to its outcome; and

- a **statement**

   o that the requested documents are not **in the possession, custody or control** of the requesting party, or

   o of the reasons why it would be **unreasonably burdensome** for the requesting party to produce such documents, and

   o of the reasons why the requesting party assumes the requested documents to be in the possession, custody or control of **another party.**

108   The requirements set out in Art. 3(3) serve a number of **purposes.** In particular, they are designed to:

---

[229] ASHFORD, Document Discovery, 97.
[230] HANOTIAU, Document Production, 117.
[231] Art. 3(3)(a)*(i)* was added by the 2010 Revision.
[232] The 1999 Rules had referred to "a description".

- permit a party to request documents which can be identified with reasonable specificity and which can be shown to be relevant to the case and material to its outcome;[233]

- prevent a "fishing expedition" by the requesting party;[234]

- prevent unnecessary hassling of the opposing party;[235]

- avoid a burdensome and costly exercise that does not seem indispensable;[236]

- have checks on the scope of a request to produce;[237]

- put the other party in a position to decide whether it wishes to comply with the request to produce voluntarily (Art. 3(4)) or to raise objections (Art. 3(5));[238]

- enable the arbitral tribunal, if there is an objection to the request, to decide whether it shall grant or reject the request, in accordance with the standards set forth in Art. 3(7).[239]

c)   Identified Document or Narrow and Specific Category

The party requesting production of a certain **individual document** must describe this document in **sufficient detail** so that it can be **identified** (Art. 3(3)(a)*(i)*). This requirements for the description of an individual document is straightforward.[240]   109

Usually, the description will consist of **three elements:**   110

(i)   the presumed **author** and/or presumed recipient of the documents,

(ii)   the presumed **date** or presumed time frame within which the document is thought to have been established, and

(iii)   the presumed **content** of the document.[241]

---

[233] IBA Review Subcommittee 2010, 8.
[234] Id., 8; Hanotiau, Document Production, 117; Shore is sceptical whether the mechanism to constrain "fishing expeditions" will prove to be successful (Shore, 77).
[235] IBA Review Subcommittee 2010, 10.
[236] Hanotiau, Document Production, 117.
[237] IBA Review Subcommittee 2010, 9.
[238] Id., 8; Kaufmann-Kohler/Bärtsch, 18.
[239] IBA Review Subcommittee 2010, 8–9; Kaufmann-Kohler/Bärtsch, 18.
[240] IBA Review Subcommittee 2010, 9.
[241] Id., 9; Kaufmann-Kohler/Bärtsch, 18. Raeschke-Kessler provides the following example with regard to the identification of an individual document: *"English licensee A, whose license was terminated after a relatively short period of time and who considered the termination to be ineffective, suspects that his German licensor B managed to conclude a new and better licensing agreement with another English company X shortly before he terminated the existing agreement. A assumes that this was the*

111   **How precise and detailed** the description of a document needs to be
       made must also be decided with a view to allowing the arbitral tribunal and
       the counterparty to assess whether the respective document is relevant to
       the case and material to the outcome of the proceedings (Art. 3(3)(b) and
       3(7)).[242]

112   A party may also request the production of a **narrow and specific cate-
       gory of documents** (Art. 3(3)(a)*(ii)*). This basically means a group of the
       same or similar documents relating to a certain topic which the requesting
       party wishes to prove.

113   A party submitting a request for a category of documents will first (as for
       an individual document) have to indicate the presumed **author** and/or the
       presumed recipient of the documents, the presumed **date** or time frame
       within which the documents were established and the presumed **content**
       of the documents.

114   The exact meaning of **"narrow and specific"** is a matter of interpreta-
       tion, under the 2010 Rules as well as under the 1999 Rules. It has been
       suggested that "narrow and specific" should be understood *"to mean nar-
       rowly tailored, i.e. reasonably limited in time and subject matter in view of
       the nature of the claims and defences advanced in the case".*[243] Requiring
       that a request is limited in time and subject matter provides a measur-
       able frame.[244] Moreover, the above interpretation makes clear that the test
       depends on the specific issues raised in a case. A request should aim at
       the production of a document which relates to certain specific issues in the
       arbitration, not a broad description of a claim or a general contention.[245]

115   The narrow and specific requirement is a **key standard** which differenti-
       ates document production in international arbitration from the document
       production rules provided for in state court litigation both in civil law and in
       common law countries.[246]

---

*actual reason for the termination. A is therefore claiming damages from B and re-
quests a procedural order [...] which requires B to produce his new licensing agreement with X. This new contract between B and X, which A believes exists, need not
be set out in only one contractual document. It could also follow from an exchange
of letters. A should therefore request the production of either the contract between
B and X or the exchange of letters between B and X, which together constitute a
contract. A should include in his request the period of time [...] during which these
documents were most probably established."* (RAESCHKE-KESSLER, Production, 418).

[242] See below, N 129–144.

[243] O'MALLEY, Document Production, 187 (with reference to: Procedural Order No. 2
       sect. 2 (ii), *International Thunderbird Gaming Corp (US) v United Mexican States*,
       unreported 2003 NAFTA/UNCITRAL).

[244] O'MALLEY, Document Production, 187, referring to "quantifiable guidelines".

[245] O'MALLEY, Document Production, 187; O'MALLEY, Procedural Rules, 45.

[246] O'MALLEY, Document Production, 187.

The possibility to request the production of documents by category prompt-   116
ed quite some discussion among the 1999 Working Party and the 2010
Review Subcommittee.[247]

The drafters of the Rules did not want to open the door to "fishing expedi-   117
tions". Yet, it was understood that a party may be unable to specifically
identify documents although they may well be relevant and material and
should be produced. In fact, *"all members of the Working Party and of the
Subcommittee, from common law and civil law countries alike, recognised
that arbitrators would generally accept such requests if they were **carefully tailored to produce relevant and material documents"**.*[248]

This can be illustrated by the following **example:** If the termination by no-   118
tice of one party (B) of a joint venture agreement is an issue in an arbitration, the other party (A) will know that the board of directors of the party B
must have made the decision to terminate the joint venture agreement in
the course of a meeting at a date close to the date of the notice, that certain documents must have been prepared for the board's consideration of
the decision to terminate and that minutes must have been taken concerning the decision. In this case the requesting party A is unable to identify the
dates or the authors of such documents, but it is still able to identify with
some specificity the nature of the documents being sought and the general
time frame in which the documents would have been prepared. Such a request may qualify as a "narrow and specific category of documents" as set
forth in Art. 3(3)(a)*(ii)*.[249]

---

[247] IBA Review Subcommittee 2010, 9.

[248] Id., 9; Kaufmann-Kohler/Bärtsch, 18.

[249] IBA Review Subcommittee 2010, 9; Raeschke-Kessler provides an example for a category
of documents as follows: *"Parties A and B are disputing whether the defendant B
has an implied contractual obligation. This is what claimant A alleges to support his
claim. According to the applicable material law, the arbitral tribunal would no longer
be able to infer an implied obligation from the contract, if the obligation was specifically discussed during negotiations and was explicitly refused by B, as B alleges and
wishes to prove. Should B succeed in proving its allegation, A's claim will have to
be dismissed. B knows that the head of the negotiation on the side of A informed its
board about each step of the negotiations and assumes that B's own refusal of that
obligation is also part of the information passed on to the board. The board protocols of A concerning the information passed from the head of A's negotiation team
to the board about the negotiations with B are 'a narrow and specific category of
documents'. B should therefore ask the arbitral tribunal, in its request to produce, to
order A to produce those board protocols concerning negotiations with B that contain
the issue of B's obligation."* (Raeschke-Kessler, Production, 418).

d)   Specific and Narrow Category in Case of Documents
Maintained in Electronic Form

119   The 2010 Review Subcommittee recognised that documents in **electronic**
        form have become more important and that their production may be bur-
        densome.[250] Hence, it introduced means for the parties to identify more
        precisely a narrow and specific requested category of documents main-
        tained in electronic form (Art. 3(3)(a)*(ii)*).

120   A party may, either on its own initiative, or at the arbitral tribunal's re-
        quest, **additionally identify** electronic documents by file name, specified
        search terms, individuals (e.g., specific authors, addressees or custodians)
        or other means of searching for such documents in an efficient and eco-
        nomic manner.[251]

121   In principle, the requested specification, regardless of whether the produc-
        tion request is aiming at electronic documents or traditional documents
        (paper documents) is done by detailed identification of single documents or
        by referring to a narrow and specific category.[252]

122   As mentioned above, the Rules are **neutral** as to whether electronic docu-
        ments should be produced or not; they simply provide a framework in case
        the parties agree on, or the arbitral tribunal orders production of electronic
        documents. They leave flexibility to the parties and the arbitral tribunal to
        deal with the specific requirements of a case.[253]

123   **Metadata** may, in appropriate circumstances, be subject to document pro-
        duction in international arbitration. This should not be the case in the large
        majority of arbitrations. However, it may be possible that metadata regard-
        ing the author, recipient or date of creation or revision of an electronic
        document may be relevant to the outcome of a specific case which turns
        on these issues.[254]

e)   Only Documents That Exist

124   A basic condition for production is that the document(s) sought **actually
        exist(s).** This requirement is stipulated for the description of a category of
        documents in Art. 3(3)(a)*(ii)* ("reasonably believed to exist"), but it is also
        relevant for a specific document in the sense of Art. 3(3)(a)*(i)*. It is also

---

[250] See also above, N 49; IBA Review Subcommittee 2010, 9.
[251] IBA Review Subcommittee 2010, 9.
[252] Cohen Kläsener/Dolgorukow, 305; Smit, 202, 204.
[253] IBA Review Subcommittee 2010, 9; Gill/Tawil/Kreindler, 29; see also above, N 56.
[254] Smit, 203; Cohen Kläsener/Dolgorukow, 305; as to metadata, see also above, N 12 and
        below, N 246.

reflected in the statement with regard to possession, custody or control as set forth in Art. 3(3)(c).[255]

A detailed description and/or detailed statement on who has **control** over   125
a document will usually provide specific indications as to why the document sought exists or at least why the document is believed with good reason to be in existence.

Specific indications as to the existence must suffice; often a party will be   126
unable to adduce proper evidence.[256]

Since document production only extends to existing documents, it is not   127
possible to request a party to **create** a new document, e.g., to break down sales figures, etc. It may, however, be possible to obtain such information and data by way of examining witnesses.[257]

The issue as to which party has to prove whether or not a document was   128
established and the consequences of any respective lack of proof must be dealt with by the arbitral tribunal in accordance with the applicable law governing the **burden of proof.**

f)   Relevance and Materiality

Art. 3(3)(b) requires that the documents requested are **relevant to the**   129
case and material to its outcome.[258] This requirement was and is central and constitutes a standard core test.

The 1999 Rules had requested that the documents sought are "relevant   130
and material to the outcome of the case", which was amended by the **2010 Revision** to require that the document is "relevant to the case and material to its outcome".[259]

---

[255] See below, N 145–155.

[256] Cf., e.g., an unpublished order by a Swiss arbitrator (quoted in HABEGGER, 30): *"The Sole Arbitrator notes at this point that Claimant has provided virtually no evidence that the various internal documents requested exist [...]. There is no concrete indication why Claimant believes that the requested documents exist; Claimant seems to rely on the general presumption that companies do establish and keep internal documents relating to their business dealings. The lack of concrete indications as to the presumed existence of these documents would in the Sole Arbitrator's view suffice to reject the requests for internal documents. The Sole Arbitrator will nevertheless examine the admissibility of Claimant's individual requests. [...]".* The position taken by the arbitrator in this case may seem rather strict. In any case, it will depend on the circumstances of a given case how specific the indications should be; in cases where the requesting party argues that a company normally has certain documents, and where this seems to be a reasonable assumption, this should suffice.

[257] BORN, 1900.

[258] This requirement is expressly set forth in Art. 2(3)(a), Art. 3(3)(b), Art. 3(7), Art. 3(9), Art. 3(11), Art. 4(9), Art. 6(3), Art. 8(5) and also in Art. 9(2)(a).

[259] See below, N 135.

131   A party filing a request to produce must, in its request, state in detail that
       and how the documents requested are relevant to the case and material to
       its outcome (Art. 3(3)(b)). The requesting party must clarify with reason-
       able particularity what facts or allegation(s) each document or category of
       documents sought is intended to establish. It must set out why it believes
       the facts it wishes to prove based on the requested document are relevant
       to the case and material to its outcome. A document may serve to support
       the allegations of the requesting party or to reject allegations made by the
       other party. In light of this, the request to produce must set out **for what
       purpose the party needs the requested documents.** Consequently,
       the content of the requested document needs to relate to the issues in the
       case, i.e. a procedural or substantive allegation or contestation made by
       the requesting party.[260]

132   A party may link its request to the **factual allegations** in the submissions
       that were filed or to factual allegations the party intends to make in its
       further submissions.[261]

133   The **relationship between the document(s) and the issue(s)** must
       be set out in sufficient specificity in order to enable the arbitral tribunal to
       understand why the requesting party needs the document sought and to
       decide if the respective document may indeed be appropriate proof for al-
       legations of the requesting party.[262]

134   The relevant and material requirement can also be seen in connection with
       the respective language of **Art. 27(4) UNCITRAL Rules,**[263] which states
       that *"the arbitral tribunal shall determine the admissibility, relevance, ma-
       teriality and weight of the evidence offered".*

135   The 2010 Revision put an emphasis on a **two-pronged test.**[264] Under the
       1999 Rules, one could get the impression that relevance and material-
       ity were a redundant statement of the same principle.[265] Under the new
       Rules, "materiality" and "relevance" are two tests to be distinguished from
       each other. Of course, *"it remains to be seen how tribunals [will] apply this
       standard."*[266]

---

[260] IBA Review Subcommittee 2010, 9–10.
[261] Hanotiau, Document Production, 116.
[262] IBA Review Subcommittee 2010, 9–10; Hanotiau, Document Production, 116; O'Malley,
      Procedural Rules, 46.
[263] Art. 25(6) UNCITRAL Rules 1976.
[264] Von Segesser, IBA Rules, 743–744; Gill/Tawil/Kreindler, 28. See above, N 130.
[265] O'Malley, Document Production, 189. Cf. also the following construction: *"The word
      'material' is clearly an attempt to delimit the relevance from being too fanciful or re-
      mote."* (Ashford, Document Discovery, 97).
[266] Von Segesser, IBA Rules, 744.

The understanding of two separate tests had already been suggested and   136
practiced under the 1999 Rules. It also reflects general practice: *"The usual
practice is to limit document production as much as possible to those documents that are strictly relevant to the issues in dispute and necessary for
the proper resolution of those issues."*[267] In this context, it has been suggested that a **relevant** document is a document that is likely to prove a
fact from which legal conclusions are drawn.[268] A **material** document is
a document required to allow complete consideration of the legal issues
presented to the arbitral tribunal.[269] It follows that, where a party is able to
prove a fact already by other means (in particular other documents), there
is no need for production of further documents.

It is difficult to imagine a document that is material to the outcome of a   137
case, but not at the same time relevant to the dispute. In contrast, there
may well be many documents relevant to the dispute, but not material to
its outcome, for example, because the respective fact has already been
proven by other means of evidence. Accordingly, it is submitted that there
are two tests set forth by the Rules, but that one of them, namely **the materiality test, is clearly the tougher test to take.**

The required relevance and materiality are to be seen in the context of the   138
burden of proof. The party submitting a request to produce actually bears
the burden of proof and needs to prove the respective fact in order to be
successful. If this additional requirement is overlooked, *"the result is an
avalanche of needless documents".*[270] In fact, the importance of the burden of proof in determining whether or not a request should be granted is
often underestimated.[271] It is for the arbitral tribunal to determine, when a
document production request is objected to, *"whether the requesting party
actually needs the documents to discharge the burden of proof. If not, the
request should be denied."*[272] In other words: *"[...]document production
must serve the purpose of bringing to the arbitral tribunal's knowledge not
just any documents relevant and material to the outcome of the dispute,
but documentary evidence without which a party would not be able to discharge the burden of proof lying upon it."*[273]

---

[267] REDFERN/HUNTER/BLACKABY/PARTASIDES, 4th ed., N 6–71.
[268] KAUFMANN-KOHLER/BÄRTSCH, 18.
[269] Id., 18; MÜLLER, IBA Rules, 62; RAESCHKE-KESSLER, Production, 427.
[270] DERAINS, Document Production, 87.
[271] HANOTIAU, Document Production, 116.
[272] DERAINS, Document Production, 87.
[273] Id., 87.

139   Accordingly, when assessing requests, the arbitral tribunal must carefully
      check that the burden of proof is actually on the requesting party.[274] If it is
      not, the arbitral tribunal must **decline the request.**

140   If a party alleges that the counterparty **failed to prove an allegation**
      it made and requests the counterparty to produce the relevant evidence,
      this request should normally be dismissed.[275] In fact, merely reminding
      a party that it has most probably not satisfied the burden of proof with
      regard to the allegation in question will cause it to provide the requested
      documents.[276]

141   The documents the production of which is sought need only be ***prima facie***
      relevant and material. In other words, they need to appear likely to contain
      information that is material to resolving what seem to be disputed issues in
      the arbitration. At the stage document production takes place, it is not pos-
      sible to be certain that particular documents will indeed contain relevant in-
      formation or that the respective piece of information will be material: *"The
      most that can be done is make prima facie judgments of likely relevance
      and materiality".*[277]

142   The arbitral tribunal may wish **to point out** that the document production
      decisions are made on the basis of *prima facie* relevance and of the par-
      ties' submissions filed so far, but not as a final decision on the ultimate
      relevance.[278]

143   Arbitral tribunals will usually **avoid making a final decision** as to the rel-
      evance and materiality of documents too early in the proceedings. In result,
      the threshold of relevance and materiality will be lowered, on the one hand,
      in order not to prejudice the arbitral tribunal's final finding and, on the oth-
      er hand, to ensure that documentary evidence that may potentially *(prima
      facie)* be relevant and material is made available by way of production.[279]

---

[274] Id., 87.
[275] Hanotiau, Document Production, 116.
[276] Id., 116.
[277] Born, 1909; Hamilton, 69 (referring to *"prima facie* relevance" or "likelihood of rele-
      vance"); Hanotiau, Document Production, 117. The level of likelihood is connected
      with the respective stage of the proceedings, see above, N 94.
[278] Hamilton, 69; Hanotiau, Document Production, 117.
[279] Habegger, 31, quoting from an unpublished order of a Swiss arbitrator as follows: *"[…]
      the requesting party's statement as to the relevance and materiality of the document
      appears to be – at the present stage of the proceedings – a reasonable position, i.e.
      that the requested document may be relevant. Thus, the Sole Arbitrator may order
      the production of documents also taking into account the requirement of procedural
      efficiency in the sense that it may appear advantageous to have certain documents
      available at the forthcoming witness hearing instead of having them available only
      at a later stage when the relevance thereof may have been finally determined."*

An arbitral tribunal may also ask the requesting party to **amend its re-**   144
quest in order to better demonstrate the relevance and materiality.[280]

g)   Possession, Custody or Control

A party filing a request to produce must state that the documents are not in   145
its **possession, custody or control** and explain why it assumes that the
documents are in the possession, custody or control of the other party. In
other words, a requesting party must set out why it is not in a position to
produce the requested documents itself, but the other party is.

This mainly aims at preventing a party from **being unnecessarily has-**   146
sled by requests of the other party.[281] As set out in Art. 3(1), a party must
submit the documents it wishes to rely on that are available to itself.[282]

The requirement that documents to be produced are within "the posses-   147
sion, custody or control" of the requested party is also demanded by arbi
tral practice in general.[283] The emphasis is on **"control"**, and control is a
practical issue; the formula extends not only to documents in the files or
archives of a party or in those of its employees, officers or directors, but to
all documents within a party's control.[284]

Some arbitrators tend to require a requesting party to provide evidence   148
or at least **specific indications** that a requested party is in possession of
the requested documents.[285] On the other hand, an arbitral tribunal may
choose to first hear the other party's comments on its alleged possession,
custody or control of the requested documents.[286]

---

[280]   HANOTIAU, Document Production, 117.
[281]   IBA REVIEW SUBCOMMITTEE 2010, 10.
[282]   With one exception, see below, N 152–154.
[283]   BORN, 1899.
[284]   Id., 1899, also pointing out that there is substantial authority in some common law
        jurisdictions regarding the meaning of "control" in the context of disclosure which is
        generally relevant in arbitration. *"The essential point is that control is not a technical
        concept, but rather a practical one which should be liberally interpreted and applied"*
        (BORN, 1899). It has also been pointed out that "possession", "custody" or "control"
        in result *"equates to the generally understood concept of 'control'. Nevertheless it
        is clumsy wording and the more modern [...] 'control' [...] is probably a neater and
        more precise descriptor."* (ASHFORD, 98).
[285]   HABEGGER, 30; see also N 126 above as to the existence of documents.
[286]   HABEGGER, 30, quoting from an unpublished order of a Swiss arbitrator as follows: *"The
        arbitral tribunal only will order the production of documents or a category of docu-
        ments if they exist and are within the possession, power, custody or control of the
        other party. If contested, the requesting party will have to show this is likely."* HABEG-
        GER, 30–31, referring to another unpublished order in which document requests were
        granted, although the requesting party had not demonstrated the likelihood of the
        possession, since the alleged possession remained unchallenged by the requested
        party; cf. also HANOTIAU, Document Production, 117.

149   It may be difficult for the arbitral tribunal to determine the **scope** of "possession, custody or control" in a specific arbitration. Generally, the scope
      will also be determined by the arbitration agreement between the parties
      and the jurisdiction of the arbitral tribunal in general.

150   Depending on the specific case and on the applicability of the so-called "group
      concept", an arbitral tribunal may consider ordering the production of documents that are not in the direct possession of the other party, but are in
      the possession of a **company that is also a member of the group** to
      which the party belongs.[287] However, in practice, a **restrictive approach**
      will have to be taken in this regard.

151   Alternatively, the requesting party and the arbitral tribunal may refer to
      Art. 3(9) which provides a basis for **production of documents by third
      parties.**[288]

152   Art. 3(3)(c)*(i)* as introduced by the 2010 Rules provides for an **exception**
      to the general rule that a request must demonstrate documents sought not
      to be in the possession, custody or control of the requesting party.[289] This
      new rule states that, where the requesting party can show that it would be
      unreasonably burdensome for it to produce the requested documents
      itself, the arbitral tribunal may order the counterparty to produce them.

153   The 2010 Review Subcommittee recognised that it is becoming increasingly
      less likely for a particular document to have been entirely deleted from a
      party's records and that such document may continue to exist electronically,
      e.g. on back-up tapes or in other forms of electronic archives. In cases
      where the document is **no longer easily retrievable** (e.g., because it is
      no longer part of a server's active data), it may be less burdensome and
      costly for the counterparty to produce it.[290]

154   What **"unreasonably burdensome"** means will, to a great extent, depend
      on the specific facts. It may be helpful to apply the rule of proportionality,[291]
      i.e. to weigh the burden imposed on the producing party against the potential use of the documents.[292] The analysis is likely to take into account
      the costs the requesting party would have to bear if it had to retrieve the
      documents itself, and the probative value of the documents. These factors
      would have to be weighed against the costs of the non-requesting party
      if it was ordered to produce the documents. Yet, the rule is that a party

---

[287] KAUFMANN-KOHLER/BÄRTSCH 19; cf. REDFERN/HUNTER/BLACKABY/PARTASIDES, N 2.39; cf. BERGER/
      KELLERHALS, N 529.
[288] See below, N 206–219.
[289] IBA REVIEW SUBCOMMITTEE 2010, 10.
[290] Id., 10.
[291] See also below, N 186.
[292] O'MALLEY, Document Production, 188.

with access to the documents must retrieve them itself, and the exception to this rule should be an exception and therefore only apply in specific circumstances.[293]

If a party has the **copy** of a document the **original** of which is **in the pos-** 155 **session of the counterparty,** then the party in possession of the copy must usually submit this copy. However, if the requesting party alleges that the copy available to it is forged and therefore differs from the original and that the content of the original is relevant to its legal position, the respective party may ask for the production of the original (cf. Art. 3(11)).

4.   No Objection by the Other Party: Obligation to Produce (par. 4)

Art. 3(4) provides that, within the time ordered by the arbitral tribunal, the 156 party to whom the request to produce is addressed shall **produce** to the other parties and, if the arbitral tribunal so orders, to it, all the documents requested that are in its possession, custody or control as to which it makes no objection.

The **2010 Revision** brought some small, but relevant amendments com- 157 pared to the text of the 1999 Rules.

With a view to procedural economy, the new Art. 3(4) sets forth that the 158 documents the requested party wishes to produce shall be transmitted **to the arbitral tribunal only if the arbitral tribunal so ordered,** *"in light of the observation that it is often not efficient for arbitrators to review all of the documents at the stage of their production".*[294] Consequently, the default mode is that documents are to be produced to the arbitral tribunal only if it so requests.[295] That the arbitral tribunal is not involved in the initial production of documents is in line with the general approach of the revised Rules to involve the arbitral tribunal only where necessary.[296] As a consequence, the evidentiary record of the arbitral tribunal will not necessarily contain all documents that were produced.[297]

---

[293] Id., 188.
[294] IBA REVIEW SUBCOMMITTEE 2010, 10; cf. also HANOTIAU, Document Production, 116.
[295] IBA REVIEW SUBCOMMITTEE 2010, 10.
[296] O'MALLEY, Document Production, 188. The 1999 Working Party had actually assumed (or hoped) that the default requirement (under the 1999 Rules) that any documents produced shall be sent to the arbitral tribunal as well should also serve as an additional limitation on the scope of documents to be requested, because any documents automatically became a part of the record and the self-interest of the parties should cause them to limit the scope of their request as they would not wish to overburden the arbitral tribunal with documents; IBA WORKING PARTY 1999, 8; IBA REVIEW SUBCOMMITTEE 2010, 10.
[297] O'MALLEY, Document Production, 188.

159   The further amendment to the 2010 Rules, i.e. the addition of the pas-
        sage **"to the other parties"** was made in consideration of multi-party
        arbitrations. The production of documents (and evidence in general) must
        be made vis-à-vis all parties, not only to the party that actually requested
        the production. It would be difficult for an arbitral tribunal to order a party
        to produce certain documents to only one of the parties but not to all
        other parties, and any excluded party would have an argument that it was
        treated unfairly.[298] As a consequence, the 2010 Rules state that document
        production (be it voluntarily or by order of the arbitral tribunal) shall be
        made to all parties.[299]

160   A party confronted with a request to produce has to decide whether it in-
        tends to **comply** with the request and wishes to produce the respective
        documents **voluntarily** or whether it wants to **object** to the production
        request.

161   If the party confronted with a request to produce does not wish to raise an
        objection **within the time limit** set by the arbitral tribunal, it is automati-
        cally obliged to produce the requested documents (Art. 3(4)). As a conse-
        quence, the arbitral tribunal simply needs to order whether the requested
        document is to be produced to it as well or only to the requesting party.

162   Art. 3(4) is based on the principle that the parties must **actively exercise**
        their **procedural rights** in the arbitration. If a party takes no action, it is
        deemed to have **waived** its right to object.

5.   Objection to Production Request (par. 5)

163   Art. 3(5) provides that if the party to whom the production request is ad-
        dressed has an **objection** to some or all of the documents requested, it
        shall state the objection **in writing** to the arbitral tribunal and to the other
        parties, within the time ordered by the arbitral tribunal. The reasons for
        such objection shall be any of those set out in Art. 9(2) or a failure to sat-
        isfy any of the requirements of Art. 3(3).

164   The **2010 Revision** amended Art. 3(5) by introducing an obligation of the
        objecting party to address objections in writing to the other parties as well,
        whilst under the 1999 Rules the objecting party was only required to ad-
        dress the arbitral tribunal. The amendment is in line with standard practice
        since an arbitral tribunal will only in exceptional circumstances entertain

---

[298] Id., 188.
[299] Id., 188.

ex parte communications.[300] Moreover, the revised Art. 3(5) expressly provides a further basis for making an objection.[301]

If a party confronted with a production request wishes to defend against   165
the request, it must state its objections in writing to the arbitral tribunal
and to the other parties.[302] A party may oppose **entirely** to a request to
produce **or in part.**

The requested party must state its objections to the arbitral tribunal **within**   166
the time ordered by the arbitral tribunal (Art. 3(5)). If the requested
party does not meet the time limit and fails to give sufficient reason for the
delay, the arbitral tribunal does not have to consider the objections when
deciding on the request. The arbitral tribunal must, however, still examine
whether the issues the requesting party wishes to prove are relevant to the
case and material to its outcome (Art. 3(7)*(i)*).

The objections are commonly divided into so-called **procedural (or for-**   167
mal) objections and **substantive** objections. This terminology is not too
precise, since the so-called procedural objections may have a substantive
element as well.

So-called **procedural (or formal) objections** are the following: The re-   168
quested party may set out that the request to produce was brought too late
since the requesting party did not meet the time limit set by the arbitral
tribunal (Art. 3(2)). Or the other party may allege that the requesting party
did not fulfil any of the requirements for the request as set out under Art.
3(3).[303] The revised wording of Art. 3(5) (and Art. 3(7)) expressly provides
for such objections.[304]

The so-called **substantive objections** are those set forth in Art. 9(2).[305]   169

The list as set out in Art. 9(2) is **not exclusive.**   170

---

[300] Id., 188.

[301] See below, N 168.

[302] IBA Review Subcommittee 2010, 10.

[303] IBA Review Subcommittee 2010, 10. It was already common practice under the 1999
Rules for parties to object to requests as being overly broad when the request did
not meet the narrow and specific category requirements. See also the Procedural
Orders 3 and 5 in a NAFTA/UNCITRAL Arbitration where the arbitral tribunal ruled
that *"[...] Claimants' 'Document Request' [was] not in conformity with Article 3 of
the IBA Rules, and the Request to Produce [was] declined."* Grand River Enterprises
v United States (Procedural Orders 3 and 5), unreported 2007 NAFTA/UNCITRAL,
available at http://www.state.gov/documents/organization/85416.pdf [last visited
23 September 2011]; see also O'Malley, Document Production, 188.

[304] O'Malley, Document Production, 188.

[305] See below, Art. 9 N 18–49.

171   A possibly relevant objection is that the **document does not exist.** Obviously, a document which has never been in existence cannot be produced. Art. 3(3) as well as Art. 9(2) presuppose that a requested document existed at some time. A party only can and only has to produce those documents that are in its possession, custody or control, but it cannot produce a non-existing document, even if it does not raise objections to a request to produce such document.[306]

6.   Invitation to Consult (par. 6)

172   Art. 3(6) provides that the arbitral tribunal, upon receipt of any objection (as per Art. 3(5)), may invite the relevant parties to **consult with each other** with a view to resolving the objection themselves.

173   This provision was introduced by the **2010 Revision.**[307] The text is completely **new.** It is in line with the general principle that the evidence-taking procedure should be conducted as efficiently as possible. Party-to-party consultation may in some cases be the more effective way of resolving objections, including those based on insufficient descriptions and other deficiencies in the form of the request.[308]

174   An invitation of the arbitral tribunal to discuss disputes over evidence imposes some burden on the parties to try to act reasonably and resolve the issue, and it may well resolve the issue, so that the arbitral tribunal does not need to decide upon the request. Accordingly, Art. 3(6) is seen as a **welcome innovation** to the Rules.[309]

175   Particularly in large and complex cases, where there are often extensive production requests by both sides and usually each party will dispute the other party's requests, a meeting between the arbitral tribunal and the parties' counsel, aiming at finding a compromise, may be **an efficient way forward.** This process may involve meetings between the parties' counsel, with the encouragement of the arbitral tribunal, in order to attempt to limit the scope of the production requests. *"Experience shows that a day spent in this manner by the tribunal and the parties often cuts through what can*

---

[306] RAESCHKE-KESSLER, Production, 422; as to non-existing documents see also above, N 124–128. In order to make the issue clear, and in order to avoid possible negative consequences or negative inferences pursuant to Art. 9(5), the party should set out within the time limit as ordered by the arbitral tribunal for objections that the respective document never existed. A document that never existed does not come within the scope of Art. 9(2)(d) which only relates to documents that existed but were lost or destroyed (see also Art. 9 N 41–42).

[307] IBA REVIEW SUBCOMMITTEE 2010, 10.

[308] Id., 10.

[309] O'MALLEY, Document Production, 189.

otherwise be a lengthy document production phase that has the potential
to delay the overall procedural schedule [...]".[310]

The arbitral tribunal may invite the parties to consult, or it may deem such   176
consultation **unnecessary.**[311]

7.   Decision and Order by the Arbitral Tribunal (par. 7)

Art. 3(7) provides that either party may request the arbitral tribunal to   177
rule on the objection, and that the arbitral tribunal shall consider the request to produce and the objection, in consultation with the parties, and
in timely fashion. Furthermore, Art. 3(7) provides that the arbitral tribunal
may **order** the party to whom such request is addressed to **produce** any
requested documents in its possession, custody or control[312] as to which
the arbitral tribunal determines that

* the issues the requesting party wishes to prove are relevant to the case
  and material to its outcome,[313] and

* none of the reasons for objection set forth in Art. 9(2) applies, and

* the requirements of Art. 3(3)[314] have been satisfied.

Any such document shall then be **produced to the other parties and to**   178
the arbitral tribunal if it so orders.

The **2010 Revision** added the third requirement set forth in Art. 3(7), i.e.   179
that the requirements of Art. 3(3) have been satisfied.[315] Moreover, the first
sentence of Art. 3(7) was added.

If the other party produces the requested documents **voluntarily** without   180
raising any objections to the request to produce, there is no need for a
particular decision by the arbitral tribunal (Art. 3(4)). The (newly added)
first sentence of Art. 3(7) clarifies that the arbitral tribunal is only required
to involve itself in the adverse document production procedure where an
objection has been made which the parties cannot resolve themselves.

---

[310] REDFERN/HUNTER/BLACKABY/PARTASIDES, N 6.112.
[311] IBA REVIEW SUBCOMMITTEE 2010, 10.
[312] See also above, N 145–155.
[313] See also above, N 129–144. See as an example regarding an objection asserting that
a particular request is not material or relevant to the case: *William Ralph Clayton
v. Government of Canada*, PCA Case No. 2009-04 (25 November 2009), Procedural
Order No. 8, available at http://www.pca-cpa.org/upload/files/Bilcon-Procedural-
OrderNo8.pdf [last visited 23 September 2011]; see also O'MALLEY, Annotated Commentary, 472.
[314] See also above, N 103–155.
[315] IBA REVIEW SUBCOMMITTEE 2010, 10.

181   If the other party raises (procedural or substantive) objections to the re-
      quest to produce,[316] and the arbitral tribunal deems consultation as set
      forth in Art. 3(6) unnecessary or if such consultation takes place but some
      objections remain, the arbitral tribunal **must decide** on the request and on
      the objection against it.[317]

182   Art. 3(7) expressly provides that the arbitral tribunal shall consider the
      request to produce and the objection **in consultation with the parties.**
      Accordingly, the arbitral tribunal will give both parties the opportunity to
      comment and state their positions. The arbitral tribunal may hold a hearing
      to deal with these issues, but this is not often the case.[318] If both parties
      expressly ask for a hearing, the arbitral tribunal will usually hold such hear-
      ing, but it may also deal with the issues by way of written statements. In
      any case, the arbitral tribunal must respect the rights of the parties as to
      fair and equal treatment and due process.

183   The decision shall take the form of a **procedural order,** by which the arbi-
      tral tribunal either denies or grants the request, in whole or in part.

184   If the arbitral tribunal grants the request, entirely or partially, it shall order
      the party to whom such request is addressed **to produce** the respective
      documents to the other parties and possibly to the arbitral tribunal itself.

185   To render such an order, the arbitral tribunal must *ex officio* be convinced
      that the issues the requesting party wishes to prove are **relevant to the
      case and material to its outcome,** that **none of the reasons for ob-
      jection** set forth in Art. 9(2) applies and that the requirements of Art. 3(3)
      have been satisfied (Art. 3(7)).[319]

186   It has been suggested that the arbitral tribunal should also take **other as-
      pects** into consideration when making its decision on document production,
      in particular:

      •   The parties' **backgrounds,** their legal cultures and their reasonable
          expectations; this may well include the same aspects with regard to the
          parties' counsel.[320]

      •   The principle of **proportionality,** balancing the potential use of the
          document(s) to be produced against the burden imposed on the pro-
          ducing party.[321] *"[...] most arbitral tribunals apply the principle of 'pro-*

---

[316] See above, N 163–171.
[317] IBA Review Subcommittee 2010, 10.
[318] Born, 1899.
[319] IBA Review Subcommittee 2010, 10.
[320] Kaufmann-Kohler/Bärtsch, 20.
[321] Id., 20.

portionality' – that is, they will limit the scope (and thus the expense) of document production to an extent that is reasonable in the context of the amount in dispute and the relative significance of the issues in respect of which document production has been requested."[322] In other words, the burden on the requested party, i.e. the efforts required of the requested party in gathering the documents, should be in proportion to the evidentiary value of the documents.[323]

- **Efficiency** of the arbitration process. Document production may often increase the duration of the arbitral proceedings and costs, which disadvantages must be balanced against the potential benefit of document production.[324]

A procedural order issued by an arbitral tribunal regarding a request to produce does not qualify as an interim or partial award. Consequently, the arbitral tribunal does not need to state the reasons for its decision in writing. However, in light of par. 3 of the Preamble, issuing a procedural order is a good way to inform the parties of the issues the arbitral tribunal regards as relevant and material. In practice, the order will provide **summary explanations** for the arbitral tribunal's rulings.[325]   187

In most jurisdictions, it will not be possible to bring an **appeal** against a procedural order before a state court.[326]   188

In general, an arbitral tribunal will not have the power to impose **coercive sanctions** (e.g. penalties, monetary fines), in contrast to a state court.[327] There may be the possibility to impose a so-called *astreinte*.[328] It is possible, but rare that an arbitral tribunal seeks judicial enforcement of its production orders in national courts.[329]   189

---

[322] REDFERN/HUNTER/BLACKABY/PARTASIDES, 4th ed., N 6–71.
[323] HAMILTON, 73; HANOTIAU, Document Production, 117.
[324] KAUFMANN-KOHLER/BÄRTSCH, 20.
[325] BORN, 1898–1899; see also above, N 102, regarding a so-called Redfern Schedule.
[326] RAESCHKE-KESSLER, Production, 424.
[327] BORN, 1918, pointing out that there is no power of arbitrators to impose coercive sanctions in virtually all jurisdictions, with few exceptions, in particular Belgium.
[328] An *astreinte* is a monetary penalty (or punitive fine), ordered by a court in case the addressee does not comply with an order, usually in the form of an order to pay a certain amount for each day of non-compliance. In France – where the *astreinte* was developed – the prevailing view is that an arbitral tribunal is entitled to impose an *astreinte*, and it has been suggested that an arbitral tribunal having its seat in Switzerland should, in general, be entitled to do so as well (BOOG, 139, 144 and 158; but the position is disputed, BERGER/KELLERHALS, 1156 and 1215). See also Art. 9 N 54 below.
[329] BORN, 1918.

C.   Review of the Document by a Neutral Expert (par. 8)

190   Art. 3(8) provides that in exceptional circumstances, if the propriety of an objection can be determined only by review of the document, the arbitral tribunal may determine it should not review the document itself. In this case, the arbitral tribunal may, after consultation with the parties, appoint an independent and impartial **expert,** bound to confidentiality, to review any such document and to report on the objection. To the extent the objection is upheld by the arbitral tribunal, the expert shall not disclose to the arbitral tribunal and to the other parties the contents of the document reviewed.

191   The **2010 Revision** did not bring any material changes to Art. 3(8) (which corresponds to Art. 3(7) of the 1999 Rules).[330]

192   A request to produce should not open the door for the requesting party to gain access to commercial or other secrets of the other party. Similarly, document production should not impair privilege. Consequently, commercial or technical **confidentiality** or special political or institutional **sensitivity** or **privilege** are listed as **objections** in Art. 9(2)(e), 9(2)(f) and 9(2)(b).[331]

193   Normally, the arbitral tribunal will not be in a position to decide whether an objection based on these grounds is valid unless and until it has had an opportunity to **review** the requested documents. Consequently, the arbitral tribunal would, as a standard procedure, first order the other party to produce the document to it but not to the requesting party in order to decide on the objection(s) raised.

194   However, this approach may **not always seem appropriate.** In particular, the arbitral tribunal may not wish to review the document itself, because it is concerned that it could not eliminate its knowledge of the document once it has reviewed it and has upheld the objection. In addition, there may also be concerns with regard to the other party's interests as to confidentiality and secrecy. Some cases may even involve a risk (or at least raise fear on

---

[330] The 2010 Revision refers to "Document" instead of "document", and changed the position of "only" in the first sentence (the 1999 Rules read: "[...] can only be determined by review [...]").

[331] See also below, Art. 9 N 43–47 and N 19–35. See Award at 5(14), *Piero Foresti v Republic of South Africa* (ICSID Case ARB(AF)/07/1), unreported 3 August 2010, available at http://ita.law.uvic.ca/documents/PieroForesti_v_SouthAfrica_Award.pdf [last visited 24 September 2011], where a neutral third party recommended by the arbitral tribunal and agreed upon by the parties acted as an independent expert; see also O'MALLEY, Document Production, 190.

the part of the requested party) that information is passed on from within the arbitral tribunal to the requesting party or to third parties.[332]

In this situation, the arbitral tribunal may appoint **an expert** in the sense of Art. 3(8).   195

Art. 3(8) provides for an **exception** from the standard procedure[333] by allowing the arbitral tribunal to appoint an **expert to assess the objection.**   196

An arbitral tribunal could also consider appointing the **secretary** to the arbitral tribunal to review the document. Another possibility is that the **chairperson** reviews the respective document *in camera*. However, these approaches may not be considered by all arbitral tribunals or all parties as appropriate, and they indeed do not seem to solve the concerns set out above.[334] In any case, if such option is chosen, the parties should be requested to declare that they will not subsequently challenge the arbitral tribunal or the award because of such procedure.[335]   197

There may be cases where, in principle, it would seem preferable to opt for an expert in the sense of Art. 3(8), but the **circumstances** do not allow for this route, in particular where time and cost factors are considered to leave no room. In this case, the arbitral tribunal may nonetheless decide to review the document itself.[336]   198

The expert must be **independent, impartial** and bound to **confidentiality.**   199

The expert does not necessarily need to be **appointed** in accordance with the terms set out in Art. 6.[337]   200

Art. 3(8) does not set out the **procedure** the expert must follow when performing his or her function. It is expressly stated that the arbitral tribunal shall consult with the parties before it appoints the expert. In practice, arbitral tribunals will invite the parties to comment on the selection of the   201

---

[332] IBA REVIEW SUBCOMMITTEE 2010, 10–11; RAESCHKE-KESSLER, Production, 423.

[333] Above, N 193.

[334] N 194; see as an example for the appointment of the secretary to the tribunal as independent expert: Procedural Order 6 at par. 1, *Dr Horst Reineccius v Bank of International Settlements,* unreported 11 June 2002, Tribunal Regarding the Bank for International Settlements, available at http://www.pca-cpa.org/upload/files/ProceduralOrderNo6.pdf [last visited 24 September 2011]; see also O'MALLEY, Document Production, 190.

[335] SACHS, 197.

[336] IBA REVIEW SUBCOMMITTEE 2010, 11.

[337] Id., 11.

expert and how he or she should perform his or her function, and will issue terms of reference to the expert.[338]

202 The expert must assess **whether the objection is valid or not.** The expert may not pass on the respective document(s) to the arbitral tribunal or to the other parties until he or she has concluded his or her assessment. It is not for the expert to decide him- or herself. The expert's function is to assess and to provide a **report on his or her findings.**[339] This report will include considerations and recommendations, but without revealing the contents of the document(s) in question.[340] It is for the arbitral tribunal to make a decision on the validity of the objection.[341]

203 If the expert regards the objection as **valid,** he or she will inform the arbitral tribunal which shall then decide in a procedural order whether it will uphold the objection and decline the production request on the basis of the expert's finding or not. If the expert considers the objection to **be invalid,** he or she will pass on the document to the arbitral tribunal which must then decide on the request to produce and the objections raised, in accordance with Art. 3(7).

204 If the objection is **upheld** by the arbitral tribunal, the document must be returned by the expert to the producing party and it will not become a part of the arbitral proceedings.[342] If the objection is **dismissed** by the arbitral tribunal, the requested party must produce the document to the arbitral tribunal and to the other parties.[343] In either case, the expert must respect the confidentiality of the documents he or she has reviewed.[344]

---

[338] As an example for the appointment of an independent expert with particular linguistic capacities after consultation of the parties: Order No. 3 at par. 2, *Guyana v Suriname,* unreported 12 October 2005 PCA, available at http://server.nijmedia.nl/pca-cpa.org/ upload/files/Order%203%20121005%20Fin.pdf [last visited 24 September 2011] and Order 1 at par. 4, *Guyana v Suriname*, unreported 18 July 2005 PCA, available at http://server.nijmedia.nl/pca-cpa.org/upload/files/Order%201%20fin%20rev.pdf [last visited 24 September 2011]; see also O'MALLEY, Document Production, 190.

[339] IBA REVIEW SUBCOMMITTEE 2010, 11; see as an example Order 4 at par. 3, *Guyana v Suriname*, unreported 12 October 2005 PCA, available at http://server.nijmedia.nl/ pca-cpa.org/upload/files/Order%204%20121005%20Fin.pdf [last visited 24 September 2011], where the Arbitral Tribunal ordered that *"the independent expert shall endeavour to report on his findings as soon as possible";* see also O'MALLEY, Document Production, 190.

[340] See Order 5 at par. 1, *Guyana v Suriname,* unreported 16 February 2006 PCA, available at http://server.nijmedia.nl/pca-cpa.org/upload/files/Order%205%20final.pdf [last visited 24 September 2011], where the Arbitral Tribunal adopted the recommendations of the independent expert; see also O'MALLEY, Document Production, 190.

[341] IBA REVIEW SUBCOMMITTEE 2010, 11.

[342] Id., 11.

[343] Id., 11.

[344] Id., 11.

The expert may also find that the objections are valid with regard to certain   205
parts of the requested document but not to the document as a whole. In this case, the expert must render the respective part of the document illegible before he or she passes the document on to the arbitral tribunal. The final decision will again be for the arbitral tribunal to take.

D.   Request to Produce Against a Third Party (par. 9)

Art. 3(9) provides that if a party wishes to obtain the production of docu-   206
ments from a person or organization which is not a party to the arbitration and from which the party cannot obtain the documents on its own, the party may, within the time ordered by the arbitral tribunal, ask the arbitral tribunal to **take whatever steps are legally available** to obtain the requested documents or seek leave from the arbitral tribunal to take such steps itself. The party shall submit such request to the arbitral tribunal and to the other parties in writing, and the request shall contain the particulars set forth in Art. 3(3). The arbitral tribunal shall decide on the request and shall take, authorize the requesting party to take, or order any other party to take such steps as the arbitral tribunal considers appropriate, if the arbitral tribunal determines that the requirements are met. These requirements are, in essence, the same as for a request to produce against a party to the arbitration, i.e. the requested document must be relevant to the case and material to its outcome, the requirements of Art. 3(3), as applicable, have to be satisfied and none of the reasons for objection set forth in Art. 9(2) apply.

The **2010 Revision** introduced the possibility for a party to seek leave of   207
the arbitral tribunal to take its own steps to obtain the document(s) from a third party. In addition, the last sentence of the revised Art. 3(9) directly refers to the general standards for document production (Art. 3(3) and 9(2)). This amendment provides for consistent application of the criteria set out in Art. 3(3) and the grounds for objection in Art. 9(2) also with regard to production from a non-party to the arbitration.[345] Art. 3(9) replaces the former Art. 3(8) of the 1999 Rules.

A party submitting a request under Art. 3(9) is required to meet the re-   208
quirements as set forth for a **request to produce** under Art. 3(3).[346]

---

[345] See as an example regarding the authenticity of an audio tape: *EDF (Services) Ltd v. Romania*, ICSID Case No. ARB/05/13 (29 August 2008), procedural order No. 3, available at http://ita.law.uvic.ca/documents/EDFPO3.pdf [last visited 24 September 2011]; see also O'Malley, Annotated Commentary, 472; O'Malley, Document Production, 191.

[346] As to these requirements, see above, N 103–155.

209   As a matter of principle, an **arbitral tribunal** does **not have the compe-
      tence** to decide on issues relating to a **third party that is not a party
      to the arbitration** since the arbitral tribunal's competence is based on
      the arbitration agreement. If the requesting party requests the production
      of documents that are in the control of a third party and if this party does
      not produce these documents voluntarily, the arbitral tribunal is not in a
      position to issue a procedural order against the third party since it does not
      have any corresponding jurisdiction.

210   In this situation, the arbitral tribunal may take the steps available in ac-
      cordance with the legal system under which it operates and ask the compe-
      tent **state court(s)** for **assistance** in taking evidence. Art. 3(9) provides
      for limited power of the arbitral tribunal; it merely requests the arbitral
      tribunal to consider the legal options that are available.[347]

211   The decisive question in this context is thus whether the relevant *lex arbi-
      tri* provides for a state court to assist an arbitral tribunal in obtaining docu-
      ment production from a party that is not a party to the arbitration.[348]

212   Certain national arbitration laws allow the parties and the arbitral tribunal
      to **request assistance** in taking evidence from a third party by a compe-
      tent state court, e.g. Art. 27 Model Law, Art. 184(2) PILS, Art. 34(2) and
      43 English Arbitration Act 1996.[349]

213   The respective state court will only grant such assistance if and to the ex-
      tent available under its **own procedural rules.**[350] If, therefore, document
      production is not available under the respective law, the state court will not
      issue such an order against a third party.

214   The court called to assist may in turn itself request **legal assistance from
      other courts** (in particular under the Hague Convention on the Taking of
      Evidence in Civil and Commercial Matters).[351]

215   As set out above, the revised Art. 3(9) provides that a party may also **seek
      leave** from the arbitral tribunal to take steps to obtain assistance of a

---

[347] O'MALLEY, Document Production, 191.
[348] Id., 191. Accordingly, a party may consider whether the seat of the arbitration should
      be in a jurisdiction in which state courts enforce document production orders of an
      arbitral tribunal; BORN, 1923.
[349] IBA REVIEW SUBCOMMITTEE 2010, 11; GIRSBERGER/VOSER, 740. In England, a party may
      apply to a court to compel the attendance of a witness and to bring with him or
      her any material documents in his or her possession; in the United States, under
      the Federal Arbitration Act, the arbitral tribunal may summon a person to attend
      before it and to produce any material documents, REDFERN/HUNTER/BLACKABY/PARTASIDES,
      N 6.127; O'MALLEY/CONWAY, 375–377. As to Art. 184(2) PILS, see PILS (Basel)-SCHNEI-
      DER, Art. 184 N 55–64.
[350] PILS (Basel)-SCHNEIDER, Art. 184 N 61.
[351] Id., Art. 184 N 63.

state court, as the arbitral tribunal considers appropriate. This reflects that national laws may empower local courts to order document production in support of arbitral proceedings, and any such application may be assisted by, or may even be conditional upon, the party obtaining permission from the arbitral tribunal.[352]

The new possibility for the parties to seek leave could be interpreted as **restricting** a party's right to take action, because the party is required to first seek leave of the arbitral tribunal before attempting to obtain court assistance in document production. However, Art. 3(9) does **not** expressly **prohibit** parties from involving a local court without first seeking leave from the arbitral tribunal.[353] Given the generally rather detailed language of the Rules, it seems fair to assume that the drafters had no intention to limit the parties' options, but rather wanted to provide for a further option.   216

Pursuant to Art. 3(9), the arbitral tribunal may only ask for assistance by the state courts if it determines that the documents would be **relevant** to the case and **material** to its outcome (Art. 3(9))[354]. This is in line with Art. 4(9) (as amended by the 2010 Revision) regarding a witness who is not willing to appear voluntarily at the request of a party.[355] Moreover, the arbitral tribunal must have come to the conclusion that the requirements of Art. 3(3), as applicable, have been satisfied.   217

In deciding upon the request, the arbitral tribunal will also take into account whether any of the **reasons for objections** set forth in Art. 9(2) apply.[356]   218

In practice, an arbitral tribunal will generally take Art. 3(9) as a **measure of last resort** only and will consider a request for assistance in involving a local state court only when it is convinced that there is indeed a need for the respective document production[357] and that it is likely that the respective state court will take action.   219

E.   Request to Produce by Arbitral Tribunal (par. 10)

Art. 3(10) provides that the **arbitral tribunal,** at any time before the arbitration is concluded, **may request** any party to produce documents, request any party to use its best efforts to take, or itself take, any steps   220

---

[352] GILL/TAWIL/KREINDLER, 30.
[353] O'MALLEY, Document Production, 192.
[354] As to relevance and materiality, see above, N 129–144.
[355] GILL/TAWIL/KREINDLER, 30. See below, Art. 4 N 80.
[356] Id., 30; as to Art. 9(2) see below, Art. 9 N 18–48.
[357] Final award, Pt II, Ch. H, par. 25, *Methanex Corp v United States of America*, unreported 3 August 2005 NAFTA/UNCITRAL, available at http://ita.law.uvic.ca/documents/MethanexFinalAward.pdf [last visited 24 September 2011]; see also O'MALLEY, Document Production, 191–192.

that it considers appropriate to obtain documents from any person or organisation. A party to whom such request is addressed may object for any of the reasons set forth in Art. 9(2). In these cases, Art. 3(4–8) shall apply correspondingly.

221   Art. 3(9) of the 1999 Rules had only entitled the arbitral tribunal to request a *party* to produce documents on its own motion. The **revised** rule (in Art. 3(10)) authorizes an arbitral tribunal to take legal steps itself or to request a party to take legal steps to obtain documents from a non-party.

222   It is generally accepted that the arbitral tribunal may on its own initiative request a party to produce documents, unless the parties have agreed otherwise.[358] The arbitral tribunal is **required** under certain arbitral rules **to establish the facts** of the case by all appropriate means,[359] which is also understood to mean that the arbitral tribunal is entitled, on its own initiative, to order a party to produce documents that have not yet been introduced as evidence.[360]

223   This power is to be seen in connection with and subject to the general rules as to what party bears the **burden of allegation and proof.** In general, the Rules do not amend the general rules in this regard, but simply provide a framework for the taking of evidence.

224   The arbitral tribunal may order document production on its own initiative only if it considers the respective document(s) to be **relevant** to the case and **material** to its outcome. The arbitral tribunal must give an opportunity to the requested party to raise **objections** against the request to produce by the arbitral tribunal. The requested party may raise the same substantive objections that are available against a request issued by one party against the other.[361] If the requested party raises such objections, the arbitral tribunal must decide on them, based on the same considerations as set out above.[362] The arbitral tribunal may order the production of the requested document by way of a procedural order only if it does not consider the objections of the party to be valid.

225   If the requested party fails to comply with the respective procedural order, the arbitral tribunal may draw **adverse inferences** pursuant to Art. 9(5).[363]

---

[358]   BERGER/KELLERHALS, N 1214.
[359]   IBA REVIEW SUBCOMMITTEE 2010, 11; see e.g., Art. 25(1) and (5) ICC Rules 2012 (former Art. 20(1) and (5) ICC Rules 1998).
[360]   IBA REVIEW SUBCOMMITTEE 2010, 11.
[361]   Id., 11.
[362]   N 163–171; IBA REVIEW SUBCOMMITTEE 2010, 11.
[363]   See below, Art. 9 N 54–69.

Arbitral tribunals are often empowered under the relevant civil procedure   226
laws to ask local state courts for **assistance** in the taking of evidence on
their own motion. Such assistance may, however, not always extend to
document production.[364]

Apart from ordering a party to produce, the arbitral tribunal may also re-   227
quest a party to use its **best efforts** to obtain documents (Art. 3(10)*(ii)*);
this may include involving a local state court's assistance.

However, *"ultimate oversight and control over this process should remain*   228
with the arbitral tribunal".[365] Yet, depending on the circumstances, a party
may be **better positioned** to take such steps, e.g. because it is based in
the country in question.[366]

A possible interpretation of Art. 3(10)*(ii)* is that an arbitral tribunal may re-   229
quest a party to obtain documents that are **in the possession of related**
entities. Arbitral tribunals have held that a party may be expected to produce documents held by entities they have a significant relationship with.
Under what circumstances this should be the case, and what "relationship"
actually means is for the arbitral tribunal to decide in the specific case. It
has been suggested that this would encompass an affiliation through which
a party could reasonably be expected to exert or have influence over another entity. Consequently, a party alleging that a document is outside of
its direct control since it is in the possession of a parent or sister company
may be requested to undertake best efforts to obtain and produce the
document under Art. 3(10).[367]

VII. Additional Documents – Second Round of Document Submission (par. 11)

Art. 3(11) provides that, within the time ordered by the arbitral tribunal,   230
the parties may submit to the arbitral tribunal and to the other parties
any **additional documents** which they intend to rely on and which they
believe have become relevant to the case and material to its outcome as a

---

[364] Kaufmann-Kohler/Bärtsch 21; cf. Berger/Kellerhals, N 1111; Redfern/Hunter/Blackaby/
Partasides, N 7.40–7.45.

[365] IBA Review Subcommittee 2010, 11.

[366] Id., 11.

[367] *"[T]he Tribunal wishes to clarify that, for a party to claim that documents are not in*
its control, it must have made 'best efforts' to obtain documents that are in the pos-
session of persons or entities with whom or which the party has a relevant relation-
ship." Procedural Order 8(1), *William Ralph Clayton v Government of Canada* (PCA
Case 2009-04), unreported 25 November 2009, available at http://www.pca-cpa.
org/upload/files/Bilcon-ProceduralOrderNo8.pdf [last visited 23 September 2011];
see also O'Malley, Document Production, 193.

consequence of the issues raised in documents, witness statements or expert reports submitted or produced, or in other submissions of the parties.

231   Under the **revised** language, a party may submit additional documents (also) if it merely intends to rely on them (in contrast to the corresponding 1999 rule in Art. 3(10), where submitting additional documents was provided for (only) if the document was believed to have become relevant etc.[368]).[369]

232   Allegations or documents submitted by the other party, written witness statements or expert reports may render it necessary for a party to submit additional documents. Thus, Art. 3(11) provides for the possibility of a **second round of document submission.**[370] The parties may therefore provide additional documentary evidence, e.g. in support of contentions and/ or arguments aiming at contradicting arguments or evidence introduced by the counterparty.

233   Again, the respective submissions must be filed within the **time limit** set by the arbitral tribunal.

VIII. Form of Submission or Production, Copies, Electronic Documents, Multiple Copies and Translations (par. 12)

A.   General Remarks

234   Art. 3(12) deals with certain issues of the **form of submission or production** of documents: the requirement of conformity of copies to originals and presentation for inspection upon request (Art. 3(12)(a)), the form of submission and production of documents maintained in electronic form (Art. 3(12)(b)), no obligation for production of multiple copies of essentially identical documents unless held otherwise (Art. 3(12)(c)), and translations of documents (Art. 3(12)(d)).

235   The **2010 Revision** brought the additions of Art. 3(12)(b) and 3(12) (c) which are helpful.[371] Moreover, the word "fully" has been omitted in the revised Art. 3(12)(a), thereby dropping the requirement that copies must "fully" conform to the originals.[372]

---

[368] See also Annex 1, Art. 3 (11).
[369] O'MALLEY, Document Production, 193.
[370] IBA REVIEW SUBCOMMITTEE 2010, 7; RAESCHKE-KESSLER, Production, 413.
[371] VON SEGESSER, IBA Rules, 745.
[372] O'MALLEY, Document Production, 193.

B.   Conformity of Copies and Presentation for Inspection (par. 12(a))

As a rule, only **copies,** not the originals of the documents, must be submit-   236
ted or produced in arbitral proceedings, in line with the practice that the
filing of copies will in most cases suffice.[373]

If copies are submitted or produced, they must of course **conform** to the   237
originals (Art. 3(12)(a)).[374]

Generally, the **presumption** is that a copy conforms to the original unless   238
it has been shown that there are serious questions as to its authenticity.[375]

The copy of an original must only conform to the document as the docu-   239
ment was **initially established** by the author.[376]

Art. 3(12)(a) applies to **all types** of production requests.   240

The arbitral tribunal may – in the specific circumstances – have reason to   241
believe that a submitted copy does not conform to the original. In this case,
it may order the party having submitted the copy to **present the original**
of the document for inspection by the arbitral tribunal and the other parties,
during an evidentiary hearing in accordance with Art. 8. If necessary, the
inspection may be carried out by forensic experts.[377]

The other parties may apply to the arbitral tribunal to issue a **procedural**   242
order to that extent if they have reason to believe that the copy submitted
does not correspond to the original.

If the party that submitted the copy fails to comply with an order to pro-   243
duce the original for inspection and fails to state valid reasons, the arbitral
tribunal may draw **negative inferences** (Art. 9(5)).[378]

---

[373] IBA Review Subcommittee 2010, 12; Craig/Park/Paulsson, 429; PILS (Basel)-Schneider, Art. 184 N 16.
[374] IBA Review Subcommittee 2010, 12.
[375] O'Malley, Document Production, 194.
[376] Raeschke-Kessler, Production, 413: *"The recipient of a letter, for example, may later add handwritten notes on that letter. These notes do not belong to the original document of the sender. If the recipient wants to introduce the letter into the arbitral proceedings as a document written by the sender, the recipient may remove from the copy his or her own handwritten notes on the original because they do not belong to the original document. A different approach applies if the recipient has written his or her own manifestations of legal importance on the document."*
[377] Redfern/Hunter/Blackaby/Partasides, N 6.134.
[378] Cf. Art. 9 N 54–57.

C.   Documents Maintained in Electronic Form (par. 12(b))

244   Pursuant to Art. 3(12)(b), documents maintained in electronic form must be submitted or produced in the **form most convenient or economical** that is reasonably useable by the recipients, unless the parties agree otherwise or, in the absence of such agreement, the arbitral tribunal decides otherwise.

245   The **2010 Review Subcommittee** recognised that the costs of taking evidence in electronic form can vary widely depending on the form in which documents must be submitted. Accordingly, the new rule contained in Art. 3(12)(b) provides that the **default form** of production of electronic documents shall be the form most convenient or economical to the producing party that is reasonably useable by the recipient.

246   The parties may have **diverging interests** regarding the form in which electronic documents must be produced. The requesting party may, for example, seek production of electronic documents with full metadata. The other party may object on the grounds that the metadata is of little evidentiary value, confidential or expensive to review. The parties may also have different views as to whether the documents should be produced in electronic or paper format.[379]

247   Art. 3(12)(b) clarifies that – unless otherwise agreed or ordered – it is **for the producing party to determine the form** in which the electronic documents are produced, and the requesting party is not entitled to request production in any particular form, subject to the *proviso* that the form chosen must be reasonably usable by the recipients.[380]

248   This default format will, in general, **not** be **the native format** with full metadata, as submissions in this format can be unduly expensive and inconvenient. In cases where electronic document production is likely to play a role in the arbitration, the question in which form the electronic documents should be produced should be addressed early on in the proceedings, in particular in the consultation provided for under Art. 2(1) and Art. 2(2)(c).[381]

D.   No Multiple Copies (par. 12(c))

249   Under Art. 3(12)(c), a party **is not obliged** to produce multiple copies of documents which are essentially identical, unless the arbitral tribunal decides otherwise.

---

[379] GILL/TAWIL/KREINDLER, 29; see also above, N 49–59.
[380] GILL/TAWIL/KREINDLER, 29.
[381] IBA REVIEW SUBCOMMITTEE 2010, 12; see also above, Art. 2 N 7.

The 2010 Review Subcommittee recognised that electronic transmission   250
and storage of documents often leads to the existence of multiple copies of
the same electronic document. Therefore, the **2010 Revision** introduced
the new rule contained in Art. 3(12)(c).

In some cases, multiple copies may be **individually relevant** to the dis-   251
pute. In other cases, the production of multiple copies may unduly increase
the costs of reviewing the documents for the other party, and even be at
odds with the parties' obligation to conduct themselves in good faith in the
taking of evidence, in accordance with par. 3 of the Preamble.[382]

E.   Translations (par. 12(d))

Art. 3(12)(d) provides that if translations of documents are submitted, they   252
must be submitted together with the **originals,** marked as translations,
and shall **identify the original language.**

The Rules do not determine whether **translations** are required in the arbi-   253
tral proceedings, whether particular documents may be translated in parts
only, how to resolve disputes regarding translations or how the submission
of translations is to be scheduled.[383]

IX.   Confidentiality (par. 13)

Art. 3(13) provides that any document submitted or produced by a party or   254
non-party in the arbitration and not otherwise in the public domain shall be
kept confidential by the **arbitral tribunal** and by the **other parties,** and
shall be used only in connection with the arbitration. This requirement shall
apply except and to the extent that production may be required of a party
for certain reasons. The arbitral tribunal may issue orders to set forth the
terms of this confidentiality. This requirement shall be without prejudice to
all other obligations of confidentiality in the arbitration.

Confidentiality under Art. 3(12) of the 1999 Rules had only covered docu-   255
ments that were produced upon request by the other party or by order of
the arbitral tribunal, whilst the revised Art. 3(13) **extends the scope of
confidentiality** to all documents, including documents that were submitted voluntarily by the parties and documents (voluntarily or involuntarily)
submitted or produced by a third party.[384]

Moreover, Art. 3(13) authorizes a party to **disclose documents** that were   256
submitted or produced in the arbitration to the extent that a party may be

---

[382] Id., 12; see also above, Preamble N 14–17.
[383] IBA REVIEW SUBCOMMITTEE 2010, 12.
[384] Id., 12–13; VON SEGESSER, IBA Rules, 745; GILL/TAWIL/KREINDLER, 29–30.

required to fulfil a legal duty, protect or pursue a right, or enforce or challenge an award in *bona fide* legal proceedings before a state court or other judicial authority.[385] In addition, the new language provides for an exception as to documents that are in the public domain. The revised language sets forth the extent and scope of the confidentiality rule in a clear manner.[386]

257   Art. 3(13) applies to **all documents produced or submitted** in the arbitral proceedings regardless of why or how they were produced and/or submitted, **by parties or by non-parties.**[387] All documents must be kept confidential by the arbitral tribunal and by the other parties, and the respective documents may be used only in connection with the arbitration, unless one of the exceptions[388] applies.[389]

258   The requirement to keep documents confidential does not apply to documents that are already in the **public domain**[390] or are made public prior to submission or production in the arbitration. The parties remain free to make their own documents public at any time.[391]

259   The 1999 Working Party as well as the 2010 Review Subcommittee discussed at length what confidentiality should be given to documents submitted and/or produced in accordance with the Rules. It generally remains a **controversial topic** to what extent confidentiality should be given to arbitral proceedings, in particular regarding intellectual property and investment treaty-based arbitrations.[392]

260   Art. 3(13) expressly provides that the requirements of confidentiality shall be without prejudice to all other obligations of confidentiality in the arbitration. This is because other rules applicable to the arbitration may also impose requirements that are relevant to confidentiality, or the parties or the arbitral tribunal may agree or determine additional rules relating to confidentiality (in this context, see also Art. 9(4) which applies to all types of evidence[393]). Consequently, the parties must, in order to determine what level of confidentiality applies to documents, look at the **institutional or ad hoc rules** pursuant to which they are conducting the arbitration, or to the **parties' agreement** or the **legal regime governing the arbitration.**[394]

---

[385]   IBA Review subcommittee 2010, 13.
[386]   O'Malley, Document Production, 194.
[387]   IBA Review Subcommittee 2010, 13; Gill/Tawil/Kreindler, 29–30.
[388]   See N 256 above.
[389]   IBA Review Subcommittee 2010, 13.
[390]   Gill/Tawil/Kreindler, 30.
[391]   IBA Review Subcommittee 2010, 13.
[392]   Id., 12–13.
[393]   Cf. Art. 9 N 50–53 below.
[394]   IBA Review Subcommittee 2010, 13.

The exception (added in the 2010 Revision) allowing disclosure of confi-   261
dential documents if required to fulfil a legal duty, protect or pursue a right,
or enforce or challenge an award in *bona fide* legal proceedings before a
state court or other judicial authority reflects **exceptions to the strict application of a confidentiality duty** as recognised under many domestic
laws.[395]

Under Art. 3(13), a "public interest" or a general "interest of justice being   262
done" does **not** constitute an exception to the confidentiality rule.[396]

The Rules take no position with respect to the confidentiality of non-docu-   263
mentary evidence such as oral testimony. However, a **transcript** recording
oral testimony would be subject to confidentiality protection as a document
submitted or produced by a non-party.[397]

In practice, arbitral tribunals often issue **protective orders** to protect the   264
parties against wider dissemination of internal documents they have submitted and/or produced. Regardless of confidentiality obligations, it seems
prudent to remove any doubt by use of express confidentiality orders.[398]

In practice, confidentiality of documents can also be increased by providing   265
for **"counsel only"** review or for **limited inspection** of documents at a
single venue only, without a right or possibility to make copies.[399]

In any case, it is advisable to **discuss issues and procedures of confi-   266
dentiality** early in consultation under Art. 2(1) (e.g., proper retention or
deletion of evidence following conclusion of the arbitral proceedings and
any challenge or enforcement proceedings).[400]

X.   Separate Issues or Phases (par. 14)

If the arbitration is divided into separate issues or phases **("bifurcation"),**   267
the arbitral tribunal may schedule the submission of documents and requests to produce separately for each issue or phase.

Art. 3(14) is a **new** addition to the Rules and allows the arbitral tribunal   268
to schedule the taking of documentary evidence in phases. The procedure
was already provided for under the 1999 Rules regarding witness testi-

---

[395] Gill/Tawil/Kreindler, 30: *"It is worth noting that the legal proceedings to enforce or
challenge an award must be bona fide and not, for example, brought solely to circumvent the confidentiality requirements."*
[396] Craig, 170.
[397] IBA Review Subcommittee 2010, 13.
[398] Born, 1917.
[399] Id., 1917.
[400] IBA Review Subcommittee 2010, 13.

mony (Art. 4(4)) and was expanded in the 2010 Revision to documentary evidence.[401]

269   Accordingly, the arbitral tribunal may organise documentary production to **correspond to the respective** phases of the arbitration in bifurcated proceedings.

270   The arbitral tribunal may, e.g., deal with the issue of **jurisdiction** separately, or there may be a separate phase regarding the **merits** or the **quantum.**[402]

271   Organising document production in accordance with the respective phase of the proceedings is also in line with the general principle of **efficiency.** It can be an important means to manage time and control costs, depending on the circumstances of the case.[403] *"This provision clearly bears the hallmark of the Rules, namely efficiency and avoiding unnecessary cost, by allowing disclosure to be limited to that which is necessary at any given stage of the arbitration."*[404] Still, the provision allows for flexibility since it is not mandatory and contemplates consultation between the arbitral tribunal and the parties.[405]

272   The parties may propose using the procedure set forth in Art. 3(14), or the arbitral tribunal may apply it on its own initiative.[406] In any case, it is for the **arbitral tribunal to decide** whether it wishes to have separate document production for separate phases.

---

[401] Id., 14.
[402] See Art. 2 N 16–22 above.
[403] IBA REVIEW SUBCOMMITTEE 2010, 14.
[404] GILL/TAWIL/KREINDLER, 29.
[405] Id., 29.
[406] IBA REVIEW SUBCOMMITTEE 2010, 14.

Article 4   Witnesses of Fact

1. Within the time ordered by the Arbitral Tribunal, each Party shall identify the witnesses on whose testimony it intends to rely and the subject matter of that testimony.

2. Any person may present evidence as a witness, including a Party or a Party's officer, employee or other representative.

3. It shall not be improper for a Party, its officers, employees, legal advisors or other representatives to interview its witnesses or potential witnesses and to discuss their prospective testimony with them.

4. The Arbitral Tribunal may order each Party to submit within a specified time to the Arbitral Tribunal and to the other Parties Witness Statements by each witness on whose testimony it intends to rely, except for those witnesses whose testimony is sought pursuant to Articles 4.9 or 4.10. If Evidentiary Hearings are organised into separate issues or phases (such as jurisdiction, preliminary determinations, liability or damages), the Arbitral Tribunal or the Parties by agreement may schedule the submission of Witness Statements separately for each issue or phase.

5. Each Witness Statement shall contain:

   (a) the full name and address of the witness, a statement regarding his or her present and past relationship (if any) with any of the Parties, and a description of his or her background, qualifications, training and experience, if such a description may be relevant to the dispute or to the contents of the statement;

   (b) a full and detailed description of the facts, and the source of the witness's information as to those facts, sufficient to serve as that witness's evidence in the matter in dispute. Documents on which the witness relies that have not already been submitted shall be provided;

   (c) a statement as to the language in which the Witness Statement was originally prepared and the language in which the witness anticipates giving testimony at the Evidentiary Hearing;

   (d) an affirmation of the truth of the Witness Statement; and

   (e) the signature of the witness and its date and place.

6. If Witness Statements are submitted, any Party may, within the time ordered by the Arbitral Tribunal, submit to the Arbitral Tribunal and to the other Parties revised or additional Witness Statements, including statements from persons not previously named as witnesses, so long as any such revisions or additions respond only to matters contained in another Party's Witness Statements,

Expert Reports or other submissions that have not been previously presented in the arbitration.

7. **If a witness whose appearance has been requested pursuant to Article 8.1 fails without a valid reason to appear for testimony at an Evidentiary Hearing, the Arbitral Tribunal shall disregard any Witness Statement related to that Evidentiary Hearing by that witness unless, in exceptional circumstances, the Arbitral Tribunal decides otherwise.**

8. **If the appearance of a witness has not been requested pursuant to Article 8.1, none of the other Parties shall be deemed to have agreed to the correctness of the content of the Witness Statement.**

9. **If a Party wishes to present evidence from a person who will not appear voluntarily at its request, the Party may, within the time ordered by the Arbitral Tribunal, ask it to take whatever steps are legally available to obtain the testimony of that person, or seek leave from the Arbitral Tribunal to take such steps itself. In the case of a request to the Arbitral Tribunal, the Party shall identify the intended witness, shall describe the subjects on which the witness's testimony is sought and shall state why such subjects are relevant to the case and material to its outcome. The Arbitral Tribunal shall decide on this request and shall take, authorize the requesting Party to take or order any other Party to take, such steps as the Arbitral Tribunal considers appropriate if, in its discretion, it determines that the testimony of that witness would be relevant to the case and material to its outcome.**

10. **At any time before the arbitration is concluded, the Arbitral Tribunal may order any Party to provide for, or to use its best efforts to provide for, the appearance for testimony at an Evidentiary Hearing of any person, including one whose testimony has not yet been offered. A Party to whom such a request is addressed may object for any of the reasons set forth in Article 9.2.**

Contents   Note

Other Rules

Art. 25(3) ICC; Art. 25 Swiss Rules; Art. 25 UNCITRAL; Art. 20 LCIA; Art. 35–36 ICSID; Art. 54 WIPO.

I.   2010 Revision

The former Art. 4(7) of the 1999 Rules provided that each witness whose   1
witness statement had been submitted had to appear for testimony at an
evidentiary hearing, unless the parties agreed otherwise. In the 2010 Revision, this provision was deleted. Instead, a **new Art. 8(1)** was introduced,
according to which each witness has to appear for testimony at the evidentiary hearing if his or her appearance is requested by the arbitral tribunal
or any party. As a consequence, the wordings of Art. 4(7) and (8) were
adapted. These amendments may have an impact on how witness statements are treated in practice.[407]

In addition, the 2010 Revision introduced further clarification on **pre-hear-**   2
ing contacts with witnesses (Art. 4(3)) and the content of the witness
statements (Art. 4(5)).

Finally, the revised Art. 4(9) provides that the arbitral tribunal may allow   3
the parties to take steps to obtain testimony from a person who is **not**
willing to appear voluntarily at such party's request (instead of taking
such steps itself).

II.   General Remarks

Few differences between **common law and civil law** procedure are   4
as striking as the attitudes toward the testimony of witnesses. The pre-

---

[407] Cf. N 57–77 below.

sentation of witnesses – in particular the role of judges and counsel – and the weight given to witness evidence are fundamentally different.[408]

5   In international arbitration, the different approaches to witness testimony are converging due to the fact that often practitioners of both systems are involved in the same case.[409] Some rules explicitly take a **mixed approach** as do the Rules: Art. 4 provides for the submission of witness statements and cross-examination and allows the arbitral tribunal to question witnesses itself and even to summon witnesses which were not named by the parties.

III.   Identification of Witnesses (par. 1)

6   Art. 4(1) provides that each Party shall **identify the witnesses** on whose testimony it intends to rely and the subject matter of that testimony within the time ordered by the arbitral tribunal. This should prevent the opposing party from being surprised by unexpected witnesses of fact.[410]

7   The provision leaves great discretion to the arbitral tribunal in what **form** and by what **time** the witnesses shall be identified. Pursuant to one common and reasonable method, the parties may be ordered to identify the evidence adduced or to be adduced to each allegation of fact in the briefs submitted. In the alternative, the parties may be allowed to make general references to evidence in their briefs and be ordered to submit a detailed list of the evidence they intend to rely on, indicating the content and relevance of each item, later in the proceedings.

IV.   Who Can Be a Witness (par. 2)

8   Internationally, a **great variety of approaches** exists with regard to the question who can be a witness. Many civil law systems traditionally have a relatively narrow definition of witnesses, excluding in particular parties and persons who have an interest in the outcome of the proceedings.[411] In contrast, common law systems usually provide a wide notion of witnesses, sometimes even including experts.[412]

---

[408] Elsing/Townsend, 62; Derains, Preuve, 783–789.
[409] Griffin, 26; Marriott, Evidence, 254; Elsing/Townsend, 63; Derains, Preuve, 789 and 797.
[410] IBA Working Party 1999, 25; Born, 1841.
[411] Griffin, 24–25; Fischer-Zernin/Junker, 21–22; IBA Working Party 1999, 26; Oetiker, Witnesses, 253; Derains, Preuve, 796.
[412] Nater-Bass in Commentary Swiss Rules, Art. 25 N 7; Bühler/Dorgan, 7–10; Raeschke-Kessler, Beweisaufnahme, 64; Derains, Preuve, 796.

Art. 4(2) states that any person may present evidence as a witness, includ-   9
ing a party or a party's officer, employee or other representative. The Rules
thereby rightly follow a broad notion widely accepted in international arbitration, pursuant to which in principle, **anyone capable of commenting
on the facts based on his or her own perception** may be a witness.[413]
This reflects the current practice in international arbitration.[414] Unlike some
institutional rules,[415] the Rules do not distinguish between witnesses and
other persons.[416]

Although the Rules in principle accept that **party-appointed experts** are   10
to be treated in a similar manner as witnesses, they do not include such
experts in the notion of witnesses (Art. 4), but provide for distinct rules
with specific requirements (Art. 5). Experts, who in contrast to witnesses
appraise objective technical data accessible to everyone, can therefore not
be named as witnesses.[417]

The broad notion of witness is tempered by the fact that the arbitral tribu-   11
nal can weigh witness testimonies within its **discretion to appraise** the
evidence presented.[418] In this respect it can and will consider in particular
the relationship of a witness with the parties. Thus, the testimony of a party's executive might be given less weight than testimony of an independent
witness of fact.[419]

V.   Interviewing Witnesses (par. 3)

Traditionally, in many jurisdictions counsel were not allowed to have con-   12
tact to their party's witnesses before the hearing.[420] This prohibition is necessarily linked to the fact that witnesses are not questioned by counsel,
but by the court in these jurisdictions. As a consequence of the absence
of pre-hearing contacts with the witnesses, witness evidence is generally
not regarded as a reliable source of evidence by counsel practising in such

---

[413] BERGER/KELLERHALS, N 1220; BLESSING, 44; NATER-BASS in COMMENTARY SWISS RULES, Art. 25
N 7; CRAIG/PARK/PAULSSON, 437–438; POUDRET/BESSON, N 656; BÜHLER/DORGAN, 7–10; KNOF,
54 and 60; GÉLINAS, 31–32; GRIFFIN, 26; LEW/MISTELIS/KRÖLL, 570; IBA WORKING PARTY
1999, 26; IBA REVIEW SUBCOMMITTEE 2010, 15; DERAINS, Témoins, 227–229; DERAINS,
Preuve, 797–798; REDFERN/HUNTER/BLACKABY/PARTASIDES, N 6.87; OETIKER, Witnesses,
253; GIRSBERGER/VOSER, 217; HASCHER, 10; BORN, 1840.

[414] BERGER/KELLERHALS, N 1220; NATER-BASS in COMMENTARY SWISS RULES, Art. 25 N 7; BLESSING,
44; PETER, Schiedsordnung, 62.

[415] E.g. Art. 25(3) ICC Rules.

[416] IBA WORKING PARTY 1999, 26.

[417] IBA WORKING PARTY 1999, 25; POUDRET/BESSON, N 656.

[418] Cf. Art. 9 N 3–16 below.

[419] BÜHLER/DORGAN 9–11; GÉLINAS, 31–33; IBA WORKING PARTY 1999, 26; OETIKER, Witnesses,
254.

[420] IBA WORKING PARTY 1999, 27.

jurisdictions. In other – mainly common law – jurisdictions, counsel are traditionally allowed to have more or less intense pre-hearing contacts with witnesses.

13   The Rules rightly do not follow the restrictive approach, but **allow for contacts** between counsel and witnesses. However, the language used is quite cautious: Art. 4(3) states that it shall *not be improper* for a party, its officers, employees, legal advisors or other representatives to *interview* its witnesses or potential witnesses. In the 2010 Revision, it was added that it shall also not be improper for a party *to discuss their prospective testimony* with the (potential) witnesses.

14   The diffidence of the wording may be explained by the fact that the possibility of pre-hearing contacts with witnesses may still be against the **ethical rules** of the national bar for certain counsel.[421]

15   According to current practice, counsel are **in general permitted** to have contact with the witnesses before the hearing.[422] In view thereof, the term "interview" used in Art. 4(3) should not be understood narrowly, but in line with the modern position that contacts between counsel and witnesses are in principle allowed and that witnesses may be prepared for the hearing. The latter is now explicitly confirmed by the reference to discussing the prospective testimony with the witness.[423] On the other hand, it is clear that counsel must in general not influence the witnesses and must in particular not coax or lead them into untrue or deliberately incomplete statements.[424]

16   Therefore, counsel must proceed with **caution in preparing witnesses** to obtain a well-balanced result. They need to keep in mind that the credibility of a witness is just as decisive for the result of evidence as the content of his or her testimony. An overly prepared witness will rapidly lose credibility. Conversely, the credibility of the underprepared witness can also suffer, in particular if the witness does not remember his or her testimony provided in a witness statement or the facts on which he or she is supposed to testify.[425]

---

[421]   IBA WORKING PARTY 1999, 27; BORN, 2309–2310.
[422]   NATER-BASS in COMMENTARY SWISS RULES, Art. 25 N 24; SCHNEIDER, Witnesses, 306; VON SEGESSER, Witness Preparation, 224; WIRTH, 13; BERGER/KELLERHALS, N 1224; CRAIG/PARK/ PAULSSON, 433 and 441; REDFERN/HUNTER/BLACKABY/PARTASIDES, N 6.140; BÜHLER/DORGAN, 12 and 20; KNOF, 60; SCHLAEPFER, 68; VAN HOUTTE, 108–113; GRIFFIN, 28; POUDRET/BESSON, N 660; HASCHER, 12; BORN, 2310.
[423]   IBA REVIEW SUBCOMMITTEE 2010, 16.
[424]   HAFTER, N 2481–2515; VON SEGESSER, Witness Preparation, 225; WIRTH, 13; REDFERN/ HUNTER/BLACKABY/PARTASIDES, N 6.140; GIRSBERGER/VOSER, 218.
[425]   BÜHLER/DORGAN, 20.

When preparing their witnesses, counsel should ask them above all and   17
from the beginning to tell the truth.[426] Further, the witnesses should be
invited to study the relevant documents once again before their oral testimony.[427] Counsel may also discuss possible questions and answers with the
witnesses[428] and acquaint them with the strategies of the parties.[429] This will
allow them to understand the context of their testimony.

Most witnesses will not be familiar with the examination situation, be it   18
direct or cross-examination. Counsel are therefore allowed to **familiarise
the witnesses with the examination techniques,** e.g. by simulating
direct examination or cross-examination by the opposing party.[430] Further,
counsel may discuss with the witnesses the general guidelines for respond-
ing to cross-examination and tribunal questions, which are in particular:[431]

- the witness should always tell the truth;

- the witness should carefully listen to the question;

- if the witness does not hear the question, he or she should ask for it to
  be repeated;

- if the witness does not understand the question, he or she should ask
  for an explanation;

- the witness should not answer compound questions;

- the witness is allowed to pause and think before answering – he or she
  should not think with his or her mouth;

- the witness should correct any factual errors in the question;

- the witness should answer only the question that is asked;

- the witness should not volunteer information;

- if appropriate, the witness may simply answer "yes" or "no";

- if necessary, the witness may explain his or her answer succinctly;

- the witness should never guess – if he or she does not know the answer,
  he or she should say so;

- the witness should never argue;

- the witness should not make speeches;

---

[426] Hafter, N 2514, with a number of further suggestions.
[427] Bühler/Dorgan, 20; Roney, 432; Madden, 438.
[428] Concurring Hafter, N 2503–2513.
[429] Roney, 432.
[430] Roney, 433; Madden, 439; Hafter, N 2508.
[431] Roney, 434; cf. Hafter, N 2514.

- the witness should avoid absolutes ("never say never or always");

- the witness should and may admit what he or she has to admit;

- the witness should have the courage to persist in what he or she does not have to admit;

- the witness should always maintain eye contact with the arbitral tribunal;

- the witness may let his or her personality come through.

19   The arbitral tribunal will be **aware** that the witnesses were prepared by counsel and will take this in due account when weighing the witness testimony.[432]

20   From the perspective of the arbitral tribunal, it is advisable to issue **supplemental procedural rules** on this issue by which the parties can be guided because under many laws and arbitration rules, it is not entirely clear to which extent the preparation of witnesses is permissible.[433] Such rules issued by the arbitral tribunal will also have the effect that both parties will apply the same criteria even if they have different legal backgrounds. Furthermore, it enables parties' counsel to point out any restrictions on contacting or preparing witnesses to which they are bound by law or codes of professional conduct. If a stricter standard applies to one party and the other party does not agree to comply with such stricter standard, the arbitral tribunal must take this into account when appraising the witness testimony.

21   Although it seldom occurs in practice, it is also entirely admissible for a party to examine the **witnesses of the opposing party** in advance of the witness hearing, for the purposes of preparation.[434] Of course, such examination serves for preparation not of the witnesses but of the counsel for the parties.

VI.   Witness Statements

A.   General Remarks (par. 4)

22   The 2010 Rules contain a new definition of the term "Witness Statement", which means a written statement of testimony by a witness of fact. Hence,

---

[432] Nater-Bass in Commentary Swiss Rules, Art. 25 N 24; Blessing, 45–46; Bühler/Dorgan, 11; IBA Working Party 1999, 27; PILS (Basel)-Schneider, Art. 184 N 25; Raeschke-Kessler, Beweisaufnahme, 64–65.

[433] Von Segesser, 223; Schlaepfer, 68; Poudret/Besson, N 660; Born, 2310.

[434] Nater-Bass in Commentary Swiss Rules, Art. 25 N 25; Blessing, 46. Critical van Houtte, 109–110.

whenever the Rules refer to witness statements, they do not mean oral statements made by a witness in an evidentiary hearing, but written witness statements.

Witness statements permit the arbitral tribunal and the parties to prepare   23
for the witness hearing more selectively and in a shorter time and therefore tend to be more **cost efficient.**[435] In many cases, the witness statements alone will contain sufficient information, so that the oral examination of many witnesses will neither be necessary from the viewpoint of the arbitral tribunal nor required by the parties.[436]

The admissibility of witness statements in international arbitration is nowa-   24
days undisputed. In fact, it is **standard practice** to present witness statements.[437] Art. 4(4), like modern institutional arbitration rules,[438] expressly allows the arbitral tribunal to order each party to submit within a specified time to the arbitral tribunal and to the other parties a written statement by each witness on whose testimony it intends to rely. It is in the full discretion of the arbitral tribunal whether to order such witness statements or not.

Although it is standard to obtain witness statements, the arbitral tribu-   25
nal should **not order or allow them without due consideration.**[439] In particular, it should be kept in mind that a serious preparation of witness statements, in particular if they are intended to fully replace the witnesses' direct examination, may involve much time and effort and thus create substantial costs for the parties.[440] This may outweigh one of the said advantages of having witness statements, i.e. cost efficiency.

Before making its decision, the arbitral tribunal should **evaluate alterna-**   26
tives for the presentation of witnesses. In certain cases, in particular if the number of witnesses and the issues on which they are to testify are limited, witness statements may be foregone entirely and the witnesses may be submitted only to direct oral examination, either by counsel or the

---

[435] WIRTH, 14; NATER-BASS in COMMENTARY SWISS RULES, Art. 25 N 21; PILS (Basel)-SCHNEIDER, Art. 184 N 24; LÉVY, Witness Statements, 96; BERGER/KELLERHALS, N 1222; CRAIG/PARK/ PAULSSON, 433; BÜHLER/DORGAN, 12–13; SCHLAEPFER, 65–66; GRIFFIN, 27; IBA WORKING PARTY 1999, 27; OETIKER, Witnesses, 254; BORN, 1830.

[436] CRAIG/PARK/PAULSSON, 434; KNOF, 64 and 71; WIRTH, 14; NATER-BASS in COMMENTARY SWISS RULES, Art. 25 N 21; GRIFFIN, 27; TALLERICO/BEHRENDT, 300–301; IBA WORKING PARTY 1999, 27; OETIKER, Witnesses, 254; GIRSBERGER/VOSER, 217.

[437] LÉVY, Witness Statements, 96; NATER-BASS in COMMENTARY SWISS RULES, Art. 25 N 21; CRAIG/PARK/PAULSSON, 432–434; REDFERN/HUNTER/BLACKABY/PARTASIDES, N 6.137; BERGER/ KELLERHALS, N 1222; KNOF, 60–61; SCHLAEPFER, 65; GRIFFIN, 27; OETIKER, Witnesses, 255; DERAINS, Témoins, 230; SHORE, 79–80; DERAINS, Preuve, 798; GIRSBERGER/VOSER, 217; BORN, 1828–1829.

[438] E.g. Art. 25(3) Swiss Rules; Art. 20(3) LCIA Rules.

[439] IBA WORKING PARTY 1999, 27; OETIKER, Witnesses, 255; SHORE, 79.

[440] WIRTH, 14; OETIKER, Witnesses, 255.

arbitral tribunal.[441] In other circumstances, it may be useful to have short witness statements which do not serve as substitute for direct oral examination, but indicate on what issues a witness may testify.[442]

27   It is submitted that the arbitral tribunal should **discuss this question with the parties** at an early stage of the proceedings. It will increase the efficiency of the proceedings if (a) the form in which witness evidence has to be presented is shaped to the requirements of the concrete case and (b) the respective rules are common ground and clear from the outset.

28   Where it is not clear at the beginning of the proceedings whether witness statements will contribute to the efficiency of the proceedings, the arbitral tribunal may **suspend its decision** until the parties have submitted their briefs and it is clear for which assertions of facts witness testimony is necessary at all.[443]

29   If the arbitral tribunal allows witness statements, it should also determine whether all witnesses have to deliver witness statements, or whether the parties can also present the testimony of certain witnesses only orally. As a rule, it is not recommended to admit both types of evidence from witnesses simultaneously.[444] If the arbitral tribunal admits witness statements, it should therefore order that only persons who submit a witness statement shall be heard as witnesses. To permit otherwise would tend to subvert the purposes of requiring witness statements.[445] This solution is provided for in Art. 4(4), pursuant to which the arbitral tribunal may order that the parties shall submit witness statements **by each witness** on whose testimony they intend to rely. Only if a party can demonstrate good reason why the submission of a witness statement was not possible should the arbitral tribunal make an exception.[446] Two necessary exceptions are already contained in Art. 4(4): the parties need not present witness statements from recalcitrant witnesses (Art. 4(9)) and from witnesses the appearance of which was ordered by the arbitral tribunal (Art. 4(10)).

B.   Submission (par. 4)

30   The witness statements must be submitted at the same time **to the arbitral tribunal and the other parties** (Art. 4(4)).

---

[441] Bühler/Dorgan, 13; Wirth, 14; Oetiker, Witnesses, 255.
[442] Cf. in this regard Oetiker, Sense and Nonsense, 29–41.
[443] Oetiker, Witnesses, 255; cf. also Wirth, 14.
[444] Lévy, Witness Statements, 100; Oetiker, Witnesses, 255.
[445] Bühler/Dorgan, 16; Oetiker, Witnesses, 255.
[446] Id., 255.

The question at what point in time the witness statements must be sub-   31
mitted is of great practical relevance. There are two main alternatives:
(a) submission of the witness statements **together with the corresponding brief** (simultaneously with the documentary evidence), or (b) **simultaneous submission** of all witness statements by both parties after conclusion of the exchange of briefs and before the witness hearing.[447]

If the witness statements are submitted together with the briefs, the ar-   32
bitral tribunal and the opposing party come to know the content of the
witnesses' testimony immediately. This can lead to an **acceleration** of
the proceedings, in particular since the opposing party can comment on
the content of the witness statements in its next brief and can have its
witnesses deal with issues raised in the witness statements of the opposing party.[448] However, the claimant will often deem it as a disadvantage if
it must disclose its witness testimony first.[449] In addition, the claimant will
usually want to submit supplementary witness statements in response to
the respondent's factual allegations and witness statements, because it
does not know, at least not definitively, the respondent's assertions of fact
at the time when it must submit its own witness statements.

If the witness statements are to be submitted simultaneously after the ex-   33
change of the briefs, the parties have the opportunity to prepare them in
full knowledge of the opposing party's assertions of facts in the briefs.
The parties, however, cannot comment in their briefs on the content of the
other party's witness statement. This disadvantage is tempered by the fact
that the parties will be given the opportunity, in any case after the witness
hearing, to comment in writing, or orally, on the result of the evidentiary
proceedings. Further, the parties will usually be allowed to submit rebuttal
witness statements in which their witnesses can make further statements
of facts in response to the other party's witness statements (Art. 4(6)).[450]

The Rules do not opt for one or the other alternative. Art. 4(4) only states   34
that the arbitral tribunal may order the submission of witness statements
within a specified time. There is no doubt that the arbitral tribunal may
set different time limits for the claimant and the respondent in line with the
sequence of briefs or provide for various rounds of submissions of witness
statements.[451]

---

[447] IBA Working Party 1999, 28; Oetiker, Witnesses, 261; Born, 1825, who states that the
second approach *"is increasingly disfavored in contemporary international arbitration"*.

[448] IBA Working Party 1999, 28; Oetiker, Witnesses, 261.

[449] Craig/Park/Paulsson, 433; von Mehren/Salomon, 287; Oetiker, Witnesses, 261.

[450] Oetiker, Witnesses, 262.

[451] Cf. also Art. 4(6) and N 50–56 below.

35   Art. 4(4), last sentence, further allows the arbitral tribunal, or the parties
      by agreement, to schedule the submission of witness statements separate-
      ly for separate issues or phases if the **evidentiary hearings** are organised
      into separate issues or phases (such as jurisdiction, preliminary determina-
      tions, liability or damages). This makes clear that several evidentiary hear-
      ings may be organised in the same proceedings and that, as a consequence,
      witness statements may also be required at different stages of the proceed-
      ings. This addendum is redundant in view of the arbitral tribunal's freedom
      to set various time limits for the submission of witness statements.

C.   Content (par. 5)

36   Art. 4(5) sets out in a rather **detailed manner** what the witness state-
      ments need to contain.

1.   Identity of the Witness (par. 5(a))

37   In order to duly perceive the content of a witness' testimony, it is **impor-
      tant to know who the witness is,** what his or her relations to the par-
      ties are and what his or her professional background is. For that purpose,
      Art. 4(5)(a) requires that each witness statement shall contain

- the full name and address of the witness,

- a statement regarding his or her present and past relationship (if any)
  with any of the parties, and

- a description of his or her background, qualifications, training and experience, if such a description may be relevant to the dispute or to the
  contents of the statement.

2.   Statement of Facts (par. 5(b))

38   The witness statement must contain a **full and detailed description of
      the facts** sufficient to serve as that witness' evidence in the matter in
      dispute (Art. 4(5)(b)). Under the 1999 Rules, this fitted in with the fact
      that the witness statements were intended to replace in full the direct
      examination of witnesses.[452] Under the revised Art. 8(1), the parties are
      explicitly allowed to request the appearance of their own witnesses. Some
      parties might be tempted to reduce the scope of the witness statements
      they submit because they may call their own witnesses for testimony. How-
      ever, it is submitted that Art. 8(1) does not qualify the rule that the witness

---

[452] Cf. HASCHER, 11.

statement must contain a full and detailed description of the facts in any respect.

Art. 4(5)(b) requires a *full* **description of the relevant facts.** It is sub-   39
mitted that this provision does not conflict with the parties' freedom to determine on what issues a certain witness is called. However, it does mean that the witness must give a full statement of his or her perception of the issues he or she is called for. Counsel will often be confronted with the situation that they would like a witness to give testimony on certain facts while not revealing other facts. If the respective facts, on the basis of a good faith assessment of counsel, cannot be separated by objective factors such as topic, time, place etc., they must either be stated in full or be fully omitted.

The requirement of **a *detailed* description of the facts** reflects the fact   40
that the witness statement will usually replace the direct examination of that witness. This will enhance the comprehensibility of the statement and will add to its plausibility. However, a too detailed narration of events after a long period of time may also jeopardize the plausibility of a witness state-ment. In this respect, it is of utmost importance to indicate the source of additional information, e.g. contemporaneous documents.[453]

In view of (I) the costs related to the preparation of comprehensive witness   41
statements, (ii) the fact that the statements are often drafted by coun-sel (and are therefore of limited authenticity) and (iii) some arbitrators' preference to have an **oral direct examination of the witnesses** or to interview the witnesses themselves, the arbitral tribunal may order, or the parties agree, that the witness statements shall not serve as the witness' evidence and therefore do not need to contain a full account of facts.[454] E.g. if the witness statement should only give an overview of the issues on which a witness can testify without replacing in full his or her direct exami-nation, the account of facts can be narrowed down to a brief summary of each issue without going into details.

The witness statement should be, if practicable, **in the witness' own**   42
words. Hence, the witnesses should draft their witness statements them-selves, or at least prepare the first draft.[455] Counsel should hold back with editing the witness statements, in particular with regard to the choice of words and style.[456]

---

[453] Cf. N 47 below.
[454] Cf. in this regard OETIKER, Sense and Nonsense, 37–41.
[455] OETIKER, Witnesses, 256.
[456] OETIKER, Witnesses, 256; PETER, Witness Conferencing, 52–53, is of the opinion that the prospect of *"witness conferencing"* enhances the quality of witness statements.

43   In practice, arbitral tribunals will, however, often encounter witness state-
      ments which were, in a more or less obvious manner, **drafted or substan-
      tially edited by counsel.**[457] On some occasions, the arbitral tribunal will
      even find that the descriptions of the relevant facts contained in different
      witness statements are identical to a large extent, using exactly the same
      language. Or the witness statements contain wording which is identical to
      parts of the briefs submitted by the parties. It is evident that the credibility
      of such witness statements will be limited compared to witness statements
      genuinely originating from the witness, unless they are accompanied by
      documentary evidence.[458]

44   Although the **problem of low credibility** of overly edited witness state-
      ments is well known among counsel and arbitrators and the suggestions
      made above are obvious, many sophisticated practitioners still undertake
      massive efforts at re-shaping witness statements.[459] One reason might be
      that the handling of numerous witness statements becomes even more
      burdensome if the witnesses are asked to do the drafting themselves. Is-
      sues of timing, inability and language skills may arise. The review of wit-
      ness statements genuinely drafted by the witnesses will take more time
      than just reviewing the amendments made by the witness to a proposed
      wording.[460] Further, it will be difficult, sometimes even impossible, to focus
      the witness statements on the pertinent issues[461] and to avoid conflicting
      language between different witness statements if they are drafted by the
      witnesses. The latter issue may be of relevance also for strategic considera-
      tions: Witness statements drafted by the witnesses, but conflicting among
      themselves, may be more harmful to the outcome of a case than uniform,
      but less credible witness statements.[462]

45   Witness statements must **not replace or complete the allegations and
      substantiation of the relevant facts** by the parties in their submissions
      to the arbitral tribunal.[463] They are means of evidence and serve to estab-
      lish the parties' allegations made in their submissions. In principle, witness
      statements should therefore limit themselves to confirm and support the
      facts alleged in the briefs, and should not refer to other facts. This being
      said, it is clear that a witness may give a full picture of his or her perception
      of the relevant facts, so that the witness statement may be broader than

---

[457] Lévy, Witness Statements, 97; Oetiker, Witnesses, 256; Derains, Témoins, 230; Shore,
      79.
[458] Veeder, Lawyer's Duty, 444; Schlaepfer, 73; Oetiker, Witnesses, 256.
[459] Veeder, Lawyer's Duty, 445; Schlaepfer, 68–69; Oetiker, Witnesses, 256.
[460] Oetiker, Witnesses, 256.
[461] Lévy, Witness Statements, 97; Schlaepfer, 69; Oetiker, Witnesses, 256.
[462] Oetiker, Witnesses, 256.
[463] Schürmann, 433–438; Lévy, Witness Statements, 99; Schlaepfer, 67.

the respective pleadings.[464] This will in particular occur if the witness statements are drafted by the witnesses on their own. Also, the witness statements should not contain speculation, legal or other argument and similar matters; although witness statements ignoring these principles will usually not be struck from evidence, they will also not advance a party's case.[465]

Furthermore, Art. 4(5)(b) requires that the **source of the witness' information** as to facts described is disclosed. The main purpose of this requirement is to reveal to the reader whether the witness knows the facts described from (a) his or her own perception of events, (b) other available information sources such as documents, or (c) oral statements of third persons (hearsay). This will allow the arbitral tribunal to appropriately weigh the evidence given. Depending on the circumstances, the description of the source of the witness' information must be fairly detailed. If this is not the case, the arbitral tribunal should address this issue in the hearing if not brought up by the other party.   46

Finally, in the 2010 Revision, a new sentence was added to Art. 4(5)(b), pursuant to which **documents on which the witness relies** and which have not already been submitted shall be provided, i.e. attached to the witness statement. On the one hand, this is a very sensible rule since it will clarify on what documents, if any, the witness bases his or her affirmations. On the other hand, this rule gives leeway to potential abuse in that a party tries to introduce additional documentary evidence by attaching it to witness statements. This danger exists in particular if the witness statements have to be submitted only after the full exchange of briefs. Hence, the arbitral tribunal should be careful in admitting such documents as documentary evidence or, even better, include a rule in the procedural rules clearly stating to which extent the parties may rely on documents submitted only in their witness statements.   47

3.   Language (par. 5(c))

In the 2010 Revision, a new requirement for the content of the witness statement was included: it must state the language in which the witness statement was **originally prepared** and the language in which the witness anticipates giving testimony at the evidentiary hearing. This conveys useful information to the arbitral tribunal. On the one hand, it may explain why the language of a witness statement originally prepared not in the witness' mother tongue contains linguistic errors or a language level which may not be attributed to the witness, but rather to the translator (or the translat-   48

---

[464] OETIKER, Witnesses, 256.
[465] BORN, 1829–1830.

ing counsel). On the other hand, it will be clear from the outset which witnesses may be heard in the language of the proceedings and which need interpretation.

4.   Affirmation of Truth and Signature (par. 5(d) and (e))

49   Pursuant to Art. 4(5)(d) and (e), the witness statement must contain an affirmation of the truth of the statement, the signature of the witness and its date and place. Hence, the witness statement under the Rules is an **unsworn voluntary declaration** of a witness which contains an affirmation of the truth of the statement and the signature of the witness.[466] Other forms such as *affidavits* (voluntary declarations of a person under oath) and *depositions* (interrogation of a party or of its witnesses by counsel of the parties in the absence of the arbitral tribunal) are not required.[467] This is reasonable, *inter alia* because the admissibility of these other forms is unclear in many jurisdictions.[468]

D.   Rebuttal Witness Statements (par. 6)

50   Art. 4(6) explicitly grants the parties the right to submit rebuttal witness statements. It is submitted that such right flows from the right to be heard, so that the parties are entitled to do so even **without an authorisation by the arbitral tribunal.** The arbitral tribunal is only called to set a respective time limit in order to ensure equal treatment of the parties and a smooth procedure. The omission of rebuttal witness statements does not limit the respective parties' right to challenge the witness statements submitted by the other parties by other means, in particular by the examination of these witnesses at the evidentiary hearing.[469]

51   The rebuttal witness statements may consist of **revised or additional witness statements.** To revise a witness statement means that the witness may add descriptions of additional facts or further elaborate on facts already described in its original witness statement. In principle, the witness may also amend its earlier description of certain facts. However, this must be done with caution since it may jeopardise the credibility of the witness. Still, it is always possible that the statements of other persons as to certain facts elicit more detailed recollections. This should be indicated by appropriate wording in an amended statement (e.g. *"In view of Mr X's witness statement, I can state more precisely as follows"*).

---

[466] GRIFFIN, 28; TALLERICO/BEHRENDT, 300; OETIKER, Witnesses, 257.
[467] IBA WORKING PARTY 1999, 28; OETIKER, Witnesses, 257.
[468] CRAIG/PARK/PAULSSON, 433.
[469] Cf. Procedural Order of 16 December 2003 in ICC Case No. 12575, in: Decisions on ICC Arbitration Procedure, ICC Bull 2010 Special Supplement, 67–68.

The rebuttal witness statements may include statements from **persons**   52
not previously named as witnesses.

The possible **scope** of the rebuttal witness statements is **limited** in two   53
respects:

Firstly, any revisions or additions in the rebuttal witness statement may   54
only respond to matters contained in a witness statement, expert
report or other submission of the other party. Hence, the parties are not
allowed to introduce new descriptions of facts unless they directly respond
to a statement submitted by the other party. This limitation is necessary
to prevent the parties from holding back certain descriptions of facts in the
first round of witness statements for strategic reasons.

Secondly, rebuttal witness statements are only allowed on **matters that**   55
have not been previously presented in the arbitration. The word "previously" refers to the time of the submission of the witness statements,
expert reports or other submissions, in which the rebutted statements are
contained. Hence, witness evidence on any issue presented in the briefs of
any party or in any other document submitted before that time must be
presented in the first round of witness statements. Art. 4(6) does not allow to present testimony on such issues only in the rebuttal witness statements. Again, this rule is directed against the strategic holding back of
witness evidence.

While the purpose of this second limitation provided for in Art. 4(6) is in   56
principle justified, it may lead to overly lengthy and numerous witness
statements. In certain circumstances, it may be more efficient to allow the
parties to include testimony on issues previously presented in the arbitration in the rebuttal witness statements only. Therefore, it is submitted that
the arbitral tribunal should apply the second limitation of Art. 4(6) with
some **flexibility** in practice.

VII. Right to Examine Witnesses Who have Submitted a Witness Statement

A.   2010 Revision: Omission of the General Duty to Appear Before the Arbitral Tribunal

The 1999 Rules provided for a **general rule** pursuant to which each wit-   57
ness whose witness statement was submitted had to appear for testimony
at an evidentiary hearing, unless the parties agreed otherwise (Art. 4(7) of
the 1999 Rules). This duty of the witnesses and the consequences of non-
compliance were extensively discussed.

58   The 2010 Rules take another approach to this issue. A new Art. 8(1) was
      introduced, pursuant to which each party must inform the arbitral tribunal
      and the other parties of the **witnesses whose appearance it requests**
      within the time ordered by the arbitral tribunal. Only if a witness' appear-
      ance was requested by a party or by the arbitral tribunal, the duty to ap-
      pear is triggered.

59   This rule is in line with the **current general practice,** according to which
      witnesses only appear if their examination was requested,[470] and with the
      fact that most parties will accept witness statements only under the condi-
      tion that they will be able to cross-examine the witnesses of the opposing
      party orally.[471] It is also reflected in some arbitration rules.[472]

60   Generally, **the parties are responsible for the appearance** of the wit-
      nesses they have called at the witness hearing.[473] If a party is not in a posi-
      tion to ensure the appearance of a witness, the arbitral tribunal may step
      in.[474] It has to be noted though that the means of the arbitral tribunal to
      summon witnesses are limited.

B.   Waiver of Appearance (par. 8)

61   As stated in the revised Art. 8(1), a witness whose witness statement was
      submitted must appear only if any party or the arbitral tribunal **requested**
      so.

62   There are **three aspects** of this rule which need to be highlighted:

63   Firstly, it was already stated that each party has the **right to cross-exam-
      ine a witness** who has submitted a witness statement. Each party is free
      to waive such right to cross-examination. In practice, the parties frequently
      waive examination of numerous witnesses, thereby contributing consider-
      ably to the efficiency of the proceedings.

64   Secondly, a **unilateral waiver** of the party entitled to cross-examination
      is in principle sufficient. However, the revised wording of Art. 8(1) makes it
      clear that *any* party, i.e. also the party who presented the respective wit-
      ness, and the arbitral tribunal may request his or her appearance. Hence,
      the unilateral waiver of the party entitled to cross-examination will lead to

---

[470] IBA Review Subcommittee 2010, 17.
[471] Craig/Park/Paulsson, 433; von Mehren/Salomon, 287; Oetiker, Witnesses, 257–258.
[472] E.g. Art. 20(4) LCIA Rules.
[473] PILS (Basel)-Schneider, Art. 184 N 26; Bühler/Dorgan, 19; Lew/Mistelis/Kröll, 572;
       Schneider, Witnesses, 309; Nater-Bass in Commentary Swiss Rules, Art. 25 N 10; Oetiker,
       Witnesses, 265; Hascher, 11.
[474] PILS (Basel)-Schneider, Art. 184 N 26; Nater-Bass in Commentary Swiss Rules, Art. 25
       N 10.

the non-appearance of such witness unless any other party or the arbitral tribunal request the appearance.

However, it is submitted that whenever the witness statements are intended   65
to substitute for the direct examination of witnesses, the parties should not be allowed to **request** that their **own witnesses,** the cross-examination of whom was waived by the opposing party, are heard.[475] This increases the incentive to submit complete and balanced witness statements. Under the 2010 Rules, the arbitral tribunal needs to include a respective procedural rule which limits the right to request the appearance of a witness pursuant to Art. 8(1) if it wants to follow this approach.

Thirdly, Art. 8(1) makes it clear that the **arbitral tribunal** is free to hear   66
any witness offered by the parties, even if none of the parties requests the appearance of such witness. This is also in line with Art. 4(10), pursuant to which the arbitral tribunal may order the hearing of any person, including one whose testimony was not offered by the parties.

Most importantly, Art. 4(8) clarifies that, if the appearance of a witness was   67
not requested pursuant to Art. 8(1), **none of the *other parties* shall be deemed to have agreed to the correctness** of the content of the witness statement.[476] In fact, the parties who did not submit the respective witness statement are at liberty to challenge its content with other means, such as documentary evidence or a testimony to the contrary of another witness.[477]

C.   Failure to Appear (par. 7)

1.   General Rule

Art. 4(7) states that, if a witness whose appearance was requested pur-   68
suant to Art. 8(1) fails without a valid reason to appear for testimony at an evidentiary hearing, the arbitral tribunal **must disregard** any witness statement related to that evidentiary hearing by the witness unless, in exceptional circumstances, the arbitral tribunal decides otherwise.[478] Accordingly, pursuant to the general rule, the witness statement of a witness who cannot be examined orally must **not be taken into account** by the arbitral tribunal. There are a number of explicit and implicit exceptions to this rather strict and inflexible rule which need to be discussed.

---

[475] Lévy, Witness Statements, 101; critical Schlaepfer, 71; Oetiker, Witnesses, 258.
[476] Bühler/Dorgan, 15; Oetiker, Witnesses, 258.
[477] Oetiker, Witnesses, 258.
[478] Equivalent rules are provided for in Art. 20(4) LCIA and Art. 54(d) WIPO. Cf. Hascher, 11.

2.   Waiver of Appearance by the Parties

69   As was already stated above, the parties may waive the appearance of a witness whose witness statement was submitted at the evidentiary hearing. As a consequence thereof, the corresponding witness statement must be regarded as a **valid means of evidence** which remains in the records.[479] However, the parties who did not request the appearance must not be deemed to have agreed to the correctness of the content of the witness statement. Rather, the arbitral tribunal must appraise the witness statement in light of the further evidence obtained.[480] This is a reasonable arrangement promoting the efficiency of the proceedings.[481]

3.   Waiver of Appearance by the Arbitral Tribunal

70   Even if the parties can request to cross-examine witnesses of the opposing party (and also to examine their own witnesses) pursuant to Art. 8(1), it is within the **power and discretion of the arbitral tribunal to deny,** in the context of an anticipated appraisal of evidence, examination of a witness called by one party if it deems the testimony of this witness to be irrelevant (Art. 9(2)(a)).[482]

71   Nevertheless, the arbitral tribunal should be **hesitant not to hear witnesses** who have delivered witness statements if this is contrary to the request of one party and should decide on the relevance of the testimony of a witness only after having heard the witness.[483] Still, this should not lead the arbitral tribunal to agree without due consideration to lengthy hearings in which numerous witnesses are examined on issues which are of no or only very limited relevance.

72   If the arbitral tribunal decides not to hear a witness whose examination was requested, the witness' written statement **remains in the file.** However, it is obvious that the arbitral tribunal will usually attribute little weight to such testimony since it declined to have the witness examined.[484]

---

[479] PILS (Basel)-SCHNEIDER, Art. 184 N 24; SCHNEIDER, Witnesses, 307–308; OETIKER, Witnesses, 258.

[480] OETIKER, Witnesses, 259; cf. LÉVY, Witness Statements, 101.

[481] BÜHLER/DORGAN, 16; OETIKER, Witnesses, 259.

[482] BERGER/KELLERHALS, N 1221; BÜHLER/DORGAN, 17; GRIFFIN, 26; LEW/MISTELIS/KRÖLL, 572; MARRIOTT, 283; POUDRET/BESSON, N 659; OETIKER, Witnesses, 259; DERAINS, Preuve, 798. Dissenting LÉVY, Witness Statements, 101. Switzerland: DFT 4P.196/2003 of 4 January 2004, ASA Bull 2004, 592, 600–601; France: CA Paris, 15 March 1984, *Soubaigne v. Limmareds Skogar*, 1985 Rev. Arb. 285; England: CA in *Dalmia Dairy Industries v. National Bank of Pakistan,* [1978] 2 Lloyd's Rep. 223, at 270.

[483] BÜHLER/DORGAN, 17–18; OETIKER, Witnesses, 259.

[484] OETIKER, Witnesses, 259.

4.   Witnesses Who Are Unavailable for Examination Because of Objective Reasons

Art. 4(7) provides that a witness statement shall only be disregarded if the   73
respective witness does not appear for testimony at an evidentiary hearing
without a valid reason. If a witness is indeed willing to appear for examination, but is unable to do so for objective reasons (such as serious illness,
overly long travel distance, etc.), it is justified as a general rule to leave the
witness statement in the records.[485] The arbitral tribunal has to take into
consideration, within the scope of its unrestricted appraisal of evidence, the
circumstance based on which the witness did not appear.[486]

This approach is **reasonable** – at least under Swiss law – even if the ap-   74
plicable rules of procedural law (arbitration agreement of the parties, arbitration rules, procedural rules issued by the arbitral tribunal) contain a
mandatory rule that witness statements be removed from the record if the
witness does not appear. If the arbitral tribunal were not to take the witness
statement of such witness into consideration, even though it is relevant,
this might amount to a violation of the right to be heard, potentially leading to the annulment of the arbitral award on the basis of Art. 190(2)(d)
PILS or the refusal of enforcement based on Art. V(1)(b) NYC. In contrast,
the violation of any rules or procedural laws that may mandate removal
from the record is not considered as a sufficient basis for successfully contesting an arbitration award under the case law of the Swiss Federal Supreme Court.[487]

5.   Unexcused Non-Appearance

Pursuant to the general rule of Art. 4(7), a witness statement has **no evi-**   75
dentiary value whatsoever if the respective witness fails to appear although his or her appearance was requested.[488] This strict position can be
justified by the already mentioned fact that the parties and the arbitral
tribunal will as a rule admit witness statements only under the reservation
that they can orally examine the witnesses to the extent desired. Only in
exceptional circumstances may the arbitral tribunal determine otherwise
(Art. 4(7)).

---

[485] E.g. DFT 4P.74/2006 of 19 June 2006, cons. 6.3.

[486] OETIKER, Witnesses, 259–260.

[487] For Art. 190(2)(d) PILS: DFT 4P.74/2006 of 19 June 2006, cons. 6.3; DFT 4P.23/2006
of 27 March 2006, cons. 4.2; DFT 4P.93/2004 of 1 July 2004, cons. 2.1; DFT 117 II
347. For Art. 190(2)(e) PILS: DFT 4P.23/2006 of 27 March 2006, cons. 4.2; DFT 128
III 191. OETIKER, Witnesses, 260.

[488] LÉVY, Witness Statements, 102; SCHNEIDER, Witnesses, 308; BÜHLER/DORGAN, 16.

76   This general rule is, however, not without controversy. According to a liberal approach, the arbitral tribunal may decide in its **free discretion** under which circumstances it will admit written statements of witnesses who refuse to appear for examination.[489] If the arbitral tribunal leaves witness statements of recalcitrant witnesses in the record, it has to make special allowance when appraising the evidence for the circumstance that their credibility is limited, for lack of an opportunity to cross-examine the witness orally.[490]

77   It is submitted that the **liberal approach should be preferred** over the strict rule of Art. 4(7). It gives the arbitral tribunal the necessary flexibility.[491] Moreover, it takes into account the circumstance that the opposing party may well wish to refer to explanations in the witness statement of a recalcitrant witness. If the statement is removed from the record, this will no longer be possible.[492] The liberal approach is also in line with case law of e.g. the Swiss Federal Supreme Court, pursuant to which Art. 182(3) PILS does not confer a right to oral cross-examination of witnesses who have submitted a written statement[493] and the violation of mandatory procedural rules is not considered as a ground for successfully contesting an arbitration award.[494]

VIII. Evidence of Recalcitrant Witnesses (par. 9)

78   Possibly, not all witnesses a party may want to rely on are under its own control. Therefore, a party wishing to present evidence from a person who will not appear voluntarily at its request may **ask the arbitral tribunal** to take whatever steps are legally available to obtain the testimony of that person or **seek leave from the arbitral tribunal** to take such steps itself (Art. 4(9)).

79   Pursuant to the wording of Art. 4(9), such request must be made **within the time ordered** by the arbitral tribunal. It is submitted that the time limit meant is the general one set for the identification of witnesses. The arbitral tribunal need not set a particular time limit for such requests.

80   In its request, the party must identify the proposed witness, describe the issues on which the witness' testimony is sought and state why such issues are relevant to the case and material to its outcome. Only if the arbitral tribunal determines in its discretion that the testimony of that witness is

---

[489] CRAIG/PARK/PAULSSON, 433; VON MEHREN/SALOMON, 288; OETIKER, Witnesses, 260.
[490] CRAIG/PARK/PAULSSON, 433; JERMINI, 608; OETIKER, Witnesses, 260.
[491] OETIKER, Witnesses, 261.
[492] Id., 261.
[493] DFT 4P.196/2003 of 4 January 2004, cons. 4.2.2.2, ASA Bull 2004, 592.
[494] Cf. N 74 above.

relevant to the case and material to its outcome, it is called to decide on the request and take the necessary steps (Art. 4(9)).[495] This **double step** avoids unnecessary efforts to ensure the appearance of a witness. Often, when the request is filed, the arbitral tribunal will not be in a position to determine the issue on a well-informed basis. It is submitted that the arbitral tribunal may therefore defer its decision until it becomes clear whether the testimony of that witness could actually be relevant to the case and material to its outcome.

The resources of the arbitral tribunal to obtain the testimony of a person   81
who will not appear voluntarily are limited. In particular, it has **no means of coercing a witness to obey a summons.**[496] Still, in some occasions, a person will be more willing to appear at an evidentiary hearing if (also) called by the arbitral tribunal and not by a party only.

Pursuant to the revised Art. 4(9), the arbitral tribunal may also **author-**   82
ize the requesting party, or order any other party, to take such steps as the arbitral tribunal considers appropriate. This new explicit competence mirrors the fact that under many *leges arbitri*, the parties are also allowed to apply to a state court for support in evidentiary matters (see e.g. Art. 184(2) PILS).[497]

Many national laws allow the arbitral tribunal or a party to call upon the   83
assistance of a state court judge.[498] In Swiss arbitral proceedings, Art. 184(2) PILS can serve as basis for applying to the state court judge for assistance with regard to witness testimony. The arbitral tribunal or the party interested in the examination of a witness may request the state court judge at the seat of the arbitration to assist in the taking of evidence by summoning recalcitrant witnesses.[499] If a recalcitrant witness is not located at the seat of the arbitration, the tribunal nevertheless has to approach the state court judge at its seat; that judge then has to prosecute the request through the channels of legal assistance.[500] As an alternative,

---

[495] IBA Working Party 1999, 29.

[496] Nater-Bass in Commentary Swiss Rules, Art. 25 N 10; Bühler/Dorgan, 18.

[497] IBA Review Subcommittee 2010, 18.

[498] Bühler/Dorgan, 18; Lew/Mistelis/Kröll, 572; IBA Working Party 1999, 29; Oetiker, Witnesses, 265. Cf. also Art. 27 Model Law.

[499] Nater-Bass in Commentary Swiss Rules, Art. 25 N 10; PILS (Zurich)-Volken, Art. 184 N 18; Berger/Kellerhals, N 1226; Oetiker, Witnesses, 265. Critical PILS (Basel)-Schneider, Art. 184 N 62, with referrals. Decisions of the President of the Geneva Civil Court of 9 May 1990, ASA Bull 1990, 283, and of 15 October 1990, ASA Bull 1994, 306. Cf. also the decision of the Neuchâtel Civil Court of 16 February 2001, ASA Bull 2003, 142, in which the judge at the seat of the arbitration ordered a witness to answer a list of questions submitted to him by the arbitral tribunal.

[500] PILS (Zurich)-Volken, Art. 184 N 22–23; Oetiker, Witnesses, 265; Cf. also Rüede/Hadenfeldt, 266.

the arbitral tribunal may ask the state court judge at its seat to request through the channels of legal assistance that the witness be heard by the state court judge at its domicile.[501]

84   Instead of using this competence, arbitral tribunals will often **take the non-appearance of a witness into account when appraising the evidence.**[502] The Swiss Federal Supreme Court has decided that an arbitral tribunal does not violate the parties' right to be heard if it does not to seek the assistance of the state court judge in summoning witnesses *ex officio* in the absence of a motion by the parties, but instead waives hearing the respective witnesses.[503] The same applies if a witness fails to appear who was summoned not by motion of a party, but by resolution of the arbitral tribunal.[504]

IX.   Witness Appearance Ordered by the Arbitral Tribunal (par. 10)

85   Pursuant to Art. 4(10), the Arbitral Tribunal may, at any time before the arbitration is concluded, order any party to provide, or to use its best efforts to provide, the **appearance for testimony** at an evidentiary hearing of any person, including one whose testimony has not yet been offered.

86   Firstly, this provision empowers the arbitral tribunal wishing to hear testimony from a particular witness to **instruct the parties to produce such witness for examination.**[505] This power allows the arbitral tribunal amongst others to order the examination of a witness whose witness statement was submitted, but whose appearance was not requested by the parties.[506] In practice, the assessment of a case and of the relevant issues by the arbitral tribunal sometimes diverges from that of all parties involved. In such situations, it is mandatory for the arbitral tribunal to ensure that evidence is given on the issues it considers to be pertinent.

87   Secondly, Art. 4(10) allows the arbitral tribunal to order the appearance for testimony at an evidentiary hearing of **persons whose testimony has not yet been offered** in the arbitral proceedings. It is submitted that this inquisitorial power is very far-reaching and should be applied cautiously by

---

[501] ASA Bull 1994, 309.

[502] PILS (Basel)-Schneider, Art. 184 N 56–57; Nater-Bass in Commentary Swiss Rules, Art. 24 N 10; Rüede/Hadenfeldt, 263–264; Bühler/Dorgan, 18; Oetiker, Witnesses, 265.

[503] DFT of 15 March 1993, ASA Bull 1993, 398, 408–409 (in DFT 119 II 271, the relevant cons. 7 is not published); DFT 4P.221/1996 of 25 July 1997, ASA Bull 2000, 96, 103–104.

[504] DFT of 28 January 1997, ASA Bull 1998, 118, 126.

[505] Griffin, 26.

[506] Cf. N 66 above.

the arbitral tribunal. It is correct that arbitral tribunals should endeavour to effectively resolve the dispute before them and not merely to settle the proceedings.[507] However, it must be left to the discretion of the parties as to which arguments and evidence they wish to present in support of their position. There is a relevant difference between the taking of evidence from witnesses which were offered, but for whom the parties waived oral examination, and from persons who were not named as witnesses by any party.

A **valid exception** based on which the arbitral tribunal should hear per-   88
sons not offered as witnesses are those rare circumstances in which an arbitral tribunal must consider certain aspects *ex officio* and the parties have not, or at least not adequately, commented on these aspects. Even in this area, however, the arbitral tribunal must be cautious, since it runs the risk of exceeding its powers.[508]

The revised Art. 4(10) allows the party to whom the arbitral tribunal ad-   89
dresses a request for the appearance of a witness to **object** for any of the reasons set forth in Art. 9(2). In this case, the arbitral tribunal must decide whether the grounds for exclusion from evidence of the requested witness are given.

---

[507] OETIKER, Witnesses, 263; cf. WIRTH, 10–11.
[508] OETIKER, Witnesses, 263.

Article 5 Party-Appointed Experts

1. A Party may rely on a Party-Appointed Expert as a means of evidence on specific issues. Within the time ordered by the Arbitral Tribunal, (i) each Party shall identify any Party-Appointed Expert on whose testimony it intends to rely and the subject-matter of such testimony; and (ii) the Party-Appointed Expert shall submit an Expert Report.

2. The Expert Report shall contain:

    (a) the full name and address of the Party-Appointed Expert, a statement regarding his or her present and past relationship (if any) with any of the Parties, their legal advisors and the Arbitral Tribunal, and a description of his or her background, qualifications, training and experience;

    (b) a description of the instructions pursuant to which he or she is providing his or her opinions and conclusions;

    (c) a statement of his or her independence from the Parties, their legal advisors and the Arbitral Tribunal;

    (d) a statement of the facts on which he or she is basing his or her expert opinions and conclusions;

    (e) his or her expert opinions and conclusions, including a description of the methods, evidence and information used in arriving at the conclusions. Documents on which the Party-Appointed Expert relies that have not already been submitted shall be provided;

    (f) if the Expert Report has been translated, a statement as to the language in which it was originally prepared, and the language in which the Party-Appointed Expert anticipates giving testimony at the Evidentiary Hearing;

    (g) an affirmation of his or her genuine belief in the opinions expressed in the Expert Report;

    (h) the signature of the Party-Appointed Expert and its date and place; and

    (i) if the Expert Report has been signed by more than one person, an attribution of the entirety or specific parts of the Expert Report to each author.

3. If Expert Reports are submitted, any Party may, within the time ordered by the Arbitral Tribunal, submit to the Arbitral Tribunal and to the other Parties revised or additional Expert Reports, including reports or statements from persons not previously identified as Party-Appointed Experts, so long as any such revisions or ad-

ditions respond only to matters contained in another Party's Witness Statements, Expert Reports or other submissions that have not been previously presented in the arbitration.

4. The Arbitral Tribunal in its discretion may order that any Party-Appointed Experts who will submit or who have submitted Expert Reports on the same or related issues meet and confer on such issues. At such meeting, the Party-Appointed Experts shall attempt to reach agreement on the issues within the scope of their Expert Reports, and they shall record in writing any such issues on which they reach agreement, any remaining areas of disagreement and the reasons therefore.

5. If a Party-Appointed Expert whose appearance has been requested pursuant to Article 8.1 fails without a valid reason to appear for testimony at an Evidentiary Hearing, the Arbitral Tribunal shall disregard any Expert Report by that Party-Appointed Expert related to that Evidentiary Hearing unless, in exceptional circumstances, the Arbitral Tribunal decides otherwise.

6. If the appearance of a Party-Appointed Expert has not been requested pursuant to Article 8.1, none of the other Parties shall be deemed to have agreed to the correctness of the content of the Expert Report.

Contents

Other Rules

Art. 25(3) ICC; Art. 25 and 27(4) Swiss Rules; Art. 27(4) UNCITRAL; Art. 21(2) LCIA; Art. 35–36 ICSID; Art. 55(c) WIPO.

I.   2010 Revision

The former Art. 5(4) of the 1999 Rules provided that each party-appointed   1
expert whose expert report had been submitted had to appear for testimony at an evidentiary hearing unless the parties agreed otherwise. In the
2010 Revision, this provision was deleted. Instead, a **new Art. 8(1)** was
introduced, according to which each party-appointed expert has to appear
for testimony at the evidentiary hearing if his or her appearance is requested by the arbitral tribunal or any party. As a consequence, the wording of
Art. 5(5) and (6) was adapted. These amendments may have an impact on
how expert reports from party-appointed experts are treated in practice.[509]

The 2010 Revision also introduced a new requirement pursuant to which   2
each party has to **identify** any party-appointed expert on whose testimony
it intends to rely and the subject-matter of such testimony before submitting the respective expert report (Art. 5(1)). Furthermore, the required
content of the expert report was substantially expanded (Art. 5(2)). In
particular, a duty to disclose the instructions to the party-appointed expert
and the requirement of a **statement of independence** were included.
Also, the former requirement of an affirmation of truth was replaced by one
of genuine belief. The fact that expert reports are sometimes rendered by
more than one person was reflected in a provision which requires the attribution of the entirety or specific parts of the expert report to each author.

Finally, Art. 5(3) now explicitly provides for the possibility to submit **rebut-**   3
tal expert reports by party-appointed experts, thereby mirroring Art. 4(6)
regarding witness statements.

II.   Reliance on a Party-Appointed Expert (par. 1)

Art. 5(1) allows a party to rely on a party-appointed expert as a **means of**   4
evidence on specific issues. Therefore, reports by party-appointed experts
must not be treated as mere submissions by parties, as the procedural
rules in certain jurisdictions provide. Rather, the party-appointed expert's

---

[509] Cf. N 43–60 below.

opinion has its own weight which depends on his or her competence and credibility.

5   The **parties are entirely free** whether to avail themselves of party-appointed experts as means of evidence or not. The arbitral tribunal neither needs to give its consent to this form of evidence, nor does it have a possibility to interfere with the submission of reports by party-appointed experts.

6   Although party-appointed experts are treated analogously to witnesses of fact (which is evidenced by the term "expert witness" widely used), in contrast to the latter, their testimony primarily relates not to observations of facts, but to **opinions.**[510] Their position can be situated somewhere between that of witnesses of fact and of parties' counsel.[511] Expert witness evidence nowadays plays a significant, often decisive role in arbitral proceedings.[512]

III. Identification of Party-Appointed Expert (par. 1)

7   Art. 5(1)(i) provides that each Party shall **identify any party-appointed expert** on whose testimony it intends to rely and the subject matter of that testimony within the time ordered by the arbitral tribunal. This should prevent the opposing party from being surprised by unexpected expert reports by party-appointed experts.

8   The provision leaves great discretion to the arbitral tribunal by what **time** the party-appointed experts shall be identified. Pursuant to one common and reasonable method, the parties may be ordered to identify the evidence adduced or to be adduced to each allegation of fact in the briefs submitted. In the alternative, the parties may be allowed to make general references to evidence in their briefs and be ordered to submit a detailed list of the evidence they intend to rely on, indicating the content and relevance of each item, later in the proceedings.

IV. Expert Report

A.   General Remarks

9   From a procedural point of view, reports from party-appointed experts are **treated in a similar fashion as witness statements.** They will in principle only stand as evidence if the party-appointed expert appears at the

---

[510] Schneider, Experts, 447.
[511] Id., 447.
[512] Nater-Bass in Commentary Swiss Rules, Art. 25 N 8; Redfern/Hunter/Blackaby/Partasides, N 6.152–6.154.

evidentiary hearing and is available for examination by the other party and the arbitral tribunal.[513] Art. 5(2) states in rather detailed manner what the expert report needs to contain. The revised Art. 6(4) provides for analogous requirements for reports by tribunal-appointed experts.[514]

B.   Submission (par. 1)

Pursuant to Art. 5(1)(ii), a party-appointed expert must submit his or her   10
expert report **within the time ordered** by the arbitral tribunal. The question when the expert report must be submitted has to be distinguished from the question when party-appointed experts must be identified.[515] It is possible that the arbitral tribunal requires the parties to identify the party-appointed experts on whose testimony they intend to rely and the subject-matter of such testimony at a relatively early stage, e.g. in the briefs, but allows the parties to submit the reports only at a later stage, e.g. together with the witness statements.

The **options** for the arbitral tribunal to tackle the issue of when the expert   11
reports must be submitted are analogous to those with regard to witness statements.[516] When scheduling the submission of expert reports, the arbitral tribunal should consider the interaction of the report with other submissions made by the parties.[517]

Although the wording of Art. 5(1)(ii) seems to imply that the party-appoint-   12
ed expert submits his or her report directly to the arbitral tribunal, this does not seem to be appropriate. Rather, the expert report should be treated like documentary evidence and witness statements and therefore be **submitted by the parties** to the arbitral tribunal and the other parties.

C.   Content (par. 2)

Art. 5(2) sets out in a rather **detailed manner** what the party-appointed   13
expert's report needs to contain.

1.   Identity of the Expert (par. 2(a))

In order to duly perceive the content of an expert report, it is important to   14
understand who the party-appointed expert is, what his or her relations to the parties, their legal advisors and the arbitral tribunal are and

---

[513] Schneider, Experts, 447.
[514] Cf. Art. 6 N 48–61 below.
[515] Cf. N 7–8 above.
[516] Cf. N 7–8 above.
[517] IBA Working Party 1999, 30.

what his or her professional background is. For that purpose, Art. 5(2)(a) requires that the party-appointed expert's report states:

- the full name and address of the expert;

- a statement regarding his or her present and past relationship (if any) with any of the parties, their legal advisors and the arbitral tribunal; and

- a description of his or her background, qualifications, training and experience.[518]

15   The 2010 Revision introduced a requirement for the party-appointed expert to disclose his or her present or past **relationship to the party's legal advisor(s) and the arbitral tribunal.** The former requirement is important to avoid that legal advisors always employ the same expert who in turn renders particularly favourable opinions.

16   In order to give the arbitral tribunal a better perception of who the expert is, he or she should also attach **a full CV** to the report.

2.   Description of Instructions (par. 2(b))

17   The opinions expressed by an expert generally depend very much on the questions put before him or her and the instructions given to the expert. In the case of a party-appointed expert, this is **not necessarily transparent.** Furthermore, the party may reshape the questions and instructions after having obtained a first (draft) opinion. Or certain opinions which do not fit in with the position of the respective party are left out in the final report.

18   Hence, the **reliability** of reports by party-appointed experts may be **increased** (and the danger of reports being overly influenced by the parties reduced) if the expert has to disclose his or her instructions. Accordingly, the newly introduced Art. 5(2)(b) requires that the party-appointed expert's report contain a description of the instructions pursuant to which he or she is providing his or her opinions and conclusions.[519] Such description should also include any amendments to the instructions.

3.   Statement of Independence (par. 2(c))

19   Pursuant to Art. 5(2)(c), the party-appointed expert's report must embrace a statement of his or her independence from the parties, their legal advi-

---

[518] Contrary to the provision regarding witnesses, Art. 5 requires that this information must always be given since it will in any case be material for the assessment of the report.

[519] HARRIS, 213.

sors and the arbitral tribunal.[520] While Art. 5(2)(a) requires mere disclosure of a past or present relationship with any of the parties, their legal advisors and the arbitral tribunal, Art. 5(2)(c) requires the expert to **evaluate any such relationships** and attest that he or she is "independent".[521]

This new provision emphasises the duty of each party-appointed expert to assess the case in an independent and neutral fashion, while it does not want to exclude experts with some connection to the participants or the subject-matter of the case.[522] This fits in with the fact that a party-appointed expert is **not a party representative** (although some of these experts seem to think that this is their role). 20

The Chartered Institute of Arbitrators recently published a **Protocol for the Use of Party-Appointed Expert Witnesses in International Arbitration** which is drawing on the reforms that have been undertaken in some common law jurisdictions with regard to expert witnesses.[523] The Protocol also requests that the expert shall be independent of the party by which he or she was appointed (Art. 4(1) of the Protocol).[524] 21

Obviously, receiving payment for services as an expert does not preclude "independence".[525] However, the expert must not have any **financial interest in the outcome** of the case or otherwise have relationships that would prevent him or her from providing an honest and frank opinion.[526] 22

4.   Statement of Facts (par. 2(d))

The expert report must contain a statement of the facts on which he or she is basing the opinions and conclusions (Art. 5(2)(d)). Since the core of the expert report is not the description of facts, but the conclusions drawn and opinions expressed, the description of facts **does not need to be *full and detailed*** as in witness statements. Rather, the representation of the facts should be made in a manner which allows comprehending and following the expert's opinions and conclusions. Still, the factual basis on which the expert draws his or her conclusions must be clearly identified. 23

---

[520] Harris, 212.
[521] IBA Review Subcommittee 2010, 19; critical Harris, 213, who pleads in favour of a test which focuses on impartiality.
[522] IBA Review Subcommittee 2010, 19.
[523] Jones, 137.
[524] Jones, 141–142.
[525] IBA Review Subcommittee 2010, 19.
[526] Id.

5.   Expert's Opinions and Conclusions (par. 2(e))

24   Most importantly, the expert report must include the expert's opinions and conclusions (Art. 5(2)(e)). The reader of the report should be enabled to clearly **distinguish** between the facts on which the opinions and conclusions are based and the opinions and conclusions themselves. Usually, it would seem appropriate for the report to provide for separate sections or sub-sections.

25   In order to allow the reader to easily perceive the content of the expert report, it may be sensible to **identify the questions** put to the expert[527] at the beginning of the report and to provide – in the sense of an executive summary – for brief and clear answers to these questions at the end of the report.

26   The statement of opinions and conclusions of an expert report must include a description of the methods, evidence and information used in arriving at the conclusions (Art. 5(2)(e)). Basically, the expert report should **state the reasoning of the expert** in a manner that may be comprehended by the parties and the arbitral tribunal.[528]

27   Finally, in the 2010 Revision, a new sentence was added to Art. 5(2)(e), pursuant to which **documents the party-appointed expert is relying on** and which have not already been submitted shall be provided, i.e. attached to the expert report. On the one hand, this is a very sensible rule since it will make clear on what documents, if any, the party-appointed expert bases its affirmations. On the other hand, this rule gives leeway to potential abuse in that a party may try to introduce additional documentary evidence by attaching it to the expert report. This danger exists in particular if the expert report is submitted only after the full exchange of briefs. Hence, the arbitral tribunal should be careful in admitting such documents as documentary evidence or, even better, include a rule in the procedural rules clearly stating to which extent the parties may rely on documents submitted only by party-appointed experts in their expert reports.

6.   Language (par. 2(f))

28   If the expert report was translated, a statement is required as to the language in which it was **originally prepared,** and the language in which the party-appointed expert anticipates giving testimony at the evidentiary hearing (Art. 5(2)(f)). This conveys useful information to the arbitral tribu-

---

[527] Cf. in this regard also Art. 5(2)(b) which requires the disclosure of the instructions to the expert, including the questions put before him or her.

[528] IBA Review Subcommittee 2010, 19.

nal. On the one hand, it may explain why the language of an expert report originally prepared not in the expert's mother tongue contains linguistic errors or, to the contrary, a language level which may not be attributed to the expert, but rather to the translator (or the translating counsel). On the other hand, it will be clear from the outset which expert may be heard in the language of the proceedings and which needs interpretation.

7.   Affirmation of Genuine Belief (par. 2(g))

In the 2010 Revision, the requirement for an expert report to contain a   29
statement of truth was (rightly) omitted. The expert report does not express facts, but (to the degree possible, objectively reasoned) opinions. In line with this, the revised Art. 5(2)(g) requires an affirmation by the party-appointed expert of his or her **genuine belief in the opinions expressed.**[529] Hence, the expert needs to declare that he or she actually believes what is stated in the report.

8.   Signature (par. 2(h))

Pursuant to Art. 5(2)(h), the expert report must **contain the signature**   30
of the expert and its date and place. If the signature is lacking, the arbitral tribunal will order the party submitting the respective expert report to obtain the signature within a short time limit. If the expert report remains unsigned, the arbitral tribunal will have to disregard it unless there are sufficient objective reasons why the party-appointed expert is not in a position to sign the report.

9.   Attribution to Several Authors (par. 2(i))

Pursuant to Art. 5(2)(i), if multiple persons sign an expert report, e.g. if   31
an organisation is hired as an expert or two experts produce a joint report, the expert report must indicate whether it is attributable as a whole to a **single author** or, if not, which specific parts thereof may be attributed to each **co-author.**[530] This information allows the arbitral tribunal and the parties to assess whether the opinions were expressed by the person who is an expert in the respective field (if several experts produce a joint expert, they will often have different fields of expertise). Furthermore, it puts the arbitral tribunal and the parties in a position to determine which experts should attend the evidentiary hearing and to prepare for questioning one or more of the co-authors.[531]

---

[529] HARRIS, 213–214.
[530] IBA REVIEW SUBCOMMITTEE 2010, 19.
[531] IBA REVIEW SUBCOMMITTEE 2010, 20.

V.   Rebuttal Expert Reports (par. 3)

32   Art. 5(3) explicitly grants the parties the right to submit rebuttal expert reports. It is submitted that such right flows from the right to be heard, so that the parties are entitled to do so even **without the authorisation by the arbitral tribunal.** The arbitral tribunal is only called to set a respective time limit in order to ensure equal treatment of the parties and a smooth procedure.

33   The rebuttal expert reports may consist of **revised or additional expert reports.** To revise an expert report means that the expert may add additional facts and/or further opinions and conclusions. In principle, the expert may also amend his or her earlier description of certain facts and/or opinions and conclusions. However, this must be done with caution since it may jeopardise the credibility of the expert. Still, it is always possible that the opinions and conclusions of other experts elicit further considerations. This should be indicated by appropriate wording in an amended report (e.g. "In view of Mr X's expert report, I can state more precisely as follows").

34   The possible **scope** of the rebuttal expert reports is **limited** in two respects:

35   Firstly, any revisions or additions in the rebuttal expert reports must **respond only to matters contained in a witness statement, expert report or other submission** of the other party. Hence, the parties are not allowed to introduce new descriptions of facts unless they directly respond to a statement submitted by the other party. This limitation is necessary to avoid that the parties hold back certain opinions and conclusions of their party-appointed experts in the first round of expert reports for strategic reasons.

36   Secondly, rebuttal expert reports are only allowed on **matters that have not been previously presented** in the arbitration. The word "previously" refers to the time of the submission of the witness statements, expert reports or other submissions, in which the rebutted opinions and conclusions are contained. Hence, expert reports on any issue presented in the briefs of any party or in any other document submitted before that time must be presented in the first round of expert reports. Art. 5(3) does not allow to present arguments on such issues only in the rebuttal expert reports. Again, this rule is directed against the strategic holding back of expert opinions.

37   While the purpose of this second limitation provided for in Art. 5(3) is in principle justified, it may lead to overly lengthy and numerous expert reports. Each party will need to anticipate whether the other party will be able, and actually will submit, expert reports on each of the matters presented

in the arbitration and then decide on the basis of this anticipation whether to submit own expert reports to contest. In certain circumstances, it may be more efficient to allow the parties to include expert reports on issues previously presented in the arbitration in the rebuttal expert reports only. Therefore, it is submitted that the second limitation of Art. 5(3) should **not be applied too strictly** in practice.

Rebuttal expert reports may also be submitted by **persons not previous-   38 ly named** as party-appointed experts. This appears to contradict the requirement pursuant to which each party must identify any party-appointed expert on whose testimony it intends to rely within the time ordered by the arbitral tribunal (Art. 5(1)). It is submitted, however, that the requirement to identify party-appointed experts does not limit the possibility to submit rebuttal expert reports by party-appointed experts which were not named before since they are commissioned in relation (and limited) to issues not previously presented.

VI.   Expert Meeting (par. 4)

By virtue of Art. 5(4), the arbitral tribunal may order that any party-ap   39 pointed experts who will submit or have submitted expert reports on the same or related issues meet and confer on such issues. The provision explicitly states that ordering such a meeting is in the **full discretion of the arbitral tribunal.** Accordingly, the parties do not have a formal right to request that such meeting be held.

The expert meeting provided for by Art. 5(4) must **not be confused with   40 so-called expert conferencing.**[532] Whereas the latter takes place at the evidentiary hearing in the presence of the arbitral tribunal and the parties, the expert meeting is held between the experts only.

The aim of the expert meeting is to reduce any differences between the   41 opinions expressed to the extent possible and therefore to **narrow down the scope of issues** on which expert evidence must be given at the evidentiary hearing. The party-appointed experts must attempt to reach agreement on the issues within the scope of their expert reports, and they must record in writing any such issues on which they reach agreement, any remaining areas of disagreement and the reasons therefore (Art. 5(4)).

Party-appointed experts are not party representatives, but a means of   42 evidence offered by the parties. Accordingly, the agreement of the party-appointed experts on certain factual findings or common conclusions **does not formally bind the parties.** They must be allowed to offer further

---

[532] Cf. Art. 8 N 31.

evidence if they do not share the findings as agreed between the party-appointed experts, although it will in practice often be difficult for a party to get around the findings shared by the expert whom it had itself appointed.

VII. Right to Examination of Party-Appointed Experts

A. 2010 Revision: Omission of the General Duty to Appear Before the Arbitral Tribunal

43   The 1999 Rules provided for a **general rule** pursuant to which each party-appointed expert whose expert report had been submitted to **appear for testimony** at an evidentiary hearing, unless the parties agreed otherwise (Art. 5(4) of the 1999 Rules).

44   The revised 2010 Rules take another approach to this issue. A new Art. 8(1) was introduced, pursuant to which each party must inform the arbitral tribunal and the other parties of the **party-appointed experts whose appearance it requests** within the time ordered by the arbitral tribunal. Only if a party-appointed expert's appearance is requested by any party or by the arbitral tribunal, the duty to appear is triggered.

45   This rule is in line with the **current general practice,** according to which party-appointed experts appear only if their examination is requested. It also takes account of the fact that most parties will only accept party-appointed expert reports to be given more weight than mere written factual allegations by the parties if the parties are granted the opportunity to challenge the expert's views.

46   Generally, **the parties are responsible for the appearance** of the party-appointed experts which they have called at the witness hearing. If a party is not in a position to ensure the appearance of a party-appointed expert, the arbitral tribunal should assume this duty (although it has to be noted that its means in this respect are limited).

B. Waiver of Appearance (par. 6)

47   As stated in the revised Art. 8(1), a party-appointed expert whose expert report had been submitted must appear only if any party or the arbitral tribunal **requests** so.

48   This explicitly includes the right of the arbitral tribunal to request the appearance **even if none of the parties** does. In many cases, it will be sensible from the arbitral tribunal's view to have the expert examined orally

since it will allow the expert to make his or her report come to life upon examination.[533]

The **unilateral waiver** of the expert's appearance by the opposite party   49
is in principle sufficient. However, the revised wording of Art. 8(1) makes it clear that *any* party, i.e. also the party who presented the respective party-appointed expert, and the arbitral tribunal may request his or her appearance. Hence, the unilateral waiver of the opposite party will lead to the non-appearance of such witness unless any other party or the arbitral tribunal requests the appearance.

Art. 5(6) clarifies that an agreement of the parties pursuant to which a   50
party-appointed expert does not need to appear for testimony at an evidentiary hearing shall not be considered to reflect an agreement as to the correctness of the content of such expert's report. This is appropriate: the parties are at liberty to **challenge expert reports by other means,** such as documentary evidence, another expert report or another expert's testimony to the contrary.

C.   Failure to Appear (par. 5)

1.   General Rule

Art. 5(5) states that, if a party-appointed expert whose appearance was re-   51
quested pursuant to Art. 8(1) fails to appear for testimony at an evidentiary hearing without a valid reason, the arbitral tribunal must **disregard its expert report** unless, in exceptional circumstances, the arbitral tribunal determines otherwise. Accordingly, pursuant to the general rule, the expert report of a party-appointed expert who cannot be examined orally must not be taken into account by the arbitral tribunal. There are a number of explicit and implicit exceptions to this rather strict and inflexible rule which need to be discussed in the following.

It was suggested that the report of a party-appointed expert who does   52
not appear at the evidentiary hearing, despite a request for appearance, might be taken into account by the arbitral tribunal as **part of the party's written argument.**[534] The arbitral tribunal should in normal cases not follow this suggestion: Firstly, the parties should plead their cases in their briefs, not by expert reports. Secondly, in the interest of due process, there should be a high incentive for a party-appointed expert to actually appear at the evidentiary hearing. This incentive would be lowered if the arbitral tribunal took the expert report into account as party pleadings in case of

---

[533] Cf. generally KREINDLER, Oral Testimony, 87.
[534] SCHNEIDER, Experts, 447.

non-appearance. Thirdly, the words of a party-appointed expert may still have a different weight than the arguments developed by counsel, even if the expert does not appear. It is therefore to be expected that a report of a non-appearing expert would have more weight than mere party pleadings. Hence, party-appointed experts should be treated as a means of evidence, not as party representatives.[535]

2.   Waiver of Appearance by the Parties

53   As was already stated above, the parties may waive the appearance of a party-appointed expert whose expert report was submitted at the evidentiary hearing. As a consequence thereof, the report of a party-appointed expert whose examination was waived by the opposing party must be regarded as a valid means of evidence which **remains in the records.** However, the arbitral tribunal must appraise this expert report in light of the further evidence obtained.

54   If the arbitral tribunal has some doubts about the accurateness of the expert report or if it wishes to examine the expert for other reasons, it **must request the appearance of the party-appointed expert** pursuant to Art. 8(1). If the expert refuses to appear, it will in general be appropriate to disregard the expert report.

3.   Waiver of Appearance by the Arbitral Tribunal

55   Even if the parties may request to cross-examine experts appointed by the opposing party (or to examine their own party-appointed experts) pursuant to Art. 8(1), it is within the power and discretion of the arbitral tribunal to **deny,** in the context of an anticipated appraisal of evidence, **the examination** of a party-appointed expert if it deems the content of his or her report to be irrelevant.

56   The arbitral tribunal should be **hesitant** not to hear party-appointed experts who have delivered an expert report, if this is contrary to the request of a party. Rather, the arbitral tribunal should allow for the examination and decide on the relevance of the expert's findings after the hearing. Still, it is submitted that the arbitral tribunal may take a stricter approach than with regard to witnesses, since the relevance and the scope of an expert report may be appraised better in advance than the scope of the testimony of witnesses of fact.

57   If the arbitral tribunal decides not to hear a party-appointed expert whose cross-examination was requested, the expert's report will **remain on file.**

---

[535] Similar BERGER/KELLERHALS, N 1228.

However, it is obvious that the arbitral tribunal will attribute little weight to such expert report since it declined to have the expert examined.

4.   Experts Who are Unavailable for Examination Because of Objective Reasons

Art. 5(5) provides that an expert report shall only be disregarded if the re-   58
spective party-appointed expert does not appear at an evidentiary hearing **without a valid reason.** If a party-appointed expert is indeed willing to appear for examination, but is unable to do so for objective reasons (such as serious illness, overly long travel distance, etc.), it is justified as a rule to leave the expert report in the record. The arbitral tribunal has to take into consideration, within the scope of its unrestricted appraisal of evidence, the circumstance that the expert has not appeared.

This approach is **reasonable** – at least under Swiss law – even if the   59
applicable rules of procedural law (arbitration agreement of the parties, arbitration rules, procedural rules issued by the arbitral tribunal) contain a mandatory rule that expert reports be removed from the record if the party-appointed expert does not appear. If the arbitral tribunal were not to take the expert report of such a party-appointed expert into consideration, even though it is relevant, this might amount to a violation of the right to be heard, potentially leading to the annulment of the arbitral award on the basis of Art. 190(2)(d) PILS or the refusal of enforcement based on Art. V(1)(b) NYC. In contrast, the violation of any rules or procedural laws mandating removal from the record is not viewed in the case law of the Swiss Federal Supreme Court as a sufficient basis for successfully contesting an arbitration award.[536]

5.   Unexcused Non-Appearance

With regard to witnesses who have produced a witness statement, it was   60
argued above that a liberal approach should be taken if they refuse to appear.[537] It is submitted that this is not the case for party-appointed experts. Unlike witnesses, party-appointed experts are under a specific contractual obligation towards their principal to appear at the evidentiary hearing. Hence, there is **no circumstance which could excuse the expert's refusal to appear.** Taking a different position would allow the parties to decide for the non-appearance of an expert for strategic considerations.

---

[536] With regard to witness statements, cf. for Art. 190(2)(d) PILS: DFT 4P.74/2006 of 19 June 2006, cons. 6.3; DFT 4P.23/2006 of 27 March 2006, cons. 4.2; DFT 4P.93/2004 of 1 July 2004, cons. 2.1; DFT 117 II 347. For Art. 190(2)(e) PILS: DFT 4P.23/2006 of 27 March 2006, cons. 4.2; DFT 128 III 191.

[537] Cf. Art. 4 N 77.

Article 6   Tribunal-Appointed Experts

1. The Arbitral Tribunal, after consulting with the Parties, may appoint one or more independent Tribunal-Appointed Experts to report to it on specific issues designated by the Arbitral Tribunal. The Arbitral Tribunal shall establish the terms of reference for any Tribunal-Appointed Expert Report after consulting with the Parties. A copy of the final terms of reference shall be sent by the Arbitral Tribunal to the Parties.

2. The Tribunal-Appointed Expert shall, before accepting appointment, submit to the Arbitral Tribunal and to the Parties a description of his or her qualifications and a statement of his or her independence from the Parties, their legal advisors and the Arbitral Tribunal. Within the time ordered by the Arbitral Tribunal, the Parties shall inform the Arbitral Tribunal whether they have any objections as to the Tribunal-Appointed Expert's qualifications and independence. The Arbitral Tribunal shall decide promptly whether to accept any such objection. After the appointment of a Tribunal-Appointed Expert, a Party may object to the expert's qualifications or independence only if the objection is for reasons of which the Party becomes aware after the appointment has been made. The Arbitral Tribunal shall decide promptly what, if any, action to take.

3. Subject to the provisions of Article 9.2, the Tribunal-Appointed Expert may request a Party to provide any information or to provide access to any Documents, goods, samples, property, machinery, systems, processes or site for inspection, to the extent relevant to the case and material to its outcome. The authority of a Tribunal-Appointed Expert to request such information or access shall be the same as the authority of the Arbitral Tribunal. The Parties and their representatives shall have the right to receive any such information and to attend any such inspection. Any disagreement between a Tribunal-Appointed Expert and a Party as to the relevance, materiality or appropriateness of such a request shall be decided by the Arbitral Tribunal, in the manner provided in Articles 3.5 through 3.8. The Tribunal-Appointed Expert shall record in the Expert Report any non-compliance by a Party with an appropriate request or decision by the Arbitral Tribunal and shall describe its effects on the determination of the specific issue.

4. The Tribunal-Appointed Expert shall report in writing to the Arbitral Tribunal in an Expert Report. The Expert Report shall contain:

    (a) the full name and address of the Tribunal-Appointed Expert, and a description of his or her background, qualifications, training and experience;

(b) a statement of the facts on which he or she is basing his or her expert opinions and conclusions;

(c) his or her expert opinions and conclusions, including a description of the methods, evidence and information used in arriving at the conclusions. Documents on which the Tribunal-Appointed Expert relies that have not already been submitted shall be provided;

(d) if the Expert Report has been translated, a statement as to the language in which it was originally prepared, and the language in which the Tribunal-Appointed Expert anticipates giving testimony at the Evidentiary Hearing;

(e) an affirmation of his or her genuine belief in the opinions expressed in the Expert Report;

(f) the signature of the Tribunal-Appointed Expert and its date and place; and

(g) if the Expert Report has been signed by more than one person, an attribution of the entirety or specific parts of the Expert Report to each author.

5. The Arbitral Tribunal shall send a copy of such Expert Report to the Parties. The Parties may examine any information, Documents, goods, samples, property, machinery, systems, processes or site for inspection that the Tribunal-Appointed Expert has examined and any correspondence between the Arbitral Tribunal and the Tribunal-Appointed Expert. Within the time ordered by the Arbitral Tribunal, any Party shall have the opportunity to respond to the Expert Report in a submission by the Party or through a Witness Statement or an Expert Report by a Party-Appointed Expert. The Arbitral Tribunal shall send the submission, Witness Statement or Expert Report to the Tribunal-Appointed Expert and to the other Parties.

6. At the request of a Party or of the Arbitral Tribunal, the Tribunal-Appointed Expert shall be present at an Evidentiary Hearing. The Arbitral Tribunal may question the Tribunal-Appointed Expert, and he or she may be questioned by the Parties or by any Party-Appointed Expert on issues raised in his or her Expert Report, the Parties' submissions or Witness Statement or the Expert Reports made by the Party-Appointed Experts pursuant to Article 6.5.

7. Any Expert Report made by a Tribunal-Appointed Expert and its conclusions shall be assessed by the Arbitral Tribunal with due regard to all circumstances of the case.

8. The fees and expenses of a Tribunal-Appointed Expert, to be funded in a manner determined by the Arbitral Tribunal, shall form part of the costs of the arbitration.

Contents   Note

Other Rules

Art. 25(4) and 37(1) ICC; Art. 27 Swiss Rules; Art. 27 UNCITRAL; Art. 21 LCIA; Art. 55 WIPO.

I.   2010 Revision

The 2010 Revision introduced a new limitation of the parties' **right to ob-**   1
ject to the expert's qualifications and independence: after the appointment of a tribunal-appointed expert, such objections may be made only for reasons of which the party becomes aware after the appointment has been made (Art. 6(2)).

2   Furthermore, Art. 6(4) now contains a comprehensive list of the required
      content of the expert report, which corresponds in most parts to the
      required content of expert reports by party-appointed experts.

II.   Appointment of Experts by the Arbitral Tribunal

A.   General Remarks (par. 1)

3   Art. 6(1), first sentence, allows the arbitral tribunal, after consulting with
      the parties, to appoint one or more independent tribunal-appointed experts
      to report to it on specific issues designated by the arbitral tribunal. The
      power of the arbitral tribunal to appoint experts is **widely recognised,**
      even in the absence of an explicit authorisation in the arbitrators' mandate
      and/or the applicable procedural rules.[538]

4   Although Art. 6(1) does not contain any provision in this regard, it is clear
      that the arbitral tribunal may appoint an expert **at its own discretion** as
      well as at the request of a party.[539]

5   In view of the fact that the parties have specifically chosen the arbitra-
      tors for deciding the dispute at hand, the arbitral tribunal should **avoid
      delegating the assessment of relevant issues** to experts. Rather, it
      should carefully scrutinise the parties' submissions in order to clearly and
      restrictively define the issues to be submitted to the expert.[540] This is par-
      ticularly true if the arbitrators were appointed because of their expertise in
      the subject matter of the dispute.

6   When considering whether to appoint an expert at its own discretion, the
      arbitral tribunal must, *inter alia,* take into account the **imminent costs**
      and the (sometimes substantial) **delay** of the proceedings.[541]

B.   Duty to Appoint an Expert

7   Pursuant to the Swiss Federal Supreme Court's standing practice, the arbi-
      tral tribunal is under a **duty to approve a party's request** that an expert
      be appointed if it is brought forward in due time and form and if the party
      undertakes to pay the necessary advance on costs, unless there are valid
      reasons pursuant to which an expert report is not necessary to decide the

---

[538] PILS (Basel)-Schneider, Art. 184 N 34; Oetiker in Commentary Swiss Rules, Art. 27 N 2;
      Weiss/Bürgi Locatelli, 484; Poudret/Besson, N 663; Redfern/Hunter/Blackaby/Partasides,
      N 6.158; Lörcher, 485; Girsberger/Voser, 220; Born, 1860.
[539] Oetiker in Commentary Swiss Rules, Art. 27 N 3; Aden, 637; Weigand-Trittmann/Duve,
      Art. 27 UNCITRAL N 2; Berger/Kellerhals, N 1232; Poudret/Besson, N 663.
[540] Schneider, Experts, 452; Oetiker in Commentary Swiss Rules, Art. 27 N 9.
[541] Weiss/Bürgi Locatelli, 483; Schneider, Experts, 455.

issue at stake.[542] If the request is brought by both parties jointly or concurrently, the arbitral tribunal should usually grant such request, although it is not bound to approve it unless the involvement of independent experts has been formally agreed by the parties.[543]

It is controversial whether the arbitral tribunal is under a **duty to appoint**   8
an expert on its own motion if it lacks certain knowledge required to properly decide the dispute.[544] A discussion on this issue was triggered by a decision of the Swiss Federal Supreme Court, finding that an arbitral tribunal which does not have the necessary technical knowledge must imperatively, and even in the absence of a party's request, appoint an expert, unless the expertise would be useless for the decision of the issues at stake.[545] It is submitted that such duty of the arbitral tribunal is irreconcilable with the nature of arbitration.[546] In fact, in two more recent decisions, the Court has answered the question in the negative, setting out that such a duty subsists only if a party requests the appointment of an expert.[547]

But even if such duty existed, the arbitral tribunal would **not be obliged**   9
to advance the fee of the expert out of the advance on costs which the parties have paid to cover the envisaged fees of the arbitral tribunal. Hence, the parties would need to pay an additional advance on costs. They would therefore be able to block an expertise ordered by the arbitral tribunal on its own motion by not advancing the respective costs.[548]

C.   Exclusion of the Arbitral Tribunal's Power

The parties may **derogate the arbitral tribunal's power** to appoint experts by agreement. If the parties stipulate such derogation, the arbitral   10
tribunal is bound thereby.[549] Despite of a derogation of the arbitral tribunal's power to appoint experts, the evidence submitted by the parties may

---

[542] DFT of 10 June 1996, ASA Bull 4/2000, 770; DFT of 11 May 1992, ASA Bull 3/1992, 397; Weiss/Bürgi Locatelli, 484–485; Müller, Case Law, 100; Poudret, 614–615; Oetiker in Commentary Swiss Rules, Art. 27 N 5; Berger/Kellerhals, N 1230; more restrictive Schneider, Experts, 454.

[543] Schneider, Experts, 454; Weiss/Bürgi Locatelli, 485; Oetiker in Commentary Swiss Rules, Art. 27 N 6.

[544] Cf. e.g. PILS (Basel)-Schneider, Art. 184 N 35; Weiss/Bürgi Locatelli, 484; Berger/Kellerhals, N 1232; Poudret/Besson, N 664.

[545] DFT of 25 May 1992, ASA Bull 3/1992, 397.

[546] Berger/Kellerhals, N 1232.

[547] DFT of 10 June 1996, ASA Bull 4/2000, 769–770; confirmed in DFT of 16 October 2003, ASA Bull 2/2004, 377–378; cf. also Poudret, 614.

[548] Weiss/Bürgi Locatelli, 484; Oetiker in Commentary Swiss Rules, Art. 27 N 4.

[549] PILS (Basel)-Schneider, Art. 184 N 34; Weiss/Bürgi Locatelli, 486; Poudret/Besson, N 663; Poudret, 616–617; Oetiker in Commentary Swiss Rules, Art. 27 N 7; Berger/Kellerhals, N 1235; Lörcher, 485–486.

include statements of party-appointed experts since they are not affected by such derogation.[550]

11   In the absence of the power to appoint experts, the arbitral tribunal must decide the case on the basis of the **evidence offered by the parties.** If the evidence produced by the parties is not sufficient to support their respective claims and defences, the arbitral tribunal should proceed on the basis of the rules on the burden of proof pursuant to the applicable law.[551] If this approach still does not allow the arbitral tribunal to come to a proper decision, it may choose to avail itself of a possible competence to decide *ex aequo et bono*[552] to circumvent the existing difficulties. As an ultimate possibility, the arbitral tribunal may decide to step down.[553] However, in view of its mandate to resolve the parties' dispute, the arbitral tribunal should avoid this *ultima ratio*.

12   The arbitral tribunal may also consider **disregarding the parties' derogation** of its power to appoint experts: Since it is accepted that procedural rules agreed upon by the parties are not mandatory procedural rules, the arbitral tribunal will thereby not expose the award to annulment.[554]

D.   Duty to Consult with the Parties (par. 1)

13   Art. 6(1), first sentence, explicitly states that the arbitral tribunal may appoint an expert only **after consulting the parties.** However, the provision does not indicate on what the arbitral tribunal needs to consult with the parties.

14   Such consultation shall include on the one hand the duty to **inform the parties** (i) that an expert will be appointed, (ii) whom the arbitral tribunal intends to appoint and (iii) what the expert shall report on. On the other hand, the arbitral tribunal must give the parties the opportunity to **express their opinion** on each of these issues. The decision remains with the arbitral tribunal.[555]

E.   Choosing the Expert

15   With regard to the choice of the expert, the arbitral tribunal is in principle **free to appoint an appropriate person.** It may ask the parties to try to

---

[550] Oetiker in Commentary Swiss Rules, Art. 27 N 7.
[551] Weiss/Bürgi Locatelli, 486; Oetiker in Commentary Swiss Rules, Art. 27 N 7.
[552] Cf. e.g. Art. 187(2) PILS.
[553] Weiss/Bürgi Locatelli, 486; Poudret/Besson, N 663; Oetiker in Commentary Swiss Rules, Art. 27 N 7; Berger/Kellerhals, N 1235.
[554] DFT 117 II 346, c. 1.b.aa; Berger/Kellerhals, N 1235; Poudret/Besson, N 663.
[555] Oetiker in Commentary Swiss Rules, Art. 27 N 8.

agree on an expert or require each party individually to identify possible experts and to submit a respective list. If the arbitral tribunal lacks knowledge of appropriate experts, it may also request specialised institutions for a proposal,[556] e.g. the ICC International Centre for Expertise, WIPO or national or international professional organisations. In any event, the arbitral tribunal must hear the parties in respect of the expert to be appointed.[557]

Experts may be appointed as **individuals, institutions or companies.**[558]   16
In particular, where complex issues are to be reported on, the appointment of an institution or a company is often appropriate.[559] The Rules do not contain any limitation in this respect. If an institution or a company is appointed, one (or several) responsible individual(s) within the company must be identified, in order to be able to comply with the parties' right to be heard amongst other matters.[560]

F.   Contractual Relationship of the Expert

Upon appointment of the expert by the arbitral tribunal, a **contractual**   17
relationship between the parties and the expert is created.[561] The position taken by some authors pursuant to which the arbitral tribunal (or its members jointly) become(s) a party to the contract with the expert[562] should not be followed. As a consequence of the contractual relationship between the parties and the expert, the parties are directly liable to the expert for his or her remuneration and the expert has a contractual liability towards the parties to duly submit the expert report.[563] On the basis of this contractual relationship, the expert may also become liable to the parties for any damage caused. Furthermore, the parties may at any time jointly, and without the possibility of interference by the arbitral tribunal, release the expert from his or her duties and/or, if the applicable law so permits, terminate the expert's contract.[564]

Under **Swiss law,** the contract between the parties and the expert must   18
be qualified either as a work contract (Art. 363–379 CO) or as an ordinary

---

[556] SCHNEIDER, Experts, 456.
[557] BERGER/KELLERHALS, N 1233; PILS (Basel)-SCHNEIDER, Art. 184 N 36; POUDRET/BESSON, N 665; KNOF, 74–75; VERMEILLE, 195–196.
[558] OETIKER in COMMENTARY SWISS RULES, Art. 27 N 10.
[559] SCHNEIDER, Experts, 456; more restrictive WEISS/BÜRGI LOCATELLI, 488.
[560] SCHNEIDER, Experts, 456; WEISS/BÜRGI LOCATELLI, 488; OETIKER in COMMENTARY SWISS RULES, Art. 27 N 10.
[561] WEISS/BÜRGI LOCATELLI, 496–497; LÖRCHER, 486.
[562] Cf. e.g. WEBER, 196.
[563] LÖRCHER, 486.
[564] OETIKER in COMMENTARY SWISS RULES, Art. 27 N 12.

mandate (Art. 394–406 CO).[565] The qualification is of some importance with regard to issues of termination and liability. Pursuant to the Swiss Federal Supreme Court, the contract qualifies as work contract only if the result of the expert's report may be verified on the basis of objective criteria; otherwise, it has to be qualified as an ordinary mandate.[566] Swiss authors usually argue that the contractual relationship between the parties and the expert is a mixed contract, containing elements of both types of contract.[567]

G.   Right of the Arbitral Tribunal to Release the Expert

19   The arbitral tribunal's competence to appoint experts includes the power to release an expert from his or her duties if it becomes clear that the expert is for some reason not in a position to properly fulfil his or her assignment. Unlike the parties, the arbitral tribunal may only base its decision to do so on **objective reasons.** In any case, the tribunal must consult with the parties before releasing an expert.[568]

H.   Scope of the Expert's Task

20   Tribunal-appointed experts are assigned to advise the arbitral tribunal on **technical questions and issues** as well as other **issues requiring special expertise** to be properly assessed and determined. The experts shall confer the necessary expertise onto the arbitral tribunal.[569]

21   Some authors allow for a **wider scope** of the expert's assignment, including the summarisation of voluminous evidence and the presentation thereof in usable form, the preservation of certain evidence and the expression of views on the claims altogether.[570] It is submitted that such tasks would go beyond the competence of an expert envisaged by Art. 6.[571] Still, it is understood that the parties may provide for, or agree to, such wider scope of the expert's tasks. For example, they may grant the expert the power to make a decision on certain factual issues which binds the parties *("Schiedsgutachten")*. However, such additional competences need to be agreed upon explicitly by the parties and may not be conferred onto the expert by the arbitral tribunal based on Art. 6 alone.[572] Or, if the arbitral

---

[565] Weber, 192; under German law, the contract is qualified as a work contract pursuant to § 631 BGB: Lörcher, 486, with references to case law.
[566] DFT 127 III 328 = ASA Bull 2/2002, 285.
[567] Weiss/Bürgi Locatelli, 495–496; PILS (Basel)-Schneider, Art. 184 N 38.
[568] Oetiker in Commentary Swiss Rules, Art. 27 N 14.
[569] Oetiker in Commentary Swiss Rules, Art. 27 N 15.
[570] PILS (Basel)-Schneider, Art. 184 N 33; Schneider, Experts, 450; cf. also Vermeille, 193.
[571] Oetiker in Commentary Swiss Rules, Art. 27 N 18.
[572] Poudret/Besson, N 666.

tribunal considers it as appropriate for an expert to summarise voluminous evidence, the parties may agree on the appointment of such expert.

III. Expert's Terms of Reference (par. 1)

Pursuant to Art. 6(1), second sentence, the arbitral tribunal shall establish the terms of reference for any tribunal-appointed expert report after consulting with the parties. The provision does not state **what the expert's terms of reference need to contain.** They should on the one hand define the tasks assigned to the expert and the issues on which the expert shall report and on the other hand set out the terms of the assignment.   22

When determining the **issues on which the expert shall report,** the arbitral tribunal must consult with the parties. It will usually be appropriate to ask the parties to suggest questions to be submitted to the expert.[573] When eventually deciding which questions suggested shall be submitted to the expert, the arbitral tribunal must bear in mind that it is not the expert's task to provide the basis for a case which a party failed to make. It is upon the parties to sufficiently substantiate their claims or defences.[574]   23

As to the terms of the expert's assignment, the tribunal must first of all determine **the expert's remuneration.** This should usually be done within the expert's terms of reference, but may also be determined in a procedural order or separately based on a budget or cost estimate of the expert.[575] The remuneration scheme also becomes part of the contract between the parties and the expert.[576]   24

Further, the arbitral tribunal should provide for the **expert's schedule,** fixing a time limit to complete his or her work.[577] Also the question of whether the expert may use auxiliary persons in completing his or her task should be resolved.[578]   25

Finally, the expert's terms of reference should contain a **confidentiality obligation** and a referral to the **duty to act to the best of his or her knowledge.**[579] These obligations become part of the contract between the parties and the expert.   26

---

[573] PILS (Basel)-Schneider, Art. 184 N 38; Berger/Kellerhals, N 1233; Lörcher, 492; Vermeille, 197–198.
[574] Schneider, Experts, 451.
[575] Schneider, Experts, 459; Weiss/Bürgi Locatelli, 494–495.
[576] Oetiker in Commentary Swiss Rules, Art. 27 N 24; Lörcher, 491.
[577] Schneider, Experts, 460; Weiss/Bürgi Locatelli, 494.
[578] Lörcher, 492.
[579] If the seat of the arbitral tribunal is in Switzerland, Art. 307 of the Swiss Criminal Code (duty of truthfulness) may be referred to; Weiss/Bürgi Locatelli, 493.

27   It will usually be appropriate for the arbitral tribunal to draw up the ex-
      pert's terms of reference **after the expert's appointment.** In certain cir-
      cumstances, it may however be more convenient to prepare the terms of
      reference beforehand, in particular if the definition of issues will facilitate
      the search of an appropriate expert.[580] Equally, it seems appropriate for the
      arbitral tribunal (or its chairperson only) to liaise with the expert during
      the preparation of the terms of reference. The arbitral tribunal may also
      choose to prepare draft terms of reference and submit them to the expert
      and the parties for comments before issuing them in their final form.[581] In
      any event, the parties must be heard regarding the content of the terms
      of reference.[582]

28   The last sentence of Art. 6(1) provides that a copy of the final terms of
      reference shall be **communicated to the parties.** Since the tribunal must
      consult with, and must hear, the parties before appointing the expert and
      issuing the expert's terms of reference, the communication of a copy of the
      final version will usually only be a formal step which concludes the expert's
      appointment.[583]

IV.   Qualification and Independence of Expert (par. 2)

A.   Description of Qualifications

29   Pursuant to Art. 6(2), the tribunal-appointed expert must submit to the
      arbitral tribunal and to the parties a description of his or her qualifications
      before accepting an appointment. It is obvious that **an expert must have
      the necessary expertise** to determine the issues which are put before
      him or her. This is particularly the case if the expert is appointed by the
      arbitral tribunal, which usually means that the arbitral tribunal will more
      heavily rely on his or her opinions and conclusions than on the ones ex-
      pressed by a party-appointed expert.

30   The information given by the tribunal-appointed expert is the **basis for
      any objection** by a party regarding his or her qualifications.

B.   Statement of Independence

31   Pursuant to Art. 6(2), first sentence, the tribunal-appointed expert, before
      accepting the appointment, must submit to the arbitral tribunal and to
      the parties a statement of his or her independence from the parties, their

---

[580] SCHNEIDER, Experts, 458; OETIKER in COMMENTARY SWISS RULES, Art. 27 N 20.
[581] PILS (Basel)-SCHNEIDER, Art. 184 N 38; SCHNEIDER, Experts, 458; OETIKER in COMMENTARY
      SWISS RULES, Art. 27 N 22; VERMEILLE, 198.
[582] POUDRET/BESSON, N 665.
[583] OETIKER in COMMENTARY SWISS RULES, Art. 27 N 28.

legal advisors and the arbitral tribunal. This is in line with the rule that an expert must be **as impartial, unbiased and independent as a judge or arbitrator.**[584]

In the statement of independence, the expert should **disclose any exist-**   32
ing facts or circumstances that may, in the eyes of the parties, give rise to doubts as to the arbitrator's impartiality or independence, or thereafter as soon as he or she learns about them. An expert who has made a disclosure considers him- or herself to be impartial and independent of the parties despite the disclosed facts and therefore capable of performing his or her duties as expert. Any doubt as to whether an expert should disclose certain facts or circumstances should be resolved in favour of disclosure.[585]

C.   Objections by the Parties

Within the time ordered by the arbitral tribunal, the parties shall inform   33
the arbitral tribunal whether they have any objections as to the tribunal-appointed expert's qualifications and independence (Art. 6(2), second sentence). In order to allow the parties to properly assess whether they have any objections, the arbitral tribunal must send them a **copy of the expert's description of his or her qualifications and his or her statement of independence.** The description of qualifications will allow the parties to assess whether the expert has the skills and expertise required in the particular case. The statement of independence will contain any referrals to possible connections to the parties and/or the arbitral tribunal which, in the view of the expert, are not detrimental to his or her independence. This will allow the parties to assess whether the expert is truly independent.

The arbitral tribunal must **decide promptly** whether to accept any such   34
objection (Art. 6(2), third sentence). If the arbitral tribunal accepts an objection by the parties, it must appoint another person as expert. If it rejects the objection, the objecting party must assess under the applicable *lex arbitri* whether it can, or as the case may be, needs to reiterate its objection before the national courts.

In the 2010 Rules, an important qualification of the parties' right to object   35
was introduced (Art. 6(2), fourth sentence): **After the appointment** of a tribunal-appointed expert, a party may only object to the expert's qualifications or independence for reasons of which the party becomes aware after

---

[584] DFT 126 III 251; Spühler/Gehri, 19; Berger/Kellerhals, N 1234; Poudret/Besson, N 667; Lörcher, 487; Born, 1862.
[585] The standard set in Part I(3) of the IBA Guidelines on Conflicts of Interest in International Arbitration may be taken as a yardstick.

the appointment has been made. Otherwise, any such objection is considered to have been waived.

36   If an objection is **legitimately** raised after the appointment, the arbitral tribunal must decide promptly what, if any, action to take. This means in particular that the arbitral tribunal is not obliged to revoke the mandate of the expert. E.g. if the qualifications of the experts prove to be insufficient after the appointment, a pragmatic solution may be the appointment of a second (sub-)expert.

V.   The Parties' Duty to Provide Information (par. 3)

A.   In General

37   The starting point of the expert's enquiry are the **pleadings and documents submitted** by the parties in the arbitration which are, depending on the tribunal's decision, transmitted to the expert in full or in extracts.[586] However, the expert is not limited to the submissions made by the parties. Rather, he or she is granted the power to request additional information and documents.

B.   The Expert's Power to Request Information and Documents

38   Pursuant to Art. 6(3), first sentence, the expert may require the parties to provide any information or access to any documents, goods, samples, property, machinery, systems, processes or site for inspection, to the extent relevant to the case and material to its outcome. For that purpose, the tribunal-appointed expert has the **same authority as the arbitral tribunal** to request such information or access (Art. 6(3), second sentence).

39   The expert's inspection right is **not limited to information and documents which were duly introduced in the proceedings.** Hence, the expert may ask for information and documents which have not been introduced in the proceedings before. This may be very far-reaching. The arbitral tribunal, therefore, has to make sure that the expert's enquiry does not go beyond the limits of the case as duly presented and introduced by the parties.

40   In principle, a party may be asked by the expert to give information or to produce documents **serving the other party's case.** It is submitted that the expert should if ever possible avoid such situations since the parties' duty under Art. 6(3) must not cause a shift of the burden of proof. It is up to the tribunal to ensure that this does not occur.

---

[586] SCHNEIDER, Experts, 460; OETIKER in COMMENTARY SWISS RULES, Art. 27 N 29.

C.   The "Relevant and Material"-Test

The scope of the expert's right to request information and documents is   41
limited firstly by the fact that such information and documents must be **relevant to the case and material to its outcome.** The test to be applied
is the same as otherwise where these criteria are used.[587]

Further, information or documents which have to be **excluded from evi-   42
dence or production** pursuant to Art. 9(2) may not be requested by the
expert (Art. 6(3), first sentence).[588]

If there is a disagreement between the expert and a party as to the rel-   43
evance, materiality or appropriateness of a request, the arbitral tribunal is
called to decide in the manner provided for in Art. 3(5–8).[589] This allows the
expert to act independently from the arbitral tribunal and puts the latter in
a position to nevertheless effectively **control** what a party is required to
produce and to ensure that the expert's report is not based on irrelevant
information and documents. However, the tribunal's competence to decide
such disputes on relevance may lead to delicate issues about a possible
bias of the arbitral tribunal, because it may need to appraise the relevance
of certain evidence at an early stage of the proceedings.[590]

D.   Providing Access to Documents etc.

The parties are under an obligation to provide the expert with access to any   44
relevant documents, goods, samples, property or sites for inspection upon
his or her request. Since the expert's right is limited to obtain *access,* the
parties are **not obliged to hand over** copies of documents or the goods
and samples to be inspected to the expert.[591]

One important consequence of this limitation is that the documents in-   45
spected by the expert **do not automatically become part of the file.**
Should the expert base its report on documents etc. not duly introduced
in the proceedings by the parties before, the party who intends to rely on
such documents must, if still possible, either introduce them properly in the
proceedings or make a request for production of such documents by the
other party. Otherwise, the documents etc. may not be directly relied on as
evidence. This is an appropriate counterweight to the expert's far-reaching
power to request access to information which the parties did not submit in
the proceedings.

---

[587] Cf. in detail Art. 3 N 129–144 above.
[588] Cf. Art. 9 N 18–48 below.
[589] Cf. Art. 3 N 164–206 above.
[590] ADEN, 639; OETIKER in COMMENTARY SWISS RULES, Art. 27 N 32.
[591] OETIKER in COMMENTARY SWISS RULES, Art. 27 N 33.

E.   Right to be Heard

46   The parties and their representatives have the **right to receive any information obtained by the expert** and to attend any inspection of documents by the expert (Art. 6(3), third sentence). Such rights are the necessary consequence of the parties' right to be heard. The arbitral tribunal
must ensure that this obligation is strictly complied with by the expert.[592]

F.   Failure to Comply with Expert's Request

47   A party's failure to comply with the expert's request has **no immediate
consequences.** Pursuant to Art. 6(3), last sentence, the tribunal-appointed expert may only record the non-compliance by a party with an appropriate request or decision by the arbitral tribunal in his or her expert report
and describe the effects of non-compliance on the determination of the
specific issue. It is then up to the arbitral tribunal to determine the consequences of such non-compliance. It can treat the failure to give certain
information or to produce certain documents to the expert in the same
way as a party's failure to produce certain documents requested by the
arbitral tribunal itself. Hence, it may infer that such information or document would be adverse to the interests of that party.[593] There is no other
sanction against a party not providing the requested information or not
producing the documents asked for to the expert.[594] Still, the applicable *lex
arbitri* may allow the arbitral tribunal to address the state courts in order to
enforce an information or production request by the expert.

VI.   Expert Report (par. 4)

A.   Submission

48   The tribunal-appointed expert must **report in writing** to the arbitral tribunal (Art. 6(4)). Although not provided for explicitly, the arbitral tribunal
may ask the expert to first submit a **draft report.**[595] This puts the arbitral
tribunal in a position to control whether each of the questions submitted to
the expert is dealt with appropriately. If this is not the case, the arbitral tribunal may return the draft report to the expert for revision. It may further
be sensible to submit the draft also to the parties for comments.[596]

---

[592] Lörcher, 492.
[593] Art. 9(6); cf. Art. 9 N 54–69 below; cf. also Berger/Kellerhals, N 1233.
[594] Oetiker in Commentary Swiss Rules, Art. 27 N 31.
[595] Weiss/Bürgi Locatelli, 495; Lörcher, 493–494; Vermeille, 202.
[596] Lörcher, 494; Vermeille, 202.

B.   Content

Art. 6(4) sets out in a rather **detailed manner** what the tribunal-appointed   49
expert's report needs to contain.

1.   Identity of the Expert (par. 4(a))

In order to duly perceive the content of an expert report, it is important   50
to **understand who the tribunal-appointed expert** and what his or her
professional background is. For that purpose Art. 6(4)(a) requires the tribunal-appointed expert's report to state:

- the full name and address of the expert;

- a description of his or her background, qualifications, training and experience.[597]

In order to give the arbitral tribunal a better perception of who the expert   51
is, the expert should also attach **a full CV** to the report.

The tribunal-appointed expert's report does not need to contain any state-   52
ment as to his or her independence. The issue of **independence** is dealt
with for tribunal-appointed experts before they may accept an appointment
(see Art. 6(2)).

2.   Statement of Facts (par. 4(b))

The expert report must contain a statement of the facts on which the ex-   53
pert is basing his or her opinions and conclusions (Art. 6(4)(d)). Since the
core of the expert report is not the description of facts, but the conclusions
drawn and opinions expressed, the description of facts **does not need to
be full and detailed** as in witness statements. Rather, the representation
of the facts should be made in a manner which allows comprehending and
following the expert's opinions and conclusions. Still, the factual basis on
which the expert draws his or her conclusions must be clearly identified.

3.   Expert's Opinion and Conclusions (par. 4(c))

Most importantly, the expert report must include the expert's opinions and   54
conclusions (Art. 6(4)(c)). The reader of the report should be enabled to
clearly **distinguish** between the facts on which the opinions and conclusions are based and the opinions and conclusions themselves. Usually, it

---

[597] Contrary to the provision regarding witnesses, Art. 6 requires that this information
must always be given since it will in any case be material for the assessment of the
report.

seems appropriate for the report to contain separate sections or sub-sections.

55   In order to allow the reader to easily perceive the content of the expert report, it may be sensible to **identify the questions** put to the expert at the beginning of the report and to provide – in the sense of an executive summary – for brief and clear answers to these questions at the end of the report.

56   The statement of opinions and conclusions of an expert report must include a description of the methods, evidence and information used in arriving at the conclusions (Art. 6(4)(c)). Basically, the expert report should **state the reasoning of the expert** in a manner that may be comprehended by the parties and the arbitral tribunal.

57   Pursuant to Art. 6(4)(c) *in fine,* **documents the tribunal-appointed expert is relying on** and which have not already been submitted must be provided, i.e. attached to the expert report. This will make clear on what documents, if any, the tribunal-appointed expert bases his or her affirmations.

4.   Language (par. 4(d))

58   If the expert report was translated, a statement is required as to the language in which it was **originally prepared,** and the language in which the tribunal-appointed expert anticipates giving testimony at the evidentiary hearing (Art. 6(4)(d)). This conveys useful information to the arbitral tribunal. On the one hand, it may explain why the language of an expert report originally prepared not in the expert's mother tongue contains linguistic errors or, to the contrary, a language level which may not be attributed to the expert, but rather to the translator (or the translating counsel). On the other hand, it will be clear from the outset which expert may be heard in the language of the proceedings and which needs interpretation.

5.   Affirmation of Genuine Belief (par. 4(e))

59   The expert report does not express facts, but (to the degree possible objectively reasoned) opinions. In line with this, Art. 6(4)(e) requires from the expert an affirmation of his or her **genuine belief in the opinions expressed** (but not a statement of truth). Hence, the expert needs to declare that he or she actually believes what is stated in the report.

6.   Signature (par. 4(f))

Pursuant to Art. 6(4)(f), the expert report must **contain the signature** of   60
the expert and its date and place. If the signature is lacking, the arbitral tribunal will need to obtain the signature from the expert. If the expert report
remains unsigned, the arbitral tribunal will have to disregard the report
unless there are sufficient objective reasons why the tribunal-appointed
expert is not in a position to sign the report.

7.   Attribution to Several Authors (par. 4(g))

Pursuant to Art. 6(4)(g), if more than one person sign an expert report,   61
e.g. if an organisation is hired as an expert or two experts produce a joint
report, it must be indicated whether the report is attributable as a whole to
a **single author** or, if not, which specific parts thereof may be attributed
to each **co-author**.[598] This information allows the arbitral tribunal and the
parties to assess whether the opinions were expressed by the person who
is an expert in the respective field (if several experts produce a joint report,
they will often have different fields of expertise). Furthermore, the arbitral
tribunal and the parties will be able to determine which experts should attend the evidentiary hearing and to prepare for the examination of one or
more of the co-authors.[599]

VII. Parties' Right to Respond to the Expert's Report (par. 5)

The arbitral tribunal has to send a copy of the expert's report to the parties   62
upon receipt (Art. 6(5), first sentence) and to grant the parties the opportunity to respond to the report in a submission by the party or through a witness statement or an expert report by a party-appointed expert (Art. 6(5)
third sentence). The parties' right to respond to the expert's report is a fundamental element of the **right to be heard**.[600] The arbitral tribunal must
send the submission, witness statement or expert report to the tribunal-
appointed expert and to the other parties (Art. 6(5), last sentence).

The Swiss Federal Supreme Court has found that the parties' right to be   63
heard is complied with if they have the **opportunity to discuss the expert's report before the arbitral tribunal**.[601] Yet, the arbitral tribunal

---

[598] IBA Review Subcommittee 2010, 19.
[599] IBA Review Subcommittee 2010, 20.
[600] PILS (Basel)-Schneider, Art. 184 N 41; Schneider, Experts, 462; Poudret, Expertise, 621; Spühler/Gehri, 19; Lew/Mistelis/Kröll, 575; Oetiker in Commentary Swiss Rules, Art. 27 N 35.
[601] DFT of 1 July 1991, ASA Bull 4/1991, 417; PILS (Basel)-Schneider, Art. 184 N 40; Poudret, 623; Poudret/Besson, N 665.

and/or the expert should consider granting the parties an opportunity to express their views on important issues for the expert's report before it is completed.[602]

64   In order to be able to duly respond to the expert report, the parties are **entitled to examine** any information, documents, goods, samples, property, machinery, systems, processes or site for inspection which the tribunal-appointed expert has examined and any correspondence between the arbitral tribunal and the tribunal-appointed expert (Art. 6(5), second sentence). This allows the parties to scrutinise relevant documents relied upon by the expert that are in the possession of the other party. This may sometimes include documents which were not introduced in the proceedings by any party. Hence, a party may obtain important additional factual knowledge by this means. Yet, as mentioned above,[603] documents relied upon by the expert, but not previously introduced into the proceedings by any party, do not automatically become part of the file. Neither the parties nor the arbitral tribunal may therefore directly rely on them. If a party wishes to base its case on such information, it must, if still possible, try to effect the production of such documents by the other party in order to introduce them properly into the proceedings.[604]

VIII. Parties' Right to Question the Expert (par. 6)

65   In principle, the expert's mandate consists only of the submission of a written report. However, at the request of a party or the arbitral tribunal, the expert may be **summoned for a hearing** (Art. 6(6), first sentence). At such a hearing, the arbitral tribunal may question the tribunal-appointed expert on the content of his or her report (Art. 6(6), second sentence). Equally, the parties or their party-appointed experts have the right to question the tribunal-appointed expert on any issue raised in his or her expert report, the parties' submissions or witness statements or the expert reports made by party-appointed experts. In many cases, it will be sensible to have the expert examined orally since it will allow the expert to make his or her report come to life upon examination.[605] It is submitted that the appearance of a tribunal-appointed expert is governed by Art. 6(6) and not Art. 8(1), although the wording of the latter seems to include tribunal-appointed experts ("any experts").

---

[602] PILS (Basel)-SCHNEIDER, Art. 184 N 40; WEISS/BÜRGI LOCATELLI, 497–498; OETIKER in COMMENTARY SWISS RULES, Art. 27 N 36.
[603] Cf. N 45.
[604] OETIKER in COMMENTARY SWISS RULES, Art. 27 N 37.
[605] Cf. generally KREINDLER, Oral Testimony, 87.

If appropriate, the arbitral tribunal may authorise the expert to **amend or**   66
extend his or her report after the hearing.[606]

IX.   Assessment of Expert Report (par. 7)

The arbitral tribunal must assess the expert report made by a tribunal-   67
appointed expert and its conclusions with due regard to all circumstances of
the case (Art. 6(7)). In this connection, it is important to recall the arbitral
tribunal's competence to **freely appraise the evidence.**

It is of particular importance that the arbitral tribunal **must not delegate**   68
its mandate to decide the dispute between the parties.[607] This means that
it must avoid assigning the direct decision of legal questions to an expert.[608]
Equally, it is crucial for the arbitral tribunal to remain independent from the
expert. It must not treat an expert as an additional member of the arbitral
tribunal. The different functions of an arbitrator and an expert must at all
times be duly distinguished.[609]

The arbitral tribunal must form its own view on the questions dealt with in   69
the expert's report and is **not bound by the expert's findings.**[610] This
is all the more important as experts often have an influential position in
arbitral proceedings.[611]

In line with this prerogative, the expert must in principle **not participate**   70
in the deliberations of the arbitral tribunal.[612] Rather, the arbitral tribunal
must obtain all information it needs from the expert for making the award
either from the written expert report or through the questioning of the expert at the evidentiary hearing.

Some authors do not categorically exclude the expert's participation in   71
the arbitral tribunal's deliberations under restricted circumstances.[613] This
raises important and difficult issues with regard to the parties' **right to be**
heard.[614] It should therefore be avoided if ever possible. Should an arbitral
tribunal nevertheless wish to have the expert participate in the deliberations (e.g. because it is impossible to convey the knowledge necessary to

---

[606] OETIKER in COMMENTARY SWISS RULES, Art. 27 N 38.
[607] OETIKER in COMMENTARY SWISS RULES, Art. 27 N 16; REDFERN/HUNTER/BLACKABY/PARTASIDES,
      N 6.157; LÖRCHER, 487.
[608] BERGER, Wirtschaftsschiedsgerichtsbarkeit, 301; LÖRCHER, 487.
[609] OETIKER in COMMENTARY SWISS RULES, Art. 27 N 16.
[610] PILS (Basel)-SCHNEIDER, Art. 184 N 42; SCHNEIDER, Experts, 463; WEISS/BÜRGI LOCATELLI,
      499; KNOF, 75.
[611] WEISS/BÜRGI LOCATELLI, 499.
[612] WEISS/BÜRGI LOCATELLI, 499–500; BERGER/KELLERHALS, N 1236; VERMEILLE, 203.
[613] SPÜHLER/GEHRI, 24; PILS (Basel)-SCHNEIDER, Art. 184 N 43; SCHNEIDER, Experts, 464.
[614] WEISS/BÜRGI LOCATELLI, 499; BERGER/KELLERHALS, N 1236.

decide the dispute in an adequate manner), it must take appropriate precautions to preserve the parties' right to be heard.[615]

X.   Cost Allocation (par. 8)

72   Pursuant to Art. 6(8), the fees and expenses of a tribunal-appointed expert must be funded as determined by the arbitral tribunal. It may in particular request a specific advance on costs from the parties. The duty to pay an advance on costs will usually be imposed on the party basing its case on facts to which the expert's report will relate. If both parties wish to rely on the expert's report to prove their case, they will be ordered to advance equal shares. The same solution will apply in case of doubt. The commencement of the expert's work is usually conditional on the payment of the advance.[616] The fees and expenses of a tribunal-appointed expert form **part of the costs** of the arbitration and will be allocated accordingly.

XI.   Appointment of an Additional Expert

73   Although this is not explicitly provided for in Art. 6, it is submitted that the arbitral tribunal's competence to appoint experts includes the competence to order an additional expert's report on issues which were already the subject of the report by an expert appointed in the first place. It may do so **upon application** of one or both parties or **on its own motion,** considering however that the parties may avoid an additional expertise ordered by the tribunal by not advancing the respective costs.

74   The arbitral tribunal will appoint an additional expert if the first expert's report is **not conclusive,** if it does not deal properly with the issues submitted to the expert or if the parties successfully challenged the conclusions of the first expert's report. The additional expert may be asked to review the first expert's report and to comment thereon or to make his or her own additional report.[617] It is clear that this must be the exception.

---

[615] Oetiker in Commentary Swiss Rules, Art. 27 N 18; similar Schneider, Experts, 464.
[616] Schneider, Experts, 459; Weiss/Bürgi Locatelli, 494–495.
[617] Oetiker in Commentary Swiss Rules, Art. 27 N 41.

Article 7   Inspection

Subject to the provisions of Article 9.2, the Arbitral Tribunal may, at the request of a Party or on its own motion, inspect or require the inspection by a Tribunal-Appointed Expert or a Party-Appointed Expert of any site, property, machinery or any other goods, samples, systems, processes or Documents, as it deems appropriate. The Arbitral Tribunal shall, in consultation with the Parties, determine the timing and arrangement for the inspection. The Parties and their representatives shall have the right to attend any such inspection.

Contents   Note

Other Rules

Art. 16(3) and 27(2) Swiss Rules; Art. 29(3) UNCITRAL; Art. 21(1)(b), Art. 22(1)(d) and (e) LCIA; Art. 33 AAA; Art. 50 WIPO.

I.   2010 Revision

In the context of the 2010 Revision, the title of Art. 7 was changed from "On- 1
site inspection" to **"Inspection"** as inspections may not only take place on site.[618] Further, Art. 7 clarifies in its revised version that the inspection may be carried out by a **tribunal-appointed or a party-appointed expert,** and it extends the list of objects capable of inspection to **samples and systems.**

II.   Introduction

Art. 7 gives the arbitral tribunal the **power to inspect or require the**   2
inspection by a tribunal-appointed or party-appointed expert of any site, property, machinery or any other goods, samples, systems, processes or documents, as it deems appropriate, unless the parties have agreed otherwise.[619] This provision reflects the view that the arbitral tribunal must be given all appropriate means in support of its decision-making process. For

---

[618] Cf. KÜHNER, 674.
[619] REDFERN/HUNTER/BLACKABY/PARTASIDES, N 6.175; LEW/MISTELIS/KRÖLL, N 22–93; RONEY/MÜLLER, 65.

example, inspections may be necessary if the arbitral tribunal needs to familiarise itself with the specific issues of the case. On-site inspections, in particular, are mostly recommended in disputes regarding the operation of industrial plants[620] or construction, engineering and mining disputes[621]. It can, however, also be considered in complex financial matters where an inspection of additional documents or processes is necessary.

3   Art. 7 gives the arbitral tribunal a **broad discretion** to order inspections. However, an opposing arbitration agreement by the parties as well as the privileges stated in Art. 9(2) may limit the arbitral tribunal's power to order inspections.

4   The arbitral tribunal should, when ordering inspections, always bear in mind the expenses such inspections are bound to cause, particularly in relation to the benefit gained.[622] The **cost-intensity** of inspections as well as the **logistical difficulties** in organising inspections attended by the arbitral tribunal, the parties and their representatives are often reasons why inspections are rarely conducted in arbitral proceedings.[623]

III. Arbitrators' Power to Order Any Kind of Inspection

A.   On Its Own Motion

5   The arbitral tribunal has the **power to order an inspection on its own motion.** The parties shall be given sufficient advance notice of any inspection the arbitral tribunal orders to conduct.[624] Art. 7 states that the arbitral tribunal shall in consultation with the parties determine the timing and arrangement for the inspection.

6   Art. 7 lists the objects that can be inspected, such as any site, property, machinery or any other goods, samples, systems, processes or documents. The **wording** of this list is **broad,** providing Art. 7 a rather ample scope.

7   Art. 7 states an efficient method of evidence-taking and confers upon **the arbitral tribunal** a **considerable amount of discretion.** Despite the arbitral tribunal's power to order the inspection of any goods or sites it deems appropriate, the arbitral tribunal also needs to consider in its decision-making process any respective **agreements between the parties,** the **chosen arbitration rules** and **applicable national laws,** as well as the

---

[620] CRAIG/PARK/PAULSSON, N 458.
[621] LEW/MISTELIS/KRÖLL, N 22–93; REDFERN/HUNTER/BLACKABY/PARTASIDES, N 6.173.
[622] REDFERN/HUNTER/BLACKABY/PARTASIDES, N 6.174.
[623] Cf. MCILWRATH/SAVAGE, N 5–226.
[624] Cf. Art. 24(2) Model Law.

costs and **time** to be spent **compared to the benefit** gained by conducting an inspection.

B.   On a Party's Request

Art. 7 states that the parties may file a request for the conduct of an inspection. According to the wording of the revised Art. 7, the parties may also appoint an expert to carry out the inspection. It is essential for the arbitral tribunal to ensure at all times that the **principle of equal treatment** is **strictly observed.**[625]   8

Art. 7 is silent on the question **until when** during the proceedings **requests for inspection** may be **filed** by the parties. In any event, parties may file requests for inspection in accordance with the procedural rules agreed upon with the arbitral tribunal. The parties should, however, further be allowed to request inspections if statements made by a party in its final submission trigger the need for any respective measures.   9

Finally, the arbitral tribunal **should always consider the necessary costs and efforts** in relation to the benefit of an inspection.[626]   10

C.   Limitations According to Art. 9(2)

The arbitral tribunal may **not order an inspection** if such order **violates Art. 9(2).** This provision expressly states that the arbitral tribunal shall exclude from evidence any document, statement, oral testimony or *inspection* for any reason of privilege as set forth in subsections (a) to (g). The decision whether there is a ground for refusal is in the sole discretion of the arbitral tribunal (by analogous application of Art. 3(5–8)).[627]   11

In addition, the arbitral tribunal shall at all times **consider the parties' private autonomy** to conduct the proceedings in line with their specific procedural expectations and needs: In particular, the arbitral tribunal shall render its decisions in consideration of the parties' agreement and the specific arbitration rules to be applied. The following arbitration rules contain provisions regarding inspections: the Swiss Rules (Art. 16(3) and 27(2)), the UNCITRAL Rules (Art. 29(3)), the LCIA Rules (in particular Art. 21(1) (b) and Art. 22(1)(d) and (e)), the AAA Commercial Arbitration Rules (in particular Art. 33) and the WIPO Rules (in particular Art. 50). The ICC Rules are silent on the question of inspections. Many national statutes also   12

---

[625] REDFERN/HUNTER/BLACKABY/PARTASIDES, N 6.176.
[626] REDFERN/HUNTER/BLACKABY/PARTASIDES, N 6.174: *"It is more common, in modern practice, for models, photographs, drawings or even videotape films to be used to fulfill the purpose that would have been served by a site inspection."*
[627] Cf. RAESCHKE-KESSLER, Beweisaufnahme, 73.

assume that the arbitrators have the power to order inspections, such as Art. 24(2) Model Law and Section 38(4) English Arbitration Act 1996. It is, however, generally accepted (subject to an agreement by the parties to the contrary) that the arbitral tribunal is authorised to undertake inspections, even where the applicable procedural rules do not explicitly say so.[628]

IV.   Parties' Right to Assist the Arbitral Tribunal in the Taking of Evidence

13   The parties or their representatives **shall generally be given the opportunity to attend the inspection.** Art. 7 is clear on this point.[629] In light of due process, a party may be excluded from attending an inspection only in exceptional circumstances. For example, if a party could gain access to business secrets of the other party due to the inspection, it might be arguable to exclude it from participating in an inspection.[630] The question remains if it is admissible (especially in light of the principle of equal treatment of the parties and the enforcement of any resulting award) to exclude only one of the parties to the arbitration.[631] In such situations, an arbitral tribunal might consider entrusting an independent expert to conduct the inspection.[632] In principle, however, the arbitral tribunal should order an inspection to be held in the presence of the parties and/or their representatives.

14   As mentioned, the parties are generally invited to attend an inspection. They may, however, also waive their right to accompany the arbitral tribunal or the tribunal-appointed or party-appointed expert. **Art. 33 AAA Commercial Arbitration Rules,** e.g., provides that in the event one or all parties are not present at the inspection, the arbitral tribunal shall make an oral or written report to the parties and afford them an opportunity to comment.

15   While the parties should attend the inspection, they cannot be forced to do so. Should a party nevertheless fail to make a particular object available for inspection without satisfactory explanation, the arbitral tribunal may **infer that the result of such inspection** would be **adverse** to the interests of that party.[633] Further, the arbitral tribunal might, in cases where it is deemed all the same necessary to conduct the inspection, ask the national

---

[628] Roney/Müller, 65; Jenkins/Stebbings, 256.
[629] Art. 7: "[...] The Parties and their representatives shall have the right to attend any such inspection."
[630] Cf. Lachmann, N 1488.
[631] Cf. Redfern/Hunter/Blackaby/Partasides, N 6.177.
[632] By analogous application of Art. 3(8).
[633] Art. 9(6).

courts for assistance if the law at the seat of the arbitration provides for such assistance.[634]

V.   Conduct of the Inspection

The arbitral tribunal shall, **in consultation with the parties, determine**   16
the timing and arrangement for the inspection. The Rules are silent
on the specific contents of such arrangement. The arbitral tribunal shall,
therefore, determine the arrangement together with the parties in advance.
It is good practice for the arbitral tribunal to issue a procedural order pri-
or to the conduct of the inspection, specifying the details.[635] Such order
should, in particular, specify the participants of the inspection, its purpose,
the objects to be inspected and the parties' rights regarding the conduct of
the inspection as well as their right to comment thereon or on the minutes
taken at the inspection, respectively.

The arbitral tribunal shall ensure that the **results** of the inspection are   17
minuted or recorded in a manner appropriate to the respective issue
in dispute.[636] If the arbitrators, in the context of the inspection, observe
a matter they deem material to the case, they should draw this to the attention of the parties and thus give them the opportunity to comment on
this issue.[637] The parties should be allowed to ask questions during the
inspection and thereafter to comment on the minutes taken. If, however,
the comments made during the inspection are also made part of the record,
the flexibility and usefulness of an inspection might be lost as a result of
the formality connected with the presence of a reporter to prepare a transcript.[638] Likewise, remarks of employees present at the site, e.g. regarding
construction equipment, machines or processes, should not be considered
as direct evidence in the proceedings.[639]

As far as the **costs** of the **inspection** are concerned, the arbitral tribunal   18
should make sure that they are covered by the parties' advance payments
or invite the parties to pay the estimated costs before conducting the inspection.

---

[634] KNOBLACH, 249.
[635] REDFERN/HUNTER/BLACKABY/PARTASIDES, N 6.177.
[636] POUDRET/BESSON, N 668; cf. BERGER/KELLERHALS, N 1237.
[637] DALE, N 13–051.
[638] REDFERN/HUNTER/BLACKABY/PARTASIDES, N 6.178.
[639] CRAIG/PARK/PAULSSON, N 458.

Article 8   Evidentiary Hearing

1. Within the time ordered by the Arbitral Tribunal, each Party shall inform the Arbitral Tribunal and the other Parties of the witnesses whose appearance it requests. Each witness (which term includes, for the purposes of this Article, witnesses of fact and any experts) shall, subject to Article 8.2, appear for testimony at the Evidentiary Hearing if such person's appearance has been requested by any Party or by the Arbitral Tribunal. Each witness shall appear in person unless the Arbitral Tribunal allows the use of videoconference or similar technology with respect to a particular witness.

2. The Arbitral Tribunal shall at all times have complete control over the Evidentiary Hearing. The Arbitral Tribunal may limit or exclude any question to, answer by or appearance of a witness, if it considers such question, answer or appearance to be irrelevant, immaterial, unreasonably burdensome, duplicative or otherwise covered by a reason for objection set forth in Article 9.2. Questions to a witness during direct and re-direct testimony may not be unreasonably leading.

3. With respect to oral testimony at an Evidentiary Hearing:

   (a) the Claimant shall ordinarily first present the testimony of its witnesses, followed by the Respondent presenting the testimony of its witnesses;

   (b) following direct testimony, any other Party may question such witness, in an order to be determined by the Arbitral Tribunal. The Party who initially presented the witness shall subsequently have the opportunity to ask additional questions on the matters raised in the other Parties' questioning;

   (c) thereafter, the Claimant shall ordinarily first present the testimony of its Party-Appointed Experts, followed by the Respondent presenting the testimony of its Party-Appointed Experts. The Party who initially presented the Party-Appointed Expert shall subsequently have the opportunity to ask additional questions on the matters raised in the other Parties' questioning;

   (d) the Arbitral Tribunal may question a Tribunal-Appointed Expert, and he or she may be questioned by the Parties or by any Party-Appointed Expert, on issues raised in the Tribunal-Appointed Expert Report, in the Parties' submissions or in the Expert Reports made by the Party-Appointed Experts;

   (e) if the arbitration is organised into separate issues or phases (such as jurisdiction, preliminary determinations, liability and damages), the Parties may agree or the Arbitral Tribunal may order the scheduling of testimony separately for each issue or phase;

(f) the Arbitral Tribunal, upon request of a Party or on its own motion, may vary this order of proceeding, including the arrangement of testimony by particular issues or in such a manner that witnesses be questioned at the same time and in confrontation with each other (witness conferencing);

(g) the Arbitral Tribunal may ask questions to a witness at any time.

4. A witness of fact providing testimony shall first affirm, in a manner determined appropriate by the Arbitral Tribunal, that he or she commits to tell the truth or, in the case of an expert witness, his or her genuine belief in the opinions to be expressed at the Evidentiary Hearing. If the witness has submitted a Witness Statement or an Expert Report, the witness shall confirm it. The Parties may agree or the Arbitral Tribunal may order that the Witness Statement or Expert Report shall serve as that witness's direct testimony.

5. Subject to the provisions of Article 9.2, the Arbitral Tribunal may request any person to give oral or written evidence on any issue that the Arbitral Tribunal considers to be relevant to the case and material to its outcome. Any witness called and questioned by the Arbitral Tribunal may also be questioned by the Parties.

Contents

Other Rules

Art. 26 ICC; Art. 25 Swiss Rules; Art. 28 UNCITRAL; Art. 19 LCIA; Art. 20, 22, 23–28, 35 and 36 AAA; Art. 53 WIPO.

I.   2010 Revision

Art. 8(1) newly provides guidance on the **appearance of witnesses** at   1
the evidentiary hearing; it also considers the use of modern communication
technology such as videoconferencing.

According to the new wording of Art. 8(2), it is not sufficient any more for   2
the arbitral tribunal to consider a question to, answer by, or appearance of
a witness to be burdensome in order to limit or exclude it, but it needs to
be **unreasonably burdensome.**

Art. 8(3)(c–d) introduce a rule on the **sequence** in which **party-appointed**   3
and tribunal-appointed experts shall be questioned. Further, Art. 8(3)
(e) considers the order of testimony to be presented in case of constella-
tions where the **proceedings** have been **bifurcated.**

In Art. 8(4), the duty to tell the truth Is extended to **expert wItnesses** In-   4
sofar as they shall **commit to state their genuine belief** in the opinions
to be expressed at the evidentiary hearing.

Finally, Art. 8(5) in its revised version specifies that the arbitral tribunal   5
may request any person to give oral or written evidence on any issue the
arbitral tribunal considers to be relevant, as referring to the **relevance to**
the case, and material, as referring to the **importance to its outcome.**

II.   Introduction

A.   Scope of Application

The **evidentiary hearing** is defined as follows in the Definitions of the   6
Rules: *"any hearing, whether or not held on consecutive days, at which the*
arbitral tribunal, whether in person, by teleconference, videoconference or
other method, receives oral or other evidence". The evidentiary hearing is
also commonly known as the main hearing. Further, for the purpose of the
comments hereinafter, the term **"witness"** includes, as explicitly stated in
Art. 8(1), **witnesses of fact as well as any experts** unless it is expressly
referred to one of them separately.

Art. 8 proposes procedural guidelines according to which the arbitral tribunal   7
and the parties to the arbitration may conduct the main hearing. Compared
to the 1999 Rules, this article has undergone significant changes; Art. 8
in its revised version largely reflects what has become **standard practice**
for evidentiary hearings in international arbitration.[640] Art. 8 does, however, not consider the possibility of preparatory hearings or any particular

---

[640] Rees, 521.

period for the submission of documentary evidence,[641] nor does it provide guidance on how to structure the post-hearing briefs. Further, Art. 8 does not provide for a fixed timeline for the evidence-taking process, nor does it mention the parties' possibility – often seen in practice – to make closing statements at the hearing after the witnesses have been examined.

8   Even though the parties to an arbitration can agree on a different procedure, it is a **common practice** in international arbitration to provide for **at least one hearing** where the parties have the opportunity to orally present their arguments and the arbitral tribunal may ask additional questions of under-standing.[642] For this purpose, Art. 8 offers a significant framework on how to organise a smooth conduct of the evidentiary hearing.

B.   Applicable Procedural Law

9   In principle, the **parties** are **free to agree upon the procedure** to present their evidence. In general, they do so in the arbitration agreement or indirectly by their choice of the institutional rules to be applied. The parties may also agree that the procedural rules of the state where the arbitral tribunal has its seat shall be applicable (although this is usually not recommended).[643]

10   The question as to the **applicable law** on the taking of evidence in arbitral proceedings **in the absence of an agreement** between the parties is con-troversial.[644] When entering into a business relationship, the parties often do not agree on a detailed arbitration agreement which would provide for a choice of law regarding procedural issues. Mostly, the parties only agree on the arbitration rules to be applied; institutional rules do, however, not always state the law applicable to the taking of evidence.[645] The arbitral tribunal is not obliged to follow the procedural rules of, or to apply the methods of evidence-taking at the seat of the arbitration.[646] It needs to be careful, however, where certain principles regarding evidence are governed by the *lex causae;* in this case, the arbitral tribunal is bound to consider the parties' choice of law.[647] Thus, the arbitral tribunal may apply the Rules as guidelines where appropriate, even if not specifically adopted by the parties. The parties' agreement for the application of the Rules may often fill in a procedural gap, particularly where the parties involved originate from juris-

---

[641] See Art. 3.
[642] REDFERN/HUNTER/BLACKABY/PARTASIDES, N 6.183; BORN, 1831.
[643] CRAIG/PARK/PAULSSON, 415.
[644] POUDRET/BESSON, N 643.
[645] CRAIG/PARK/PAULSSON, 415.
[646] BERGER, Arbitration, 427.
[647] POUDRET/BESSON, N 644.

dictions with distinctive rules governing the evidence procedure. Moreover, the parties have strong interests to avoid surprises and render the procedure of taking and presenting evidence more foreseeable.[648] Therefore, the parties' choice of a set of arbitration rules or of the Rules is recommendable and beneficial to the smooth conduct of presenting and taking evidence.

III. Appearance of Witnesses (par. 1)

Art. 8(1) holds that each witness whose **appearance** has been **requested**   11
by any party or by the arbitral tribunal shall appear for testimony at the evidentiary hearing.[649] This new provision helps avoiding that witnesses who have provided uncontroversial witness statements are required to attend an oral hearing.[650] Each witness shall appear in person unless the arbitral tribunal allows the use of videoconference or similar technology with respect to a particular witness.

If a witness whose appearance has been requested fails to appear for testi-   12
mony at the evidentiary hearing without a valid reason, the arbitral tribunal shall disregard this person's witness statement unless exceptional circumstances justify the absence (Art. 4(7)). In such cases, the arbitral tribunal may, however, also seek **judicial assistance** by the competent **state court** due to the arbitral tribunal's lack of power to impose sanctions on a recalcitrant witness.[651] If the uncooperative witness is not domiciled at the seat of the arbitration, the arbitral tribunal nevertheless has to approach the state court judge at its seat; the competent judge then may issue a request for legal assistance for the attention of the competent state court at the domicile of said witness.[652]

If a party fails without satisfactory explanation to make witness testimony   13
available, the arbitral tribunal may also take the **non-appearance of a witness** into account when appraising the evidence[653] and consequently **infer** that such **evidence** would be **adverse** to the interests of that party (Art. 9(6)).

IV. Leading Role of the Arbitral Tribunal (par. 2)

Generally, the Rules set forth a pragmatic approach as to the evidence-tak-   14
ing proceedings. According to Art. 8(2), the **arbitral tribunal** shall at all

---

[648] Berger, Arbitration, 428; Raeschke-Kessler, Festschrift Briner, 662.

[649] See also Art. 4 N 57–89.

[650] Newmark, 168; cf. Kühner, 674.

[651] Berger/Kellerhals, N 1226.

[652] Oetiker, Witnesses, 265.

[653] Id.

times have **complete control over the evidentiary hearing**, a method similar to civil law court procedure.[654] The power of the arbitral tribunal to manage and control the evidentiary hearing is also widely recognised by arbitration rules.[655]

15   Pursuant to Art. 8(2), the **arbitral tribunal** may **refuse** to hear or **limit** oral evidence on subjects it deems to be **irrelevant, immaterial, unreasonably burdensome,**[656] **duplicative** or **otherwise covered** by a reason for objection as set forth in **Art. 9(2).** Under the revised Rules, it is not sufficient for refusal or restriction if the piece of evidence is burdensome as such, but it must be unreasonably burdensome. It lies within the arbitral tribunal's discretion to determine whether or not a ground for any restriction or exclusion of evidence is given either on a party's request or on its own motion.[657]

16   Within the subject permitted, the arbitral tribunal may additionally forbid a party's **question** to a witness during direct and re-direct testimony which is **unreasonably leading.** A question is leading if it is asked in such a way as to suggest the answer.[658] The opposing party may further raise an objection if its witness is asked a leading or irrelevant question or a question touching upon privileged matters (see Art. 9); it is within the arbitral tribunal's discretion to decide whether the objection should be sustained, overruled or reserved.[659]

17   The parties should thus aim at only submitting **evidence** that is **relevant to the case and material to its outcome** and not duplicative. The parties should, for the sake of efficiency of the proceedings, avoid submitting any evidence giving rise to unnecessary costs and time efforts.

18   Even though the arbitral tribunal is given broad discretion under the Rules to decide on the evidence-taking procedure, one might expect that it would rather hear a witness (albeit with a limitation of the testimony to a specific subject) than to exclude him or her from the hearing.[660] Further, the **arbitral tribunal** will mostly **consult with the parties** before the evidentiary

---

[654] IBA Review Subcommittee 2010, 23.

[655] See, e.g., Art. 26(3) ICC Rules; Art. 14(2) LCIA Rules (unless otherwise agreed by the parties); Art. 15(1) Swiss Rules; Art. 17(1) UNCITRAL Rules; Art. 20(1) Vienna Rules; Art. 38(a) WIPO Rules.

[656] Berger (Arbitration, 429) states the following as an example of when evidence may turn out to be burdensome: *"There are cases in the international practice where the files are so voluminous that they have to be transmitted to the arbitrators by van and each member of the tribunal does not get to the point of defense until he is nearly at page 5,000."*

[657] See also Raeschke-Kessler, Festschrift Geimer, 863–864.

[658] Hanotiau, Conduct of Hearings, 374.

[659] Id.

[660] Bühler/Dorgan, 17; Hanotiau, Conduct of Hearings, 373 fn. 22.

hearing takes place and, if need be, issue a procedural order in this respect. Accordingly, there is often a clear understanding between the parties and the arbitral tribunal what the main issues of the evidence-taking procedure are and where the parties run a risk of any question being restricted or even excluded by the arbitral tribunal.

V.   Sequence of Witness and Expert Presentation (par. 3)

Art. 8(3) is a guideline to facilitate the conduct of the hearings, giving a   19
general framework of the **default order** in which the witnesses and experts are to be presented and questioned. Art. 8(3) reflects the common
law approach of how to structure the evidentiary hearing.[661] The arbitral
tribunal may, however, on its own motion or at a party's request, deviate
from this order (Art. 8(3)(f)).

The Rules do not state whether witnesses who have not yet testified may   20
attend other testimonies. According to some institutional arbitration rules,
the arbitral tribunal may decide that witnesses of fact not being a party to
the arbitration shall not attend the testimony given by other witnesses before the arbitral tribunal **("sequestration of witnesses").**[662] It is further
generally acknowledged that witnesses of fact who have not yet testified
may be excluded from attending other witnesses' examinations.[663] Where a
fact witness is at the same time a party's representative, the party's right
to be in the hearing room may prevail over the exclusion of the witness.[664]
Expert witnesses are generally allowed to stay in the hearing room during
all testimonies.[665]

A.   Sequence of Direct Testimony (par. 3(a))

Art. 8(3)(a) starts with the **direct examination** of the witnesses, giving   21
the claimant an opportunity to first present the testimony of its witnesses.
Art. 8(3)(a), as an exception to the principle in Art. 8(1), refers to the
claimant's witnesses of fact only, since Art. 8(3)(c) clarifies that the claimant's party-appointed experts are called thereafter.[666]

The claimant will either refer to the submitted written witness statement   22
or wish to question its witnesses orally. As mentioned before, the arbitral
tribunal may limit the subjects on which a witness may be questioned

---

[661] Cf. KNOBLACH, 213.
[662] See Art. 28(3) UNCITRAL Rules; Art. 25(4) Swiss Rules; Art. 54(f) WIPO Rules;
CRAIG/PARK/PAULSSON, 440.
[663] BORN, 1846; BÜHLER/DORGAN, 27.
[664] BÜHLER/DORGAN, 27; GÉLINAS, 43; HANOTIAU, Conduct of Hearings, 375.
[665] HANOTIAU, Conduct of Hearings, 375.
[666] REES, 522.

(Art. 8(2)), provided that the **party's right to be heard** is not violated. The respondent's witnesses shall follow, whereby the arbitral tribunal shall ensure that the parties' interests are **treated** and considered **equally** and both parties have enough time to present their witnesses.[667]

23   It has become common practice in international arbitration for parties to agree either on a **dispension of direct examination altogether** and to rely on the written witness statement previously filed, or to allow the witness to make a **short statement** summarising the contents of his or her witness statement in order to save time and costs.[668]

24   Further, there is a growing tendency in international arbitration to allow parties and their counsel to **prepare a witness for his or her questioning** at the hearing;[669] this preparation must, however, not interfere with the witness's ability and duty to testify truthfully.[670]

B.   Sequence of Cross-Examination and Re-Direct Examination (par. 3(b))

25   **Cross-examination** is well established in international arbitration.[671] During cross-examination, the witness has the duty to also answer questions on issues he or she was not primarily summoned for, provided the arbitral tribunal does not consider such questions as violating Art. 8(2). In other words, cross-examiners are not limited to issues covered in direct examination, but may also question the witness on issues not referred to in the written witness statement in order to rebut the latter.[672]

26   It is possible that new facts come to light when the witness is questioned by the opposing party. Therefore, the party relying on and presenting the witness may re-examine its own witness on these new issues to correct the testimony given by the witness in response to the questions of the other party or to have it reformulated in a more favourable way for the party's legal position **("re-direct examination").**[673] Even though Art. 8(3) does not mention it explicitly, the arbitral tribunal may also give the other party an opportunity to examine the witness once again on any additional

---

[667] Bühler/Dorgan, 17.
[668] Griffin, 27; Redfern/Hunter/Blackaby/Partasides, N 6.202; Tackaberry/Marriott, N 2–794; cf. van den Berg, 163. See also Art. 4 N 23–29.
[669] See in more detail Art. 4 N 16–19.
[670] Griffin, 28.
[671] Bühler/Dorgan, 26.
[672] Cf. Griffin, 28.
[673] Cf. Oetiker, Witnesses, 268; van den Berg, 164.

issues which may have arisen during re-direct examination **("re-cross-examination").**[674]

The arbitral tribunal will again need to bear in mind the parties' right to be 27 treated equally and, therefore, it must consider the **time exposure.**[675] The equal treatment of the parties, however, does not implicitly mean equal allocation of time. Depending on the specific issues of the case, it may be fair and just to offer one party more time to present its arguments.[676]

C. Sequence of Testimony for Party-Appointed Experts (par. 3(c))

The claimant shall ordinarily first present the testimony of its **party-ap-** 28 **pointed experts** followed by the respondent. The party who was first to present its party-appointed experts shall have the opportunity, after the presentation of the experts by the other party, to ask additional questions, but only on the matters raised in the other party's questioning.

D. Questioning of Tribunal-Appointed Experts (par. 3(d))

The arbitral tribunal, the parties, and any party-appointed expert may 29 question a **tribunal-appointed expert;** questions are, however, only allowed on issues raised in the tribunal-appointed expert report, in the parties' submissions or in the expert reports submitted by the party-appointed experts.

E. Bifurcation of Arbitral Proceedings (par. 3(e))

If the arbitral tribunal ordered a **bifurcation of the proceedings,** the par- 30 ties may agree on, or the arbitral tribunal may order the separate **scheduling of testimony** for each issue or phase. This makes sense because, when dealing with a bifurcation of the proceedings, e.g. into a jurisdiction and a liability phase, some witnesses or experts may only be able to give testimony on the question of liability, but not on questions concerning the possible jurisdiction of the arbitral tribunal.

F. Variations of Sequence/Witness Conferencing (par. 3(f))

The order of questioning witnesses and experts as described above may, 31 upon a party's request or on the arbitral tribunal's own motion, be varied

---

[674] HANOTIAU, Conduct of Hearings, 374; cf. OETIKER, Witnesses, 268; BERGER/KELLERHALS, N 1223.
[675] See "Böckstiegel Method" at N 44 below.
[676] OETIKER, Witnesses, 268; BÜHLER/DORGAN, 24.

freely. The arbitral tribunal is also given the power to order the questioning of the parties' witnesses at the same time and in confrontation with each other. This manner of presenting witness testimony is known as **"witness conferencing"**.[677] Witness conferencing may prove to be an efficient method of taking evidence, which *"consists of assembling all the witnesses around one table and confronting them with each other's statements"*.[678] It may be particularly helpful where witnesses of both parties worked together on the disputed project and where the party-appointed experts presented contradicting expert reports.[679] Thus, witness conferencing or **"hottubbing"** may help the arbitral tribunal to better understand contradictions and to determine the weight and credibility of certain testimony.[680] As witness conferencing is best used in addition to traditional cross-examination, it is generally more time-consuming.[681] Further, the advantages gained from witness conferencing are highest when the arbitral tribunal is well-prepared; witness conferencing thus puts a higher burden on the arbitral tribunal with respect to preparation and conduct of the hearing.[682]

32   As to the sequence of examination in general, the **arbitral tribunal may examine** the witnesses on the main points **first** in order to directly address the significant issues and thereafter leave any further examination to the parties.[683] In addition, even though it is more common in modern international arbitrations for the closing submissions to be in writing ("post-hearing briefs"), the parties may be given the opportunity to present some form of oral **closing statement** after the witness testimony has been heard.[684]

G.   Arbitral Tribunal's Power to Ask Questions (par. 3(g))

33   The **arbitral tribunal** has a **wide discretion** in asking the witnesses and experts questions at any time during the evidentiary hearing. Arbitrators may not only ask questions of fact, but also questions as to the credibility of a witness if required by the specific circumstances of the case.[685]

---

[677] POUDRET/BESSON, N 658; see also BERGER/KELLERHALS, N 1221, 1223. For a detailed assessment of witness conferencing see PETER, Witness Conferencing, 47–58; RAESCHKE-KESSLER, Witness Conferencing, 415–428.

[678] POUDRET/BESSON, N 658; RAESCHKE-KESSLER, Festschrift Briner, 662.

[679] BERGER/KELLERHALS, N 1223; cf. REDFERN/HUNTER/BLACKABY/PARTASIDES, N 6.217–6.219; for a list showing the pros and cons of witness conferencing see SUTCLIFFE/WIRTH, 41–42.

[680] VON SEGESSER, IBA Rules, 750.

[681] BORN, 1850–1851.

[682] HANOTIAU, Conduct of Hearings, 377.

[683] OETIKER, Witnesses, 267; cf. BÜHLER/DORGAN, 25.

[684] REDFERN/HUNTER/BLACKABY/PARTASIDES, N 6.229–6.230.

[685] REDFERN/HUNTER/BLACKABY/PARTASIDES, N 6.206; cf. BÜHLER/DORGAN, 9–10.

VI.   Witnesses' Affirmation of Telling the Truth (par. 4)

The Rules remain silent on the question whether or not the arbitral tribu-   34
nal has the power to take an **oath.** Particularly in common law countries,
arbitrators are permitted to do so; in other jurisdictions, however, as in
most civil law states, national law forbids arbitrators from administering an
oath.[686] The arbitral tribunal, therefore, may not *a priori* assume that it has
such a power.[687] Moreover, the arbitral tribunal will have to check its competences from case to case based on the applicable laws or customs at the
seat of the arbitration *(lex arbitri)* or at the place of the hearing.[688]

If no oath can be administered, Art. 8(4) describes the possibility for a   35
witness to affirm, in a manner determined appropriate by the arbitral
tribunal, that he or she **commits to telling the truth** or, in the case of an
expert witness, his or her genuine belief in the opinions to be expressed
at the evidentiary hearing.[689] This affirmation by the witness is important,
because in some jurisdictions providing false testimony before an arbitral
tribunal may entail criminal sanctions.[690] It is thus suggested that these instructions by the arbitral tribunal be recorded in the minutes of the hearing
or in the transcript in order to furnish adequate proof later.[691]

When presenting evidence, the parties in most arbitral proceedings submit   36
affidavits or simple witness statements which are solely signed by the respective witness.[692] If the witness has submitted a **witness statement** or
an expert report, the **witness shall confirm** it. The parties may agree, or
the arbitral tribunal may order, that the witness statement or the expert
report shall serve as that witness's direct testimony (Art. 8(4)). It can be
derived there from that, in general, witnesses should still be questioned
orally even if they have filed a witness statement.[693]

VII.   Witnesses or Experts Requested by the Arbitral
Tribunal (par. 5)

Art. 8(5) grants the arbitral tribunal a wide discretion reminiscent of in-   37
quisitorial powers: the **arbitral tribunal** may **request any person to**

---

[686] Born, 1848–1849.
[687] For Germany see also Raeschke-Kessler, Beweisaufnahme, 74.
[688] Raeschke-Kessler, Beweisaufnahme, 74; Bühler/Dorgan, 24.
[689] *"Often, the arbitral tribunal will also simply admonish the witness to tell the truth,
      and sometimes it will additionally advise the witness of criminal sanctions applying
      at the seat of the arbitration or at the physical place of the hearing."* (IBA Review
      Subcommittee 2010, 24); Griffin, 28.
[690] Berger/Kellerhals, N 1225; cf. Oetiker, Witnesses, 269.
[691] Berger/Kellerhals, N 1225.
[692] Redfern/Hunter/Blackaby/Partasides, N 6.138; Roney/Müller, 63.
[693] Knoblach, 182.

give oral or written **evidence** on any issue the arbitrators consider to be relevant to the case and material to its outcome. Any witness called and questioned by the arbitral tribunal may also be questioned by the parties.

38   The arbitral tribunal is therefore also empowered to order the testimony of an expert who was not chosen by the parties in analogy to appointing an expert pursuant to Art. 6.[694] The choice of an **independent expert** may help avoiding a "battle of experts" appointed by the parties in dispute.[695]

VIII. Some Practical Aspects of Managing the Evidentiary Hearing

39   Most arbitration laws and institutional arbitration rules do not contain specific provisions on how to structure the evidentiary hearing. This allows for flexible solutions taking into account the particular circumstances in the proceedings. Nevertheless, the parties are well-advised to **agree on a procedure** to be applied **as soon as possible** in the arbitral proceedings. Ideally, rules on which party will start examining the witnesses, how the hearing is recorded, who has to organise an interpreter if a witness does not testify in the language of the arbitration etc. are determined by the arbitral tribunal in consultation with the parties at the outset of the arbitral proceedings, e.g. at the first organisational hearing. For this purpose, **Art. 8** refers to **appropriate and practice-oriented guidelines** that have proved to be reconcilable with parties having either a common law or a civil law background.

40   From an **organisational standpoint,** the arbitral tribunal needs to deal with the following aspects when preparing a hearing:

- the **date** of the hearing;
- the appropriate **location** of the hearing;
- the arrangement of any necessary **transcripts** and/or **interpreters;**
- the **sequence** of witnesses;
- the **time management.**

41   The arbitral tribunal shall in consultation with the parties determine the date of the hearing as well as the appropriate hearing location or any other administrative arrangements. Therefore, it is recommended for the arbitral tribunal, after the written submissions and the evidence have been exchanged, to convene a **pre-hearing meeting** or **telephone conference**

---

[694] BERGER, Wirtschaftsschiedsgerichtsbarkeit, 299–300.
[695] BERGER, Wirtschaftsschiedsgerichtsbarkeit, 300.

with the parties and their representatives in order to prepare the conduct of the evidentiary hearing as efficiently as possible.[696]

Bearing in mind that the arbitral proceedings are mostly conducted in a   42
language different from the parties' and their witnesses' native language, the arbitral tribunal must ensure an uninterrupted conduct of the hearings. Where the arbitral tribunal wishes to hear a specific witness who may not be able or does not wish to testify in the language of the arbitral proceedings, the arbitral tribunal must provide for an **interpreter.** If the arbitral tribunal chooses not to do so, it is the responsibility of the party presenting the witness to arrange for the interpretation of that witness's testimony.[697] The interpreter needs to be independent from the parties.[698]

It is generally recognised that witness testimony should be tape-record-   43
ed and that the **verbatim transcripts** prepared by a professional court reporter should be served to the parties.[699] If one party requests that a transcript be taken, the arbitral tribunal may order such transcript notwithstanding the other party's objection, in particular when the specific case is complex and of a certain magnitude or where the statements of witnesses are anticipated to contradict.[700] The specific circumstances of a case (such as cost-sensitivity) must, however, be considered and may demand for other methods of recording, e.g. the taking of internal minutes of the testimony or the issuing of a summary of the witnesses' testimonies both by the arbitral tribunal or its secretary, respectively.[701]

The parties are free to determine the time to be allocated to the conduct   44
of the evidentiary hearing. In terms of time- and cost-efficiency, however, the parties may want to agree on a specific timeline before the hearing. The **"Böckstiegel Method"**[702] is a well-known method of managing time in hearings; it involves allocating a fixed amount of time to each party and then providing the parties with broad freedom to use their allocated time as they wish.[703] Consequently, within the time allotted, each party is free to decide how much of its total time it wishes to spend on the examination of which witness and expert.[704] Needless to say, also when applying this

---

[696] REDFERN/HUNTER/BLACKABY/PARTASIDES, N 6.193; RONEY/MÜLLER, 67; TACKABERRY/MARRIOTT, N 2–761.
[697] See also BÜHLER/DORGAN, 21.
[698] BÜHLER/DORGAN, 21; OETIKER, Witnesses, 270.
[699] REDFERN/HUNTER/BLACKABY/PARTASIDES, N 4.173; FOUCHARD/GAILLARD/GOLDMAN, N 1288; CRAIG/PARK/PAULSSON, 440; RONEY/MÜLLER, 68; BORN, 1849–1850.
[700] CRAIG/PARK/PAULSSON, 440.
[701] See BÜHLER/DORGAN, fn. 75; CRAIG/PARK/PAULSSON, 440; OETIKER, Witnesses, 271–272.
[702] Named after its "father", the renowned German arbitrator Karl-Heinz Böckstiegel.
[703] RONEY/MÜLLER, 67.
[704] BÖCKSTIEGEL, 7.

method, a certain extent of flexibility must remain in order to adapt the procedures to the specific circumstances of the case.

45   Arbitral proceedings are generally private and the **hearings** thus **not open to the public.**[705] Besides the parties and their representatives, the parties may consent to the presence of additional persons whose attendance may be convenient, e.g. any specialists such as engineers, provided that they are not requested to appear as witnesses or experts.[706]

---

[705] REDFERN/HUNTER/BLACKABY/PARTASIDES, N 6.189.
[706] REDFERN/HUNTER/BLACKABY/PARTASIDES, N 6.189; RONEY/MÜLLER, 67.

Article 9   Admissibility and Assessment of Evidence

1. The Arbitral Tribunal shall determine the admissibility, relevance, materiality and weight of evidence.

2. The Arbitral Tribunal shall, at the request of a Party or on its own motion, exclude from evidence or production any Document, statement, oral testimony or inspection for any of the following reasons:

   (a) lack of sufficient relevance to the case or materiality to its outcome;

   (b) legal impediment or privilege under the legal or ethical rules determined by the Arbitral Tribunal to be applicable;

   (c) unreasonable burden to produce the requested evidence;

   (d) loss or destruction of the Document that has been shown with reasonable likelihood to have occurred;

   (e) grounds of commercial or technical confidentiality that the Arbitral Tribunal determines to be compelling;

   (f) grounds of special political or institutional sensitivity (including evidence that has been classified as secret by a government or a public international institution) that the Arbitral Tribunal determines to be compelling; or

   (g) considerations of procedural economy, proportionality, fairness or equality of the Parties that the Arbitral Tribunal determines to be compelling.

3. In considering issues of legal impediment or privilege under Article 9.2(b), and insofar as permitted by any mandatory legal or ethical rules that are determined by it to be applicable, the Arbitral Tribunal may take into account:

   (a) any need to protect the confidentiality of a Document created or statement or oral communication made in connection with and for the purpose of providing or obtaining legal advice;

   (b) any need to protect the confidentiality of a Document created or statement or oral communication made in connection with and for the purpose of settlement negotiations;

   (c) the expectations of the Parties and their advisors at the time the legal impediment or privilege is said to have arisen;

   (d) any possible waiver of any applicable legal impediment or privilege by virtue of consent, earlier disclosure, affirmative use of the Document, statement, oral communication or advice contained therein, or otherwise; and

(e) the need to maintain fairness and equality as between the Parties, particularly if they are subject to different legal or ethical rules.

4. The Arbitral Tribunal may, where appropriate, make necessary arrangements to permit evidence to be presented or considered subject to suitable confidentiality protection.

5. If a Party fails without satisfactory explanation to produce any Document requested in a Request to Produce to which it has not objected in due time or fails to produce any Document ordered to be produced by the Arbitral Tribunal, the Arbitral Tribunal may infer that such document would be adverse to the interests of that Party.

6. If a Party fails without satisfactory explanation to make available any other relevant evidence, including testimony, sought by one Party to which the Party to whom the request was addressed has not objected in due time or fails to make available any evidence, including testimony, ordered by the Arbitral Tribunal to be produced, the Arbitral Tribunal may infer that such evidence would be adverse to the interests of that Party.

7. If the Arbitral Tribunal determines that a Party has failed to conduct itself in good faith in the taking of evidence, the Arbitral Tribunal may, in addition to any other measures available under these Rules, take such failure into account in its assignment of the costs of the arbitration, including costs arising out of or in connection with the taking of evidence.

Contents Note

Other Rules

Art. 22(3) ICC; Art. 24(1–2) Swiss Rules; Art. 27(1) and 27(4) UNCITRAL; Art. 22(1)(f) LCIA; Rule 34(1) ICSID; Art. 48(a) and 52 WIPO.

I.   2010 Revision

In Art. 9(3), the Review Subcommittee provided additional non-binding 1
guidance on determining the applicable **privileges** under Art. 9(2)(b), by referring in particular to the following criteria: (i) the confidentiality of documents or communications for the purpose of providing legal advice, (ii) the confidentiality of settlement negotiations, (III) the expectations of the parties, (iv) waiver of privilege, and (v) the need to maintain fairness and equality between the parties.

In addition, the new Art. 9(7) specifically grants arbitral tribunals the dis- 2
cretion to sanction parties for **breaches of good faith** in the assignment of the costs of arbitration.

II.   Assessment of Evidence by Arbitral Tribunals (par. 1)

A.   Introduction

As Rusty Park once remarked, *"arbitrators decide cases neither by flipping* 3
a coin nor by cutting a baby in half, but by weighing evidence".[707] The principle that arbitrators have discretion to determine the evidentiary weight of evidence is **generally accepted**[708] and expressly codified, for example, in Art. 27(4) of the UNCITRAL Rules and Art. 24(2) of the Swiss Rules.

---

[707] PARK, Elephants and Pornography, 270.
[708] BORN, 1851–1852; REDFERN/HUNTER/BLACKABY/PARTASIDES, N 6.143; BERGER/KELLERHALS, N 1238.

B.   Admissibility of Evidence

4   What is or is not admissible as evidence **may vary** significantly from one jurisdiction to another. In some but not all countries, corporate officers can testify for their company, and approaches to hearsay can be diverse among jurisdictions.[709]

5   Restrictions on the admissibility may result from **mandatory provisions** of the *lex fori* or from international public policy, such as the prohibition to rely on evidence obtained through illegal means.[710]

6   To protect an award from annulment, arbitrators are generally careful not to exclude evidence in a way that could arguably prejudice one side's right to present its case. The general practice in international arbitration is to admit evidence freely, leaving it to the arbitrators to assess its weight, and the technical rules of evidence known to common law counsel are largely absent from international arbitration.[711] The **predisposition** of many arbitrators **for admitting evidence** does not mean that an arbitrator should allow undue surprise, misleading questions or testimony with little probative value. But it does mean that counsel should be encouraged to think carefully before making objections.[712] And counsel should trust that arbitrators are able to understand the probative value of testimony.

7   Swiss doctrine and jurisprudence consistently hold that the principle of equal treatment and the right to be heard are not violated if the arbitral tribunal, within its discretion to evaluate evidence, only accepts evidence that is offered **in due form and time**.[713]

C.   Burden of Proof

8   Even though rarely codified,[714] it is widely accepted in international arbitration that each party shall have the burden of proof regarding the facts relied on to support its claim or defence.[715] According to civil law, the burden of proof is governed by the applicable substantive law, while common law

---

[709] PARK, Elephants and Pornography, 270.

[710] PILS (Basel)-SCHNEIDER, Art. 184 N 13–14; BERGER/KELLERHALS, N 1207.

[711] BORN, 1853–1854 with further references; BÜHLER/DORGAN, 28; BERGER/KELLERHALS, N 1205; cf. also par. 13 of the Procedural Order of 12 May 2003 in ICC Case No. 12169, in: Decisions on ICC Arbitration Procedure, ICC Bull 2010 Special Supplement, 35: *"The Tribunal is not bound by any strict rules of evidence"*.

[712] PARK, Elephants and Pornography, 271.

[713] DFT 119 II 386; DFT of 11 May 1992, ASA Bull 3/1992, 397; BERGER/KELLERHALS, N 1208–1209; NATER-BASS in COMMENTARY SWISS RULES, Art. 25 N 28.

[714] Cf. however Art. 27(1) UNCITRAL Rules and Art. 24(1) Swiss Rules.

[715] BORN, 1857; PILS (Basel)-SCHNEIDER, Art. 184 N 12; REDFERN/HUNTER/BLACKABY/PARTASIDES, N 6.92.

qualifies this principle as an issue of procedural law.[716] In practice, this distinction does not play such an important role, because the burden of proof is **less important** in international arbitration than in state court proceedings. As KARRER points out, arbitrators should not strive to find a resolution with as little effort as possible, but should attempt to hear sufficient evidence to get a good picture of the relevant events on the basis of which an award is rendered.[717] Justice will rarely be "seen to be done"[718] if a case is decided on the basis of the parties' burden of proof.[719]

Only **factual and contested** assertions need to be proven. Under common   9
law, the substance matter of foreign law may also require proof, since it is
the common law view that foreign law constitutes a factual assertion.[720]

D.   Standard of Proof

While the burden of proof *(Beweislast)* determines *which party* needs to   10
prove a certain allegation, the standard of proof *(Beweismass)* defines the
criteria to consider something as proven, i.e. the required ***level of proof.***
If a strict proof is not possible, civil law tradition will generally require a
degree of probability "verging on certainty",[721] while common law arbitrators usually content themselves with a preponderance of evidence.[722] In
arbitration practice, it has been suggested that the standard of proof to be
achieved is close to the so-called "balance of probability".[723] According to
this principle, a fact is considered as proven if the arbitral tribunal is in a
position to say "we think it more probable than not", whereas, if the probabilities are equal, the burden of proof will persist.[724]

A **higher standard** of proof is often required for important or delicate   11
questions such as bribery or other criminal actions.[725] The arbitral tribunal

---

[716] PILS (Basel)-SCHNEIDER, Art. 184 N 11.
[717] KARRER, 108; cf. also BORN, 1857 with further references.
[718] The aphorism *"Not only must justice be done; it must also be seen to be done"* has its basis in a judgment by Lord Hewart CJ in a leading English case on the impartiality of judges, *R v Sussex Justices,* Ex parte *McCarthy* ([1924] 1 KB 256, [1923] All ER 233).
[719] KARRER, 108.
[720] NATER-BASS in COMMENTARY SWISS RULES, Art. 24 N 5.
[721] The German term under Swiss law is *"mit an Sicherheit grenzender Wahrscheinlichkeit";* cf. DFT 130 III 132 cons. 3.2; ZPO (Basel)-GUYAN, Art. 157 N 7–8 (mentioning a numeric probability of 90%). Where mere causality must be proven (e.g. for tort claims), "preponderant probability" *(überwiegende Wahrscheinlichkeit)* is sufficient according to Swiss practice; cf. DFT 132 III 719–720 cons. 3.1; ZPO (Basel)-GUYAN, Art. 157 N 9 (mentioning a numeric probability of 75%).
[722] VON MEHREN, 127–128.
[723] BORN, 1857–1858; REINER, 335.
[724] Denning J in *Miller v. The Minister of Pensions,* [1947] 2 All ER 372.
[725] BORN, 1858–1859.

in ICC Case No. 6401[726] stated for example that bribery must be proven by "clear and convincing evidence".

E.   Weight of Evidence

12   In general, arbitral tribunals tend to give less weight to uncorroborated witness testimony than to evidence contained in **contemporary documents.**[727] Arbitrators also give greater weight to the evidence of a witness that has been tested by cross-examination or by an examination by the arbitrators themselves.[728]

13   In the process of assessing and weighing the evidence, arbitral tribunals further distinguish between **direct** (or "primary") **and indirect** ("secondary" or "circumstantial") **evidence.** Direct evidence will naturally be given more weight than indirect evidence.[729] Sometimes, however, direct evidence will not be available to prove a certain allegation.

14   In determining the weight to be given to indirect evidence, arbitral tribunals will look at the **reasons for non-production** of direct evidence. In cases of revolutions, nationalisations, armed conflicts and civil unrest, for example, documents and other physical evidence are often lost or destroyed.[730]

15   In the absence of direct evidence, arbitral tribunals will often presume or infer facts on the basis of other proven or accepted factual knowledge, which effectively **shifts the burden of proof** to the other party.[731]

16   In the well-known ***Corfu Channel* case** of the International Court of Justice, the Court admitted indirect evidence with regard to an allegation by the United Kingdom that Albania knew about the laying and presence of mines in the Corfu Channel and thus was responsible for damage and loss of life caused by the explosion of mines in Albanian territorial waters. The ICJ acknowledged that the United Kingdom could not produce any direct evidence to prove its allegation, due to the exclusive territorial control of Albania over the respective waters, and inferred that Albania was aware of the mines. The judges noted that indirect evidence *"is admitted in all systems of law, and its use is recognized by international decisions. It must be regarded as of special weight when it is based on a series of facts linked together and leading logically to a single conclusion".*[732]

---

[726] International Arbitration Report 1/1992, B 19; cf. also REDFERN/HUNTER/BLACKABY/PARTASIDES, N 6.93–6.95.

[727] Cf. BROWER/BRUESCHKE, 186–188, regarding the practice of the US-Iran Claims Tribunal.

[728] REDFERN/HUNTER/BLACKABY/PARTASIDES, N 6.144.

[729] PIETROWSKI, 380.

[730] Id., 381.

[731] Id.

[732] 1949 ICJ Rep. 18.

F.   Stay of Proceedings

The possibility of absence of evidence is a risk inherent in civil procedure.   17
Therefore, **evidentiary problems** such as pending parallel proceedings in
the course of which additional evidence may be expected to emerge can
usually not justify a stay of proceedings.[733] A party which was not able to
offer conclusive evidence in time has the opportunity to obtain a revision
of the arbitral award, provided that the further conditions for a revision are
fulfilled.[734]

III.   Exclusion of Evidence (par. 2)

Art. 9(2) contains a catalogue of provisions allowing the arbitral tribunal, at   18
the request of a party or on its own motion, to limit or exclude certain evidence. The list of examples should **not** be considered as **conclusive.** For
example, a party should be allowed to raise an objection that the formal
requirements for a document production request under Art. 3(3) have not
been met by the other side or that certain allegations contained in production requests (e.g. as to the availability of evidence) are incorrect.[735]

A.   Legal Privilege (par. 2(b) and 3)

1.   Introduction

The issue of evidentiary privileges in international arbitration, in par-   19
ticular the attorney-client privilege,[736] has been a hotly debated topic in
recent years. The **reasons for the complexity** of this matter are the
following:[737]

a) the nature and concept of evidentiary privileges is different in civil law
   and common law;

b) there are essential differences in the qualification of privileges as substantive or procedural matters in common and civil law;[738]

c) there are no established conflict of law rules for the determination of the
   law applicable to privileges in international arbitration.

---

[733] DFT 119 II 390; PILS (Basel)-Schneider, Art. 184 N 50.
[734] Cf. DFT 119 II 390.
[735] Müller, IBA Rules, 67–68.
[736] Art. 9(2)(b) also applies to other forms of privilege such as the rights of witnesses
to refuse testimony or communications between doctors and patients. The issues
discussed below are applicable *mutatis mutandis* to these types of privileges.
[737] Berger, Evidentiary Privileges, 501–502.
[738] Von Schlabrendorff/Sheppard (763–765) submit that legal privileges are both procedural and substantive in character.

20   In addition, arbitral tribunals are faced with two basic policy considerations
      in the area of privilege. First, arbitrators should admit an appropriate privi-
      lege objection raised in good faith. In other words, *"disregarding privileges
      and other rules while ordering the production of privileged documents is
      simply not right as a matter of principle"*.[739] Secondly, the need for pre-
      dictability to safeguard the **parties' legitimate expectations** as to the
      application of a certain privilege standard is particularly strong in this field
      because parties rely on privileges.[740] In other words, a "trial by ambush"
      must be avoided:

> *"Parties are likely to be surprised, to say the least, to learn that their
> agreement to arbitrate could have the effect of imposing on them a
> general obligation to disclose all relevant documents including internal
> communications and legal advice which would not be subject to disclo-
> sure under their own domestic national procedures."*[741]

21   Because the parties may have relied on different privileges with different
      protection levels, it has been suggested to develop **best practice stand-
      ards** by institutions such as the IBA instead of *ad hoc* decision-making
      by arbitrators in a given case, in order to avoid unequal treatment of the
      parties.[742]

22   In common law jurisdictions, the **justification** for the attorney-client privi-
      lege focuses on the client who needs to be protected from comprehen-
      sive discovery rights,[743] while the attorney secrecy in civil law jurisdictions
      originates in the secrecy obligation of attorneys who are subject to criminal
      sanctions if they violate the professional duty of confidentiality, i.e. in the
      integrity of the legal profession.[744]

23   This **conceptual difference** has important implications:[745]

      a) While the common law attorney-client privilege covers any communica-
         tion (excluding facts) between client and attorney which have the main
         purpose of providing legal services and may be invoked by clients and
         attorneys, the civil law attorney secrecy covers everything the attorney
         knows about the client's affairs (including facts) and may be invoked by
         attorneys only.

---

[739] HEITZMANN, 218; cf. also BORN, 1912–1913.
[740] VON SCHLABRENDORFF/SHEPPARD, 765–766.
[741] SINDLER/WÜSTEMANN, 621.
[742] VOSER, 118.
[743] Regarding differences between the U.S. and the U.K., see HEITZMANN, 208–209.
[744] BERGER, IBA Rules, 172; see also the comparison chart in MEYER-HAUSER/SIEBER, 164–
      165.
[745] MEYER-HAUSER/SIEBER, 148.

b) Whereas the attorney-client privilege is said to belong to the client, the attorney secrecy must be claimed by the attorney.

c) Finally, the scope of the different concepts is not the same. Information protected under one concept may not be protected by the other, which may become particularly relevant in connection with information shared by in-house counsel.[746]

2.   In-House Counsel

In the U.S. and England, the attorney-client privilege applies to in-house   24
counsel, provided that the relevant communication relates to legal advice and not to general business matters.[747] The **situation** in Continental Europe **is diverse.** While the attorney secrecy does not apply to in-house counsel in Switzerland, France, Sweden and Italy, the secrecy extends to both outside and in-house counsel in Belgium, the Netherlands and Spain.[748] In Germany, the legal situation appears to be far from settled.[749]

Under **EU law,** the current rules on privilege date from the ECJ's judg-   25
ment in *AM&S Europe Ltd v. Commission,*[750] which was confirmed in the ECJ's recent *Akzo Nobel* decision[751]. Essentially, written communications are privileged if they are made between a company and an "independent" lawyer (defined by the ECJ as *"lawyers who are not bound to the client by a relationship of employment"*[752]) who is qualified to practice in the EU, and are made for the purpose and in the interest of the company's rights of defence in relation to Commission proceedings. Under the *Akzo Nobel* test, therefore, in-house counsel and even outside counsel not qualified in the EU will not be covered by any rules on privilege.

Some commentators point out that the restrictive practice of the Commis-   26
sion and the European Courts will simply result in written evidence becoming more and more rare.[753] Because of the growing size of legal departments and the expectations of business people that they can turn to their in-house counsel for advice without any fear of disclosure, industry and

---

[746] See N 24–27 below.
[747] *Upjohn v. United States,* 449 U.S. 383, 392 (1981); *Waterford v. The Commonwealth* (1987) 163 CLR 54.
[748] BERGER, IBA Rules, 172–173 with further references; HEITZMANN, 210. Regarding the situation in Switzerland, see also MEYER-HAUSER, N 45–46.
[749] BERGER, IBA Rules, 173.
[750] [1982] ECR 1575.
[751] *Akzo Nobel Chemicals v. Commission,* C-550/07 P, 14 September 2010.
[752] *Akzo Nobel Chemicals v. Commission,* par. 41.
[753] HEITZMANN, 211.

company lawyer associations are petitioning for a **revision** of the *AM&S* and *Akzo* case law.[754]

27   Against this background, one may imagine situations where a request for production of communications of Swiss in-house counsel is made and granted, and the documents are produced because the respective party does not consider any privilege to be applicable. Sometime later, an identical request is made with respect to U.S. in-house counsel and met by a claim for privilege. Whatever approach the arbitral tribunal takes, the parties will be **treated unequally.** Therefore, it is important for an arbitral tribunal to decide early in the proceedings how privilege claims will be addressed.[755]

3.   Conflict of Law Issues

28   The Rules remain silent on the question of which privilege rules or which conflict rules should be applied by arbitral tribunals in determining what information is privileged. It is generally acknowledged that there are no established rules in this area, and the possible **connecting factors** are numerous:[756]

- the applicable procedural law;

- the applicable substantive law;

- the law of the jurisdiction where enforcement of any order or award will be sought;

- the law of the jurisdiction where the party or lawyer claiming protection resides;

- the law of the place where the information was created;

- the law of the place where the information was sent from, or to;

- the law where the record of the communication is stored;

- the law where the lawyer with whom the communication took place is admitted.

29   The matter is further complicated by the fact that common law jurisdictions tend to qualify evidentiary privileges as a substantive issue (i.e. subject to the law applicable to the merits), while civil law jurisdictions are inclined to qualify them as a procedural matter (subject to the *lex arbitri*).[757] Irrespective of the legal qualification of privilege claims, it is generally ac-

---

[754] HEITZMANN, 211–212, with further references.
[755] SINDLER/WÜSTEMANN, 629; see also Art. 2 N 11 above.
[756] SINDLER/WÜSTEMANN, 620; MEYER-HAUSER, N 181; VON SCHLABRENDORFF/SHEPPARD, 769–771.
[757] MEYER-HAUSER, N 149–153.

knowledged that arbitral tribunals should do justice to the legitimate expectations of the parties when rendering choice of law decisions.[758] Because neither classification (as substantial or procedural law) is satisfactory[759] and the connecting factors listed above do not provide the necessary predictability and certainty, arbitral practice has resorted to the **"closest connection"** or "centre of gravity" test, i.e. an application of the law of the place where the entire attorney-client relationship has its predominant effects.[760] Typically, this will be the law of the state where the attorney-client relationship was established and which prevails even when the arbitral procedure is conducted in another country.[761] Where a party and its attorney are based in different countries, the *party's* (and not the attorney's) expectations are decisive in this connection. Therefore, it is the law of the jurisdiction where the party had its place of business when the relevant communication took place which will be applied in most cases (and not the place where the attorney is admitted to the Bar).[762] In case of witness testimony, it is the law of the witness's domicile which must be applied.[763]

It must be taken into consideration, however, that an application of the   30
closest connection test will still not prevent an unfair treatment of the parties under certain circumstances.[764] Therefore, the doctrine advocates an application in arbitral proceedings of the **"most favourable privilege"** rule which has its origin in Art. 11 of the 1970 Hague Convention on the Taking of Evidence.[765] This rule authorises courts to apply the law of the party which accords the broadest protection to any given privilege issue.[766]

---

[758] BERGER, Evidentiary Privileges, 508.

[759] MEYER, 367–370.

[760] MEYER-HAUSER, N 190–195; BORN, 1914. This solution is also in line with Art. 187(1) PILS which provides that the arbitral tribunal shall decide the case according to the rules of law chosen by the parties or, in the absence thereof, according to the rules of law with which the case has the closest connection. See also Art. 4 of the 1980 Rome Convention on the Law Applicable to Contractual Obligations, discussed by HEITZMANN, 219–220. The closest connection test also corresponds to the "most significant relationship" test favoured in the U.S. (American Law Institute, Restatement of Law, Second, Conflict of Laws, § 188); cf. VON SCHLABRENDORFF/SHEPPARD, 768–769.

[761] MEYER-HAUSER, N 195.

[762] BERGER, Evidentiary Privileges, 511–512. On the other hand, BORN favours, from the perspective of predictability, an application of the law where the lawyer is qualified to practice, because a lawyer will often be more sensitive and alert to issues of privilege than the client, and will most naturally consider them from the perspective of his or her legal system (BORN, 1914).

[763] BERGER, Evidentiary Privileges, 512.

[764] See N 27 above.

[765] The most favourable privilege rule has also been enacted in the EU under Art. 14(1) of EC Regulation 1206/2001 enhancing judicial cooperation; cf. HEITZMANN, 220–223.

[766] MEYER-HAUSER/SIEBER, 186; SINDLER/WÜSTEMANN, 637; BERGER, Evidentiary Privileges, 518; VON SCHLABRENDORFF/SHEPPARD, 771–774. See also Art. 7 of the ICDR Guidelines for Arbitrators Concerning Exchange of Information, stipulating that the arbitral tribunal should give *"preference to the rule that provides the highest level of protection"* if

Such an approach best takes into account the parties' expectations because they can be confident that information privileged under their own laws would never have to be produced. This solution also corresponds with the underlying principle of Art. 9(2)(g) which authorises arbitral tribunals to exclude evidence based on considerations of equality and fairness.[767]

4.   List of Elements to Consider (par. 3)

31   While Art. 9 of the 1999 Rules remained silent as to what specific considerations arbitral tribunals might take into account when dealing with a privilege issue, the new par. 3 contains a **checklist** of five specific elements which were deemed relevant.[768]

32   Apart from the attorney-client privilege (Art. 9(3)(a)) and the parties' expectations (Art. 9(3)(c)) which were already discussed above,[769] the Rules specifically mention that arbitral tribunals may take into account the confidentiality of documents created or statements made in connection with or for the purpose of settlement negotiations (Art. 9(3)(b)). This provision acknowledges a respective transnational privilege principle,[770] also referred to as "without prejudice" privilege. Furthermore, there is an unanimous view today in international ADR practice that a general mediation privilege exists.[771] The basic policy consideration underlying the **settlement privilege** is also accepted in arbitration practice.[772] The broad language of Art. 9(3)(b) ("in connection with and for the purpose of") makes it clear that not only documents submitted during negotiations, but also internal documents prepared for settlement discussions are privileged.[773] Finally, it must be kept in mind that the right to rely on the settlement privilege is subject to the good faith obligation under par. 3 of the Preamble. Therefore, a party cannot invoke the settlement privilege if it has introduced a statement or document during settlement negotiations solely for the purpose of shielding this information from the other side in subsequent arbitration.[774]

---

the parties, their counsel or their documents would be subject under applicable law to different rules of privilege.

[767] See N 48–49 below.
[768] BERGER, IBA Rules, 171.
[769] N 19–30 (attorney-client privilege) and N 20 (parties' expectations).
[770] BERGER, Settlement Privilege, 269–272, referring among others to the decisions of the Iran-US Claims Tribunal in *The Islamic Republic of Iran v. United States,* Decision No. 12-A1-FT (3 August 1983), 1 Iran-US CTR 189, 190; and to *Mobil Oil Iran v. The Islamic Republic of Iran,* Partial Award No. 311-74/76/81/150-3 (14 July 1987), 16 Iran-US CTR 3, 55. Cf. also BORN, 1914–1916.
[771] BERGER, Settlement Privilege, 266–269, with further references.
[772] BERGER, Settlement Privilege, 270–271, referring to the final award in ICC Case No. 6653 (1993), Collection of ICC Awards III (1991–1995), 512–529, at 516.
[773] BERGER, Settlement Privilege, 272–273.
[774] Id., 273–274.

Art. 9(3)(d) stipulates that arbitral tribunals may take into account **waiv-**   33
ers of any applicable legal privilege by way of consent, earlier disclosure,
affirmative use of the document or statement, or otherwise. Because the
privilege belongs to the party under U.S. and English law, a party may
claim full protection for documents in its possession. In the civil law context, however, only information in the lawyer's possession is protected. The
same information or advice attracts no protection in the hands of the client.[775] While the privilege may be waived by a party under both systems, a
civil law attorney may continue to rely on the respective secrecy in some
jurisdictions despite a waiver by the party.[776]

Art. 9(3)(e) states that arbitral tribunals may take into account the need to   34
maintain **fairness and equality** between the parties, particularly if they
are subject to different legal or ethical rules, and thus specifies the general
rule under Art. 9(2)(g). The best way to maintain fairness and equality
between the parties with respect to rules of legal privilege is to apply the
"most favourable privilege" rule discussed above.[777]

The revision has **deliberately omitted** specific directions as to which privi-   35
lege rule should apply to each party in all cases, or which conflict-of-law
rules should be employed, because it was impossible to find a short common denominator for the standards in the various jurisdictions and arbitral
tribunals should continue to be afforded a certain amount of flexibility and
discretion in matters of legal privilege.[778]

B.   Other Reasons to Exclude Evidence (par. 2(a–g))

1.   Lack of Relevance or Materiality (par. 2(a))

The principle that an arbitral tribunal may exclude evidence for lack of suf-   36
ficient relevance or materiality is well established in arbitration practice[779]
and Swiss law[780]. Arbitral tribunals in Switzerland may reject a request for
the taking of evidence and/or close the proceedings if any remaining requests for the taking of evidence appear to be irrelevant or inappropriate
to prove a certain fact.[781] Similarly, arbitral tribunals may refuse to accept
further evidence if they **anticipate,** based on the present evidence, that

---

[775] SINDLER/WÜSTEMANN, 616 in relation to Swiss law, referring to a decision of the Swiss
Federal Supreme Court of 6 June 1988, DFT 114 III 108.
[776] See Art. 13(1) of the Swiss Federal Act on Lawyers (BGFA); for U.K. law cf. *Three
Rivers DC* [2004] UKHL 48, [2005] 1 A.C. 610 at 635.
[777] See N 30 above; BERGER, IBA Rules, 176; CARTER, 179.
[778] VON SEGESSER, IBA Rules, 751; CARTER, 179.
[779] PETROCHILOS, N 5.125 p. 220.
[780] DFT 106 II 171; 116 II 644; PILS (Basel)-SCHNEIDER, Art. 184 N 50.
[781] DFT 4P.23/2006 of 27 March 2006, cons. 3.1; BERGER/KELLERHALS, N 1239.

such further evidence would not change the conclusions.[782] Such anticipated assessment of evidence can only be reviewed in annulment proceedings under the limited scope of public policy violations.[783]

2. Legal Impediment (par. 2(b) and 3)

37 Besides the attorney-client privilege and **other types of evidentiary privileges,**[784] there are further legal impediments which can be invoked in international arbitrations, such as the seizure of assets or freezing orders. The guidelines under Art. 9(3) also apply to these legal impediments.

3. Unreasonable Burden to Produce (par. 2(c))

38 Article 9(2)(c) permits the arbitral tribunal to exclude from production or from evidence any documents or evidence which would be **unreasonably burdensome** to produce. This may involve the following situations:

a) production of documents which, because of their sheer **quantity,** would create an unreasonable burden on the respective party to produce (including so-called "fishing expeditions");[785]

b) documents in the possession, custody or control of a party which nevertheless are unreasonably **difficult** for the party **to obtain;**[786]

c) potential **witnesses** who have left a company and cannot be located despite reasonable efforts such as inquiries with former work colleagues and Internet research;[787]

d) the evidence already submitted or produced is **sufficient** to prove the requesting party's allegations.[788]

39 The issue of an unreasonable burden to produce will often come up in connection with **e-discovery.** In this field, it is particularly important for the

---

[782] DFT 4P.23/2006 of 27 March 2006, cons. 3.1 with reference to DFT 130 II 425 cons. 2.1 at 429. In this case, the arbitral tribunal had decided not to conduct any evidence-taking, thus implicitly rejecting all the parties' respective requests. Cf. also DFT 4P.115/2003 of 16 October 2003, cons. 4.2, in ASA Bull 2/2004 364, at 377–378 with reference to DFT 119 Ib 505–506, concerning the refusal by an arbitral tribunal to order any new examinations by an expert witness; BERGER/KELLERHALS, N 1239.

[783] DFT 4P.23/2006 of 27 March 2006, cons. 3.1 with further references; DFT 4P.115/2003 of 16 October 2003, cons. 4.2, in ASA Bull 2/2004 364, at 378; BERGER/KELLERHALS, N 1241.

[784] As set forth in fn. 736 above.

[785] IBA REVIEW SUBCOMMITTEE 2010, Art. 9 par. 7.

[786] Id.

[787] Investigations by private detectives would probably be considered as unreasonable unless they concern a key witness with exclusive knowledge in a large case.

[788] RAESCHKE-KESSLER, Production, 429; cf. also N 36 above.

arbitrators to limit the scope of production, because there is a high risk of overreaching requests where electronic data are concerned. The arbitrators should apply rather high standards as to relevancy and materiality and invite the requesting party to demonstrate carefully why a particular electronic document is necessary and more beneficial than other more easily accessible data.[789] In order to reduce the burden on the producing party, one could also consider shifting the costs of the production to the requesting party.[790]

With respect to physical evidence, however, arbitral tribunals are best advised to apply Art. 9(2)(c) with some **reservation.**[791]   40

4.   Loss or Destruction (par. 2(d))

An arbitral tribunal may conclude that a party's lack of access to evidence   41
arises from destruction of that evidence and may draw appropriate inferences from non-production of such evidence. The doctrine lists **six requirements for drawing adverse inferences** from the destruction of evidence:[792]

1) an act of destruction must be shown to have occurred;

2) the destroyed evidence must be relevant to the dispute;

3) the destruction must be intentional;

4) the destruction must have occurred when legal proceedings were pending or foreseeable;

5) the destruction must be attributable to that party or to its agents; and

6) the party must have had a duty to preserve the destroyed evidence.

The routine destruction of documents is an important matter in connec-   42
tion with **electronic evidence.** Under the new U.S. e-discovery Federal Rules,[793] failure to manage how electronic information is maintained and periodically destroyed on a computer system is subject to sanctions. Any U.S. organisation that destroys electronic information in the regular course of its business should maintain written retention and destruction policies in

---

[789] MEIER, 188.

[790] As it was apparently done in the case *Zubulake v. UBS Warburg,* 217 F.R.D. 309 (S.D.N.Y. 2003); cf. MEIER, 188.

[791] Cf. MÜLLER, IBA Rules, 69.

[792] SHARPE, 558, with further references.

[793] See E-Discovery Amendments to the Federal Rules of Civil Procedure and Committee Comments, available at www.uscourts.gov/RulesAndPolicies/FederalRulemaking/ Overview.aspx. The new rules are applicable to all pending and future cases filed in the federal court system as of 1 December 2006.

order to regularise the process and increase the likelihood of falling within the safe harbour against sanctions.[794]

5.   Commercial and Technical Confidentiality (par. 2(e))

43   Art. 9(2)(e) restates the generally acknowledged principle that parties should not gain unauthorised access to **trade secrets.**[795] Such confidential information includes for example:

- research & development information;

- recipes;

- information subject to banking secrecy;

- price calculations;

- sources of supply;

- distribution channels;

- agreements with suppliers and customers.

44   Art. 9(4) clarifies that arbitral tribunals may make necessary **arrangements** to protect confidential information.[796]

6.   Political or Institutional Sensitivity (par. 2(f))

45   When an early draft of the Rules during the **1999 Revision** referred only to "commercial and technical confidentiality", certain international political organisations pointed out that this term might not include confidentiality within such organisations.[797]

46   Politically sensitive evidence includes e.g. technical data on weapons, algorithms used for encryption programmes, certain information of national banks, and confidential information of international organisations such as the UN, the World Bank or the IMF.[798] The respective documents or data are usually classified as confidential, secret or top secret.[799] **National security privileges** (also referred to as "public interest immunity") have been acknowledged by many international arbitral tribunals.[800]

---

[794] Smit/Robinson, 117.
[795] Cf. e.g. Art. 162 of the Swiss Criminal Code. It might have been helpful to specify in the Rules that the importance of confidential documents should be weighed against the level of confidentiality; cf. Knoblach, 303.
[796] See N 50–53 below.
[797] IBA Review Subcommittee 2010, Art. 9 par. 8.
[798] Cf. Raeschke-Kessler, Production, 429.
[799] Berger, Evidentiary Privileges, 504.
[800] Id.

Whether an arbitral tribunal is actually bound to an **exclusion of evidence** for reasons of national security[801] may be **questionable.**[802] It is certainly appropriate, however, to take such restrictions and the resulting difficulties for the producing party into consideration when the evidence is weighed.[803]   47

7.   Considerations of Procedural Economy, Proportionality, Fairness or Equality (par. 2(g))

The **catch-all provision** of Art. 9(2)(g) is intended to assure procedural   48
economy, proportionality, fairness and equality to all sides in the case.[804]
With this provision, the drafters intended among others to ensure that arbitral tribunals provide the parties with a fair and effective hearing.[805] The 2010 Revision has added the criteria of procedural economy and proportionality to those of fairness and equality, thereby placing more emphasis on the requirement of efficiency in evidence-taking.

The principle of equal treatment of the parties is a **fundamental right**   49
codified in many arbitration codes and rules.[806]

IV.   Confidentiality Protection (par. 4)

Art. 9(4) clarifies that arbitral tribunals may take certain precautions to   50
prevent confidential evidence from unwarranted disclosure. The most elaborate provisions on confidentiality protection among the major arbitration rules can be found in Art. 52 of the **WIPO Rules.** Confidentiality protection is also mentioned e.g. in Art. 22(3) ICC Rules and Art. 20(6) ICDR International Arbitration Rules.

Art. 52 WIPO Rules provides the following **steps** in connection with applica-   51
tions for protective measures:

1) A party invoking the confidentiality of any information it wishes or is required to submit shall make an **application** to have the information classified as confidential by notice to the arbitral tribunal (with a copy to the other party), including the reasons for which it considers the information to be confidential.

---

[801] As proposed by Schlosser, N 835.
[802] PILS (Basel)-Schneider, Art. 184 N 14.
[803] Id.; see also Pietrowski, 404–405.
[804] IBA Review Subcommittee 2010, Art. 9 par. 9.
[805] Id.
[806] Art. 18 Model Law, Art. 182(3) PILS, Art. 22(4) ICC Rules, Art. 17(1) UNCITRAL Rules, Art. 15(1) Swiss Rules; cf. Petrochilos, N 4.85–4.91.

2) The arbitral tribunal determines whether the stated reasons are **valid,** i.e. whether a disclosure would cause serious harm to the invoking party.

3) If the information is classified as confidential, the arbitral tribunal decides under which **conditions** and to whom the confidential information may be disclosed (in part or in whole).

4) The arbitral tribunal shall require any person to whom the confidential information is to be disclosed to sign an appropriate **confidentiality undertaking.**

5) In exceptional circumstances, the arbitral tribunal may, after consultation with the parties, designate a **confidentiality advisor** who will determine in lieu of the arbitral tribunal whether the information is to be classified and will decide on the respective conditions.

6) The arbitral tribunal may also appoint the confidentiality advisor as an expert to **report to the arbitral tribunal,** on the basis of confidential information, on specific issues designated by the arbitral tribunal, without disclosing the confidential information to the other party or to the arbitral tribunal.

52　　The Rules mention the possibility to appoint an **independent expert** in connection with objections to document production requests (Art. 3(8)).[807] The same procedure should apply for confidentiality matters.[808] The appointment of a confidentiality advisor is also recommended by the ICC in its Draft Best Practice Note on the European Commission Acting as Amicus Curiae in International Arbitration Proceedings, i.e. in EC-competition-law-related arbitral proceedings.[809]

53　　**Other possibilities** to protect confidential information are to make certain documents available "for attorneys' eyes only" or to display documents without the possibility of taking copies.[810]

V.　Adverse Inference (par. 5–6)

A.　Introduction

54　　Often, parties in international arbitration depend on evidence under the control of the other party to prove certain allegations. Because arbitrators

---

[807] See Art. 3 N 190–205 above.
[808] Müller, IBA Rules, 68.
[809] See par. 50 of the Note, reprinted in Andenas/Alpa (eds.), European Business Law Review Special Edition 2008 – Arbitrating Competition Law Issues, at 216.
[810] Cf. Knoblach, 154–156.

lack the power to compel production and judicial assistance[811] is often cumbersome and too time-consuming, a party relying on documents from the other side would be heavily disadvantaged if the latter could simply refuse production without facing any consequences. While some arbitral tribunals may revert to the imposition of financial penalties to compel production (e.g. by so-called *astreintes*[812]), drawing adverse inferences is certainly a more effective and less invasive method to cope with the **retention of harmful information.** Some parties will simply not be impressed by monetary sanctions, which are in any event difficult to enforce against recalcitrant parties.

By threatening to draw adverse inferences and thus encouraging appropriate disclosure, arbitrators ensure a complete evaluation of the merits and thus a **better enforceability** and voluntary compliance with respective awards.[813] Ultimately, adverse inferences thereby promote efficiency and fairness in international arbitration.[814]

55

While the instrument of adverse inference is generally acknowledged by the doctrine,[815] **legal provisions** on this concept, apart from the Rules, are rare. Art. 44 of the International Arbitration Rules of the Zurich Chamber of Commerce authorised arbitral tribunals to *"take into consideration the conduct of the parties during the procedure, in particular a refusal to cooperate in the administration of proof".*[816]

56

The primary source of case law on adverse inferences is the **Iran-United States Claims Tribunal** ("Claims Tribunal").[817] Because of the turmoil in Iran following the Islamic revolution and the ensuing lack of documentary evidence, the Claims Tribunal has been regularly confronted with requests

57

---

[811] Which constitutes an alternative to drawing negative inferences, cf. Art. 184(2) PILS.

[812] Lévy, Astreintes; Berger/Kellerhals, N 1156; Wyss, 199–200. Lévy and Wyss submit that this sanction, which is of French origin, may also be ordered by arbitrators sitting in Switzerland (Lévy, Astreintes, 29; Wyss, 199). See also Art. 3 N 189 above.

[813] Cf. Sharpe, 550, and Art. 41 ICC Rules, instructing arbitral tribunals to undertake every effort to ensure that their award is enforceable.

[814] Sharpe, 550.

[815] Born, 1855–1856 and 1919–1921; Poudret/Besson, N 650; PILS (Basel)-Schneider, Art. 184 N 21; Berger/Kellerhals, N 1240; Craig/Park/Paulsson, 456.

[816] The ZCC Rules have been replaced by the Swiss Rules which do not contain any respective provision.

[817] In Swiss case law, one of the rare references to the Rules can be found in a decision on adverse inference by the Swiss Federal Supreme Court of 25 July 1997 (ASA Bull 1/2000, 96–104). The arbitral tribunal's refusal to draw an adverse inference from the non-appearance of certain witnesses was upheld by the Supreme Court, taking into account Art. 6 of the 1983 "Supplementary Rules Governing the Presentation and Reception of Evidence in International Commercial Arbitration" which preceded the 1999 Rules.

to draw adverse inferences because certain important documents were destroyed, lost or not produced by the parties.[818] These factors, combined with the vast number of decisions rendered by the Claims Tribunal over the last decades, provide a key source of information on the procedural issue of adverse inference. Some of the most important cases shall be discussed below.

B.   General Requirements

58   Before drawing adverse inferences, arbitral tribunals must ensure that they are applying this principle appropriately, with due regard to the circumstances of the case. The doctrine has identified the following **general requirements** for drawing adverse inferences:[819]

a) the party seeking the adverse Inference must produce all available evidence corroborating the inference sought;

b) the requested evidence must be accessible to the other party;

c) the inference sought must be reasonable, consistent with facts in the record and logically related to the likely nature of the evidence withheld;

d) the party seeking the adverse inference must produce *prima facie* evidence; and

e) the other party must know, or have reason to know, of its obligation to produce evidence rebutting the adverse inference sought.

C.   Production of all Corroborating Evidence by Requesting Party

59   Arbitral tribunals will be reluctant to draw an adverse inference if the requesting party itself has access to **corroborating evidence** but has failed to produce it.

60   In the **Levitt case,** the Claims Tribunal refused to draw an adverse inference, despite Iran's non-production of certain documents, because the claimant did not even keep a copy of the main contract documents in its New York office, but stored all relevant documents in Teheran. In addition, the claimant failed to produce certain key employees as witnesses which

---

[818] Sharpe, 551. It has been estimated that parties complied with only approximately half of the Claims Tribunal's production orders; Caron/Caplan/Pellonpää, 578.

[819] See Brower/Brueschke, 194–197, and the detailed comments by Sharpe, summarised in the following (N 58–69).

could have corroborated its allegations related to the document production requests.[820]

D.   Evidence Accessible to the Other Party

In the **Edwards case,** the claimant failed to convince the Claims Tribunal   61
that the respondents had come into actual possession of some important business records the claimant had abandoned when he fled Iran in November 1979.[821]

Arbitral tribunals similarly may refuse to draw adverse inferences if certain   62
evidence is under the control of **uncooperative third parties,** as in the INA Corporation case where the claimant was not held accountable for the failure of organisations over which it had no control to provide certain requested information.[822] An exception must apply, however, to situations where the evidence is held by a parent, subsidiary or related company and thus may be deemed to be accessible to the other party.[823]

E.   Reasonable Inference

Inferences drawn by arbitral tribunals must be reasonable, i.e. in conform-   63
ity with the arbitrators' common understanding of commercial practice. The **Claims Tribunal** has developed the following reasonable inferences:[824]

---

[820] *William J. Levitt v. Islamic Republic of Iran,* Award No. 520-210-3 (29 August 1991), 27 Iran-US CTR 145, sect. 109 and 121. The fact that one witness had a financial dispute with the claimant and did not testify because of this was regarded as the claimant's internal problem and therefore considered irrelevant. The respective approach is criticised by BORN in that the criteria for applying an adverse inference *"are applied in an unrealistic fashion which approaches a denial of justice"* (BORN, 1920–1921).

[821] *George Edwards v. Government of the Islamic Republic of Iran,* Award No. 451-251-2 (5 December 1989), 23 Iran-US CTR 290, sect. 11, citing *H.A. Spalding, Inc. v. Ministry of Roads and Transport of the Islamic Republic of Iran,* Award No. 212-437-3 (24 February 1986), 10 Iran-US CTR 22, at 31.

[822] *INA Corporation v. Government of the Islamic Republic of Iran,* Award No. 184-161-1 (12 August 1985), 8 Iran-US CTR 373, at 381. Government agencies and private companies failed to provide notifications or confirmations which could have had an influence on the valuation of the claimant's shares in a nationalised company.

[823] CREMADES, 53.

[824] BRUNETTI, 376–377.

a) in the absence of contemporaneous objections, **invoices** or payment documents presented during the term of a contract are presumed to be correct,[825] payable[826] or evidencing satisfaction of payment[827];

b) the **failure to dispute** an account for a lengthy period of time places a burden on the respondent to demonstrate that the account was inaccurate;[828]

c) a party which **delays** detailing its **objection** to a claim for payment bears the burden of proving its justification;[829]

d) where a party's invoices typically contain **substantiating documentation,** the absence of such documentation presumably invalidates those invoices.[830]

F.   Consistence with Facts in the Record

64   Adverse inferences must lead to conclusions consistent with facts in the record. In the ***Corfu Channel* case,** for instance, the ICJ refused to draw from the refusal of the United Kingdom to produce certain naval orders any conclusions *"differing from those to which the actual events gave rise"*.[831]

G.   Logical Relation to Evidence Withheld

65   A party seeking an adverse inference must establish a **logical connection** between the nature of the documents withheld and the inference derived there from.

66   In the ***Riahi* case,**[832] the claimant failed to produce certificates for 510 bearer shares. At the claimant's request, the arbitral tribunal twice ordered

---

[825] *Houston Contracting Co. v. National Iranian Oil Co.,* Award No. 378-173-3 (22 July 1988), 20 Iran-US CTR 3 at 24–25; *Lockheed Corp. v. Government of Iran,* Award No. 367-829-2 (9 June 1988), 18 Iran-US CTR 292 at 308.

[826] *RAM International Industries v. Air Force of the Islamic Republic of Iran,* Award No. DEC 118-148-2 (28 December 1993), 29 Iran-US CTR 383 at 390–391; *Rockwell International Systems, Inc. v. Government of the Islamic Republic of Iran,* Award No. 438-430-1 (5 September 1989), 23 Iran-US CTR 150.

[827] *Behring International, Inc. v. Islamic Republic of Iran Air Force,* Award No. 523-382-3 (29 October 1991), 27 Iran-US CTR 218 at 234.

[828] *DIC of Delaware, Inc. v. Teheran Redevelopment Corp.,* Award No. 176-255-3 (26 April 1985), 8 Iran-US CTR 144 at 164.

[829] *Howard Needles Tammen and Bergendorff v. Government of the Islamic Republic of Iran,* Award No. 244-68-2 (8 August 1986), 11 Iran-US CTR 302 at 327.

[830] *Iran National Airlines Co. v. Government of the United States of America,* Award No. 335-B9-2 (30 November 1987), 17 Iran-US CTR 214 at 221.

[831] *United Kingdom v. Albania,* judgment of 9 April 1949, [1949] ICJ Rep. 4, at 32.

[832] *Frederica Lincoln Riahi v. Government of the Islamic Republic of Iran,* Award No. 600-485-1 (27 February 2003), YB Comm. Arb. 1993, 464. Criticised by Born, at 1920.

the respondent to produce the respective company's share register. When the respondent failed to produce the share register, the majority of the arbitral tribunal refused to draw an adverse inference, concluding that Iranian law does not require transfers of bearer shares to be entered into share registers, and it was not convinced that the share register of the company would show that the claimant owned the 510 bearer shares. Judge Brower questioned this conclusion in his dissenting opinion, concluding that it was unjust and inequitable to reward the respondent for its calculated flouting of two separate production orders of the arbitral tribunal.

H.   *Prima Facie* Evidence by Requesting Party

Arbitral tribunals should not draw any negative inference if the requesting party has failed to introduce *prima facie* **evidence** for its claim, i.e. evidence that is, under the circumstances, reasonably consistent, complete and detailed.   67

I.   Sufficient Opportunity for Requested Party to Produce

Whenever possible, arbitral tribunals should inform parties that adverse inferences may be drawn against them from their failure to comply with disclosure obligations.[833] Otherwise, the party against whom the adverse inference is drawn would not have an opportunity to rebut it, which could raise due process concerns.[834] A respective **announcement** should be included in the terms of reference or the constitutional order, as the case may be, and repeated in any production order.   68

The **Avco case** illustrates the danger of failing to advise the parties of their evidentiary obligations.[835] At a pre-hearing conference, the chairperson stated that the claimant could submit an auditor's report in lieu of hundreds of invoices. Three years later, however, the arbitral tribunal (with a new chairperson and with the Iran-appointed member now participating) rejected the claimant's invoice claims presented on this basis. Dissenting, Judge Brower concluded that the arbitral tribunal had *"misled the Claimant, however unwittingly, regarding the evidence it was required to submit, thereby depriving Claimant, to that extent, of the ability to present its case"*.[836] The claimant successfully raised this defence to prevent enforcement of the award in U.S. courts.[837]   69

---

[833] Nater-Bass in Commentary Swiss Rules, Art. 24 N 20.
[834] Webster, 51.
[835] *Avco Corp. v. Iran Aircraft Industry,* Award No. 377-261-3 (18 July 1988), 19 Iran-US CTR 200.
[836] Id. at 231.
[837] *Iran Aircraft Industry v. Avco Corp.,* 980 F.2d 141 (2d Cir. 1992).

VI.　Cost Sanctions for Bad Faith Conduct (par. 7)

70　The new Art. 9(7) authorises arbitral tribunals to impose costs based on bad faith conduct and constitutes a **specific implementation** of the good faith principle under par. 3 of the Preamble. Although this provision does not necessarily attribute powers to arbitral tribunals that they did not have already, it may be expected to increase the frequency with which parties request costs on this basis.[838]

71　In the past, arbitral tribunals have **regularly taken into account** a party's bad faith conduct for the allocation of costs,[839] e.g. when the respective party caused unjustified delays or obstructed the proceedings,[840] requested excessive compensation,[841] or concluded an agreement contrary to *bonos mores*[842].

---

[838] Cohen Kläsener, 161.

[839] See *ReliaStar Life Insurance Co. of NY v. EMC National Life,* 564 F. 3d 81 (2d Cir. 2009), where the arbitral tribunal awarded respondent ReliaStar all legal fees because the claimant's conduct had been "lacking in good faith", notwithstanding that the contract explicitly required each party to bear its own attorneys' fees; Park, Accuracy, 30; cf. also Gotanda, 42–43.

[840] ICC Case No. 8486 (1996), Collection of ICC Arbitral Awards IV (1996–2000) 321–332, at 331, YB Comm. Arb. 1999, 172. In this case, the respondent made none of the advance payments required, filed its counterclaim belatedly, refused to sign the terms of reference, did not participate in the oral hearings, and appointed its counsel at the last moment, i.e. shortly before comments on the evidence were due. Cf. also PILS (Basel)-Wirth, Art. 189 N 65.

[841] ICC Case No. 6527 (1991), Collection of ICC Arbitral Awards III (1991–1995) 185–194, at 194, YB Comm. Arb. 1993, 44, 52.

[842] ICC Case No. 6248 (1990), Collection of ICC Arbitral Awards III (1991–1995) 239–255, at 254–255, YB Comm. Arb. 1994, 124, referring to a decision of the Zurich Commercial Court of 9 May 1968, published in SJZ 1968, 354.

Annex 1:
Comparison IBA Rules 1999 and 2010

The Rules

Preamble

1. These IBA Rules on the Taking of Evidence
   in International ~~Commercial~~ Arbitration
   ~~(the "IBA Rules of Evidence")~~ are intended
   to ~~govern in~~<ins>provide</ins> an efficient ~~and,~~
   economical ~~manner~~<ins>and fair process for</ins> the
   taking of evidence in international
   ~~commercial~~ arbitrations, particularly those
   between Parties from different legal
   traditions. They are designed to supplement
   the legal provisions and the institutional ~~or,~~
   ad hoc <ins>or other</ins> rules ~~according to which the~~
   ~~Parties are conducting their~~<ins>that apply to the</ins>
   <ins>conduct of the</ins> arbitration.

2. Parties and Arbitral Tribunals may adopt the
   IBA Rules of Evidence, in whole or in part, to
   govern arbitration proceedings, or they may
   vary them or use them as guidelines in
   developing their own procedures. The
   Rules are not intended to limit the
   flexibility that is inherent in, and an
   advantage of, international arbitration, and
   Parties and Arbitral Tribunals are free to
   adapt them to the particular circumstances
   of each arbitration.

3. ~~Each Arbitral Tribunal is encouraged to identify to the Parties, as soon as it considers it to be appropriate, the issues that it may regard as relevant and material to the outcome of the case, including issues where a preliminary determination may be appropriate.~~

3. The taking of evidence shall be conducted on the ~~principle~~principles that each Party shall act in good faith and be entitled to know, reasonably in advance of any Evidentiary Hearing or any fact or merits determination, the evidence on which the other Parties rely.

Article I Definitions

In the IBA Rules of Evidence:

"*Arbitral Tribunal*" means a sole arbitrator or a panel of arbitrators ~~validly deciding by majority or otherwise~~;

"*Claimant*" means the Party or Parties who commenced the arbitration and any Party who, through joinder or ~~otherwise~~other wise, becomes aligned with such Party or Parties;

"*Document*" means a writing, communication, picture, drawing, program or data of any kind, whether recorded or

maintained on paper, or by electronic means,
audio or, visual recordings or any other
mechanical or electronic means of storing or
recording informationmeans;

"'Evidentiary Hearing"' means any hearing,
whether or not held on consecutive days, at
which the Arbitral Tribunal, whether in
person, by teleconference, videoconference
or other method, receives oral or other
evidence;

"'Expert Report"' means a written statement by
a Tribunal- Appointed Expert or a Party-
Appointed Expert submitted pursuant to the
IBA Rules of Evidence;

"'General Rules"' mean the institutional or, ad
hoc or other rules accordingthat apply to
which the Parties are conducting theirthe
conduct of the arbitration;

'IBA Rules of Evidence' or 'Rules' means these
IBA Rules on the Taking of Evidence in
International Arbitration, as they may be
revised or amended from time to time;

"'Party"' means a party to the arbitration;

"'Party-Appointed Expert" means an expert
witness presented by a' means a person or
organization appointed by a Party in order to

report on specific issues determined by the Party;

~~"~~'*Request to Produce*~~"~~' means a <u>written</u> request by a Party ~~for a procedural order by which the Arbitral Tribunal would direct~~<u>that</u> another Party ~~to~~ produce ~~documents~~<u>Documents</u>;

~~"~~'*Respondent*~~"~~' means the Party or Parties against whom the Claimant made its claim, and any Party who, through joinder or ~~otherwise~~<u>other wise</u>, becomes aligned with such Party or Parties, and includes a Respondent making a counter- claim;

~~"~~'*Tribunal-Appointed Expert*~~"~~' means a person or organization appointed by the Arbitral Tribunal in order to report to it on specific issues determined by the Arbitral Tribunal<u>;</u> <u>and</u>

<u>'*Witness Statement*' means a written statement of testimony by a witness of fact</u>.

Article ~~2~~<u>1</u> Scope of Application

1. Whenever the Parties have agreed or the Arbitral Tribunal has determined to apply the IBA Rules of Evidence, the Rules shall govern the taking of evidence, except to the extent that any specific provision of

them may be found to be in conflict with any mandatory provision of law determined to be applicable to the case by the Parties or by the Arbitral Tribunal.

2. <u>Where the Parties have agreed to apply the IBA Rules of Evidence, they shall be deemed to have agreed, in the absence of a contrary indication, to the version as current on the date of such agreement.</u>

3. In case of conflict between any provisions of the IBA Rules of Evidence and the General Rules, the Arbitral Tribunal shall apply the IBA Rules of Evidence in the manner that it determines best in order to accomplish the purposes of both the General Rules and the IBA Rules of Evidence, unless the Parties agree to the contrary.

4. In the event of any dispute regarding the meaning of the IBA Rules of Evidence, the Arbitral Tribunal shall interpret them according to their purpose and in the manner most appropriate for the particular arbitration.

5. Insofar as the IBA Rules of Evidence and the General Rules are silent on any matter concerning the taking of evidence and the Parties have not agreed ~~otherwise~~<u>other wise</u>, the Arbitral Tribunal ~~may~~<u>shall</u>

conduct the taking of evidence as it deems
appropriate, in accordance with the
general principles of the IBA Rules of
Evidence.

Article 2 Consultation on Evidentiary Issues

1. The Arbitral Tribunal shall consult the
Parties at the earliest appropriate time in
the proceedings and invite them to consult
each other with a view to agreeing on an
efficient, economical and fair process for
the taking of evidence.

2. The consultation on Evidentiary issues
may address the scope, timing and manner
of the taking of evidence, including:

   (a) the preparation and submission of
       Witness Statements and Expert
       Reports;
   (b) the taking of oral testimony at any
       Evidentiary Hearing;
   (c) the requirements, procedure and format
       applicable to the production of
       Documents;
   (d) the level of confidentiality protection to
       be afforded to evidence in the arbitration;
       and
   (e) the promotion of efficiency, economy
       and conservation of resources in
       connection with the taking of evidence.

3. The Arbitral Tribunal is encouraged to identify to the Parties, as soon as it considers it to be appropriate, any issues:
(a) that the Arbitral Tribunal may regard as relevant to the case and material to its outcome; and/or
(b) for which a preliminary determination may be appropriate.

Article 3 Documents

1. Within the time ordered by the Arbitral Tribunal, each Party shall submit to the Arbitral Tribunal and to the other Parties all ~~documents~~Documents available to it on which it relies, including public ~~documents~~Documents and those in the public domain, except for any ~~documents~~Documents that have already been submitted by another Party.

2. Within the time ordered by the Arbitral Tribunal, any Party may submit to the Arbitral Tribunal and to the other Parties a Request to Produce.

3. A Request to Produce shall contain:
(a) (i) a description of a~~each~~ requested ~~document~~Document sufficient to identify it, or *(ii)* a description in sufficient

detail (including subject matter) of a
narrow and specific requested category
of ~~documents~~Documents that are
reasonably believed to exist; in the case
of Documents maintained in
electronic form, the requesting Party
may, or the Arbitral Tribunal may
order that it shall be required to,
identify specific files, search terms,
individuals or other means of searching
for such Documents in an efficient and
economical manner;

(b) ~~a description of~~(b) a statement as to
how the ~~documents~~ Documents
requested are relevant to the case and
material to ~~the~~its outcome ~~of the case~~;
and

~~(c)~~(c) (i) a statement that the ~~documents~~
Documents
requested are not in the possession,
custody or control of the requesting Party~~,~~
~~and of the reason~~ or a statement of the
reasons why it would be unreasonably
burdensome for the requesting Party to
produce such Documents, and (ii) a
statement of the reasons why ~~that~~the
requesting Party assumes the
~~documents~~Documents requested ~~to be~~are
in the possession, custody or control of
~~the other~~another Party.

4. Within the time ordered by the Arbitral
   Tribunal, the Party to whom the Request

to Produce is addressed shall produce to the ~~other Parties and, if the~~ Arbitral Tribunal ~~and~~so orders, to ~~the other Parties~~it, all the ~~documents~~Documents requested in its possession, custody or control as to which it makes no objection~~is made~~.

5. If the Party to whom the Request to Produce is addressed has ~~objections~~an objection to some or all of the ~~documents~~Documents requested, it shall state ~~them~~the objection in writing to the Arbitral Tribunal and the other Parties within the time ordered by the Arbitral Tribunal. The reasons for such ~~objections~~objection shall be any of those set forth in Article ~~9.2.~~9.2 or a failure to satisfy any of the requirements of Article 3.3.

6. Upon receipt of any such objection, the Arbitral Tribunal may invite the relevant Parties to consult with each other with a view to resolving the objection.

7. Either Party may, within the time ordered by the Arbitral Tribunal, request the Arbitral Tribunal to rule on the objection. The Arbitral Tribunal shall then, in consultation with the Parties and in timely fashion, consider the Request to Produce

and the ~~objections~~objection. The Arbitral
Tribunal may order the Party to whom
such Request is addressed to produce ~~to~~
~~the Arbitral Tribunal and to the other Parties~~
~~those~~any requested ~~documents~~Document
in its possession, custody or control as to
which the Arbitral Tribunal determines
that *(i)* the issues that the requesting Party
wishes to prove are relevant <u>to the case</u> and
material to ~~the~~its outcome ~~of the case, and~~;
(ii) none of the reasons for objection set
forth in Article 9.2 ~~apply~~applies; and *(iii)* the
requirements of Article 3.3 have been
satisfied. Any such Document shall be
produced to the other Parties and, if the
Arbitral Tribunal so orders, to it.

8. In exceptional circumstances, if the
    propriety of an objection can ~~only~~ be
    determined <u>only</u> by review of the
    ~~document~~Document, the Arbitral Tribunal
    may determine that it should not review
    the ~~document~~Document. In that event, the
    Arbitral Tribunal may, after consultation
    with the Parties, appoint an independent
    and impartial expert, bound to
    confidentiality, to review any such
    ~~document~~Document and to report on the
    objection. To the extent that the objection
    is upheld by the Arbitral Tribunal, the
    expert shall not disclose to the Arbitral
    Tribunal and to the other Parties the

contents of the ~~document~~Document
reviewed.

9. If a Party wishes to obtain the production of
    ~~documents~~Documents from a person or
    organization who is not a Party to the
    arbitration and from whom the Party
    cannot obtain the ~~documents~~Documents
    on its own, the Party may, within the time
    ordered by the Arbitral Tribunal, ask it to
    take whatever steps are legally available to
    obtain the requested ~~documents. The Party~~
    ~~shall identify the documents in sufficient~~
    ~~detail and state why such documents are~~
    ~~relevant and material to the outcome of~~
    ~~the case~~Documents, or seek leave from
    the Arbitral Tribunal to take such steps
    itself. The Party shall submit such request
    to the Arbitral Tribunal and to the other
    Parties in writing, and the request shall
    contain the particulars set forth in Article
    3.3, as applicable. The Arbitral Tribunal
    shall decide on this request and shall take
    ~~the necessary steps if,~~ authorize the
    requesting Party to take, or order any
    other Party to take, such steps as the
    Arbitral Tribunal considers appropriate
    if, in its discretion, it determines that *(i)*
    the ~~documents would be relevant and~~
    ~~material~~Documents would be relevant to
    the case and material to its outcome, *(ii)*
    the requirements of Article 3.3, as
    applicable, have been satisfied and *(iii)*

none of the reasons for objection set forth in Article 9.2 applies.

10. ~~The Arbitral Tribunal, at~~At any time before the arbitration is concluded, the Arbitral Tribunal may *(i)* request ~~a Party to produce to the Arbitral Tribunal and to the other Parties any documents that it believes to be relevant and material to the outcome of the case. A Party may object to such a~~any Party to produce Documents, *(ii)* request any Party to use its best efforts to take or *(iii)* itself take, any step that it considers appropriate to obtain Documents from any person or organization. A Party to whom such a request for Documents is addressed may object to the request ~~based on~~for any of the reasons set forth in Article 9.2. ~~If a Party raises~~In such ~~an objection, the Arbitral Tribunal shall decide whether to order the production of such documents based upon the considerations set forth in Article 3.6 and, if the Arbitral Tribunal considers it appropriate, through the use of the procedures set forth in Article 3.7.~~cases, Article 3.4 to Article 3.8 shall apply correspondingly.

11. Within the time ordered by the Arbitral Tribunal, the Parties may submit to the Arbitral Tribunal and to the other Parties any additional ~~documents~~Documents on which they intend to rely or which they

believe have become relevant to the case
and material to its outcome as a
consequence of the issues raised in
~~documents~~Documents, Witness
Statements or Expert Reports submitted
or produced ~~by another Party~~, or in other
submissions of the Parties.

12. With respect to the form of submission or
    production of Documents:
    ~~11. If~~(a) copies ~~are submitted or produced,~~
    they ~~must~~of Documents shall conform
    ~~fully~~to the originals. ~~At~~ and, at the
    request of the Arbitral Tribunal, any
    original ~~must~~shall be presented for
    inspection~~.~~;
    (b) Documents that a Party maintains in
    electronic form shall be submitted or
    produced in the form most convenient
    or economical to it that is reasonably
    usable by the recipients, unless the
    Parties agree otherwise or, in the
    absence of such agreement, the Arbitral
    Tribunal decides otherwise;
    (c) a Party is not obligated to produce
    multiple copies of Documents which are
    essentially identical unless the Arbitral
    Tribunal decides otherwise; and
    (d) translations of Documents shall be
    submitted together with the originals and
    marked as translations with the original
    language identified.

13. ~~All documents~~Any Document submitted
    or produced by a Party ~~pursuant to the~~
    ~~IBA Rules of Evidence (or by a~~or non-Party
    ~~pursuant to Article 3.8)~~in the arbitration
    and not otherwise in the public domain
    shall be kept confidential by the Arbitral
    Tribunal and ~~by~~ the other Parties, and
    ~~they~~ shall be used only in connection with
    the arbitration. This requirement shall
    apply except and to the extent that
    disclosure may be required of a Party to
    fulfil a legal duty, protect or pursue a legal
    right, or enforce or challenge an award in
    bona fide legal proceedings before a state
    court or other judicial authority. The
    Arbitral Tribunal may issue orders to set
    forth the terms of this confidentiality. This
    requirement ~~is~~shall be without prejudice
    to all other obligations of confidentiality
    in the arbitration.

14. If the arbitration is organised into
    separate issues or phases (such as
    jurisdiction, preliminary determinations,
    liability or damages), the Arbitral
    Tribunal may, after consultation with the
    Parties, schedule the submission of
    Documents and Requests to Produce
    separately for each issue or phase.

Article 4 Witnesses of Fact

1. Within the time ordered by the Arbitral Tribunal, each Party shall identify the witnesses on whose testimony it ~~relies~~intends to rely and the subject matter of that testimony.

2. Any person may present evidence as a witness, including a Party or a Party's officer, employee or other representative.

3. It shall not be improper for a Party, its officers, employees, legal advisors or other representatives to ~~interview~~inter view its witnesses or potential witnesses and to discuss their prospective testimony with them.

4. The Arbitral Tribunal may order each Party to submit within a specified time to the Arbitral Tribunal and to the other Parties ~~a written statement~~Witness Statements by each witness on whose testimony it ~~relies~~intends to rely, except for those witnesses whose testimony is sought pursuant to ~~Article 4.10 (the "Witness Statement").~~Articles 4.9 or 4.10. If Evidentiary Hearings are ~~organized on~~organised into separate issues or phases (such as jurisdiction, preliminary determinations, liability ~~and~~or damages),

the Arbitral Tribunal or the Parties by
agreement may schedule the submission
of Witness Statements separately for each
~~Evidentiary Hearing~~issue or phase.

5. Each Witness Statement shall contain:
   (a) the full name and address of the witness,
       a statement regarding his or her present
       and past relationship (if any) with any of
       the Parties, and a description of his or her
       background, qualifications, training and
       experience, if such a description may be
       relevant ~~and material~~ to the dispute or to
       the contents of the statement;
   (b) a full and detailed description of the
       facts, and the source of the witness's
       information as to those facts, sufficient to
       serve as that witness's evidence in the
       matter in dispute. Documents on which
       the witness relies that have not already
       been submitted shall be provided;
   (c) a statement as to the language in which
       the Witness Statement was originally
       prepared and the language in which the
       witness anticipates giving testimony at
       the Evidentiary Hearing;
   (d) an affirmation of the truth of the
       ~~statement~~Witness Statement; and
   (de) the signature of the witness and its date
       and place.

6. If Witness Statements are submitted, any
   Party may, within the time ordered by the

Arbitral Tribunal, submit to the Arbitral Tribunal and to the other Parties revised or additional Witness Statements, including statements from persons not previously named as witnesses, so long as any such revisions or additions ~~only~~ respond only to matters contained in another Party's Witness ~~Statement~~ ~~or~~Statements, Expert ~~Report and such~~ ~~matters~~Reports or other submissions that have not been previously presented in the arbitration.

7. ~~Each witness who has submitted a Witness Statement shall appear for testimony at an Evidentiary Hearing, unless the Parties agree otherwise.~~

7. If a witness ~~who has submitted a Witness Statement does not appear~~whose appearance has been requested pursuant to Article 8.1 fails without a valid reason to appear for testimony at an Evidentiary Hearing, ~~except by agreement of the Parties~~, the Arbitral Tribunal shall disregard ~~that~~any Witness Statement related to that Evidentiary Hearing by that witness unless, in exceptional circumstances, the Arbitral Tribunal ~~determines otherwise~~decides other wise.

8. If the ~~Parties agree that~~appearance of a
    witness ~~who~~ has ~~submitted a Witness
    Statement does not need to appear for
    testimony at an Evidentiary Hearing, such
    an agreement shall not be considered to
    reflect an agreement as~~not been requested
    pursuant to Article 8.1, none of the other
    Parties shall be deemed to have agreed to
    the correctness of the content of the
    Witness Statement.

9. If a Party wishes to present evidence from
    a person who will not appear voluntarily
    at its request, the Party may, within the
    time ordered by the Arbitral Tribunal, ask
    it to take whatever steps are legally
    available to obtain the testimony of that
    person~~.~~~~The~~, or seek leave from the
    Arbitral Tribunal to take such steps itself.
    In the case of a request to the Arbitral
    Tribunal, the Party shall identify the
    intended witness, shall describe the
    subjects on which the witness's testimony
    is sought and shall state why such subjects
    are relevant to the case and material to
    ~~the~~its outcome ~~of the case~~. The Arbitral
    Tribunal shall decide on this request and
    shall take ~~the necessary steps~~ if, authorize
    the requesting Party to take or order any
    other Party to take, such steps as the
    Arbitral Tribunal considers appropriate
    if, in its discretion, it determines that the

testimony of that witness would be relevant to the case and material to its outcome.

10. ~~The Arbitral Tribunal may, at~~At any time before the arbitration is concluded, the Arbitral Tribunal may order any Party to provide for, or to use its best efforts to provide for, the appearance for testimony at an Evidentiary Hearing of any person, including one whose testimony has not yet been offered. A Party to whom such a request is addressed may object for any of the reasons set forth in Article 9.2.

Article 5 Party-Appointed Experts

1. A Party may rely on a Party-Appointed Expert as a means of evidence on specific issues. Within the time ordered by the Arbitral Tribunal, ~~a Party~~ (i) each Party shall identify any Party-Appointed Expert on whose testimony it intends to rely and the subject-matter of such testimony; and (ii) the Party-Appointed Expert shall submit an Expert Report.

2. The Expert Report shall contain:
   (a) the full name and address of the Party-Appointed Expert, a statement regarding his or her present and past relationship (if any) with any of the Parties, their legal advisors and the Arbitral Tribunal, and a

description of his or her background, qualifications, training and experience;

(b) a <u>description of the instructions pursuant to which he or she is providing his or her opinions and conclusions;</u>

(c) a <u>statement of his or her independence from the Parties, their legal advisors and the Arbitral Tribunal;</u>

(d) a statement of the facts on which he or she is basing his or her expert opinions and conclusions;

(e~~e~~) his or her expert opinions and conclusions, including a description of the ~~method~~<u>methods</u>, evidence and information used in arriving at the conclusions<u>. Documents on which the Party-Appointed Expert relies that have not already been submitted shall be provided</u>;

(d) ~~an affirmation of the truth of the Expert Report; and~~<u>f) if the Expert Report has been translated, a statement as to the language in which it was originally prepared, and the language in which the Party-Appointed Expert anticipates giving testimony at the Evidentiary Hearing;</u>

(g) <u>an affirmation of his or her genuine belief in the opinions expressed in the Expert Report;</u>

(e<u>h</u>) the signature of the Party-Appointed Expert and its date and place~~.~~<u>; and</u>

(i) <u>if the Expert Report has been signed by more than one person, an attribution of</u>

the entirety or specific parts of the Expert
Report to each author.

3. If Expert Reports are submitted, any Party
    may, within the time ordered by the
    Arbitral Tribunal, submit to the Arbitral
    Tribunal and to the other Parties revised
    or additional Expert Reports, including
    reports or statements from persons not
    previously identified as Party-Appointed
    Experts, so long as any such revisions or
    additions respond only to matters
    contained in another Party's Witness
    Statements, Expert Reports or other
    submissions that have not been previously
    presented in the arbitration.

4. The Arbitral Tribunal in its discretion
    may order that any Party-Appointed
    Experts who will submit or who have
    submitted Expert Reports on the same or
    related issues meet and confer on such
    issues. At such meeting, the Party-
    Appointed Experts shall attempt to reach
    agreement on ~~those~~the issues ~~as to which
    they had differences of opinion in~~within the
    scope of their Expert Reports, and they shall
    record in writing any such issues on which
    they reach agreement~~.~~

4. ~~Each Party-Appointed Expert shall appear
    for testimony at an Evidentiary Hearing,
    unless the Parties agree otherwise and the
    Arbitral Tribunal accepts this agreement.~~,

~~any remaining areas of disagreement and the reasons therefore.~~

5. If a Party-Appointed Expert ~~does not appear~~whose appearance has been requested pursuant to Article 8.1 fails without a valid reason to appear for testimony at an Evidentiary Hearing~~, except by agreement of the Parties accepted by the Arbitral Tribunal~~, the Arbitral Tribunal shall disregard ~~his or her~~any Expert Report by that Party-Appointed Expert related to that Evidentiary Hearing unless, in exceptional circumstances, the Arbitral Tribunal ~~determines otherwise~~decides otherwise.

6. If the ~~Parties agree that~~appearance of a Party-Appointed Expert ~~does not need to appear for testimony at an Evidentiary Hearing, such an agreement shall not be considered to reflect an agreement as~~has not been requested pursuant to Article 8.1, none of the other Parties shall be deemed to have agreed to the correctness of the content of the Expert Report.

Article 6 Tribunal-Appointed Experts

1. The Arbitral Tribunal, after ~~having consulted~~consulting with the Parties, may

appoint one or more independent Tribunal-Appointed Experts to report to it on specific issues designated by the Arbitral Tribunal. The Arbitral Tribunal shall establish the terms of reference for any Tribunal-Appointed Expert ~~report~~Report after ~~having consulted~~consulting with the Parties. A copy of the final terms of reference shall be sent by the Arbitral Tribunal to the Parties.

2. The Tribunal-Appointed Expert shall, before accepting appointment, submit to the Arbitral Tribunal and to the Parties a description of his or her qualifications and a statement of his or her independence from the Parties, their legal advisors and the Arbitral Tribunal. Within the time ordered by the Arbitral Tribunal, the Parties shall inform the Arbitral Tribunal whether they have any objections as to the Tribunal-Appointed Expert's qualifications and independence. The Arbitral Tribunal shall decide promptly whether to accept any such objection. After the appointment of a Tribunal- Appointed Expert, a Party may object to the expert's qualifications or independence only if the objection is for reasons of which the Party becomes aware after the appointment has been made. The

Arbitral Tribunal shall decide promptly what, if any, action to take.

3. ~~Subject to the provisions of Article 9.2, the Tribunal-Appointed Expert may request a Party to provide any relevant and material information or to provide access to any relevant documents, goods, samples, property or site for inspection.~~

3. <u>Subject to the provisions of Article 9.2, the Tribunal-</u> Appointed Expert <u>may request a Party to provide any information or to provide access to any Documents, goods, samples, property, machinery, systems, processes or site for inspection, to the extent relevant to the case and material to its outcome.</u> The authority of a Tribunal-Appointed Expert to request such information or access shall be the same as the authority of the Arbitral Tribunal. The Parties and their representatives shall have the right to receive any such information and to attend any such inspection. Any disagreement between a Tribunal-Appointed Expert and a Party as to the relevance, materiality or appropriateness of such a request shall be decided by the Arbitral Tribunal, in the manner provided in Articles 3.5 through ~~3.7.~~<u>3.8.</u> The Tribunal-Appointed Expert shall record in the ~~report~~<u>Expert Report</u> any non-compliance by a Party with an

appropriate request or decision by the
Arbitral Tribunal and shall describe its
effects on the determination of the
specific issue.

4. The Tribunal-Appointed Expert shall
   report in writing to the Arbitral Tribunal
   in an Expert Report. The ~~Tribunal-Appointed Expert shall describe in the report the method, evidence and information used in arriving at the conclusions.~~Expert Report shall contain:
   (a) the full name and address of the
       Tribunal- Appointed Expert, and a
       description of his or her background,
       qualifications, training and experience;
   (b) a statement of the facts on which he or
       she is basing his or her expert opinions
       and conclusions;
   (c) his or her expert opinions and
       conclusions, including a description of
       the methods, evidence and information
       used in arriving at the conclusions.
       Documents on which the Tribunal-
       Appointed Expert relies that have not
       already been submitted shall be provided;
   (d) if the Expert Report has been translated,
       a statement as to the language in which it
       was originally prepared, and the language
       in which the Tribunal-Appointed Expert
       anticipates giving testimony at the
       Evidentiary Hearing;

(e) an affirmation of his or her genuine belief in the opinions expressed in the Expert Report;

(f) the signature of the Tribunal-Appointed Expert and its date and place; and

(g) if the Expert Report has been signed by more than one person, an attribution of the entirety or specific parts of the Expert Report to each author.

5. The Arbitral Tribunal shall send a copy of such Expert Report to the Parties. The Parties may examine any ~~document~~ information, Documents, goods, samples, property, machinery, systems, processes or site for inspection that the Tribunal-Appointed Expert has examined and any correspondence between the Arbitral Tribunal and the Tribunal-_-Appointed Expert. Within the time ordered by the Arbitral Tribunal, any Party shall have the opportunity to respond to the ~~report~~Expert Report in a submission by the Party or through a Witness Statement or an Expert Report by a Party-Appointed Expert. The Arbitral Tribunal shall send the submission, Witness Statement or Expert Report to the Tribunal-Appointed Expert and to the other Parties.

6. At the request of a Party or of the Arbitral Tribunal, the Tribunal-Appointed Expert shall be present at an Evidentiary Hearing.

The Arbitral Tribunal may question the
Tribunal-Appointed Expert, and he or she
may be questioned by the Parties or by
any Party- Appointed Expert on issues
raised in his or her Expert Report, the
Parties' submissions or inWitness
Statement or the Expert Reports made by
the Party- Appointed Experts pursuant to
Article 6.5.

7. Any Expert Report made by a Tribunal-
Appointed Expert and its conclusions shall
be assessed by the Arbitral Tribunal with
due regard to all circum- stances
circumstances of the case.

8. The fees and expenses of a Tribunal-
Appointed Expert, to be funded in a
manner determined by the Arbitral
Tribunal, shall form part of the costs of
the arbitration.

Article 7 On Site Inspection

Subject to the provisions of Article 9.2, the
Arbitral Tribunal may, at the request of a
Party or on its own motion, inspect or require
the inspection by a Tribunal- Appointed
Expert or a Party-Appointed Expert of any site,
property, machinery or any other goods or
process, or documents, samples, systems,
processes or Documents, as it deems

appropriate. The Arbitral Tribunal shall, in consultation with the Parties, determine the timing and arrangement for the inspection. The Parties and their representatives shall have the right to attend any such inspection.

Article 8 Evidentiary Hearing

1. <u>Within the time ordered by the Arbitral Tribunal, each Party shall inform the Arbitral Tribunal and the other Parties of the witnesses whose appearance it requests. Each witness (which term includes, for the purposes of this Article, witnesses of fact and any experts) shall, subject to Article 8.2, appear for testimony at the Evidentiary Hearing if such person's appearance has been requested by any Party or by the Arbitral Tribunal. Each witness shall appear in person unless the Arbitral Tribunal allows the use of videoconference or similar technology with respect to a particular witness.</u>

2. The Arbitral Tribunal shall at all times have complete control over the Evidentiary Hearing. The Arbitral Tribunal may limit or exclude any question to, answer by or appearance of a witness ~~(which term includes, for the purposes of this Article, witnesses of fact and any Experts)~~, if it considers such question, answer or

appearance to be irrelevant, immaterial, unreasonably burdensome, duplicative or otherwise covered by a reason for objection set forth in Article 9.2. Questions to a witness during direct and ~~redirect~~re-direct testimony may not be unreasonably leading.

3. With respect to oral testimony at an Evidentiary Hearing:

~~2. The~~(a) the Claimant shall ordinarily first present the testimony of its witnesses, followed by the Respondent presenting the testimony of its witnesses~~, and then by the presentation by Claimant of rebuttal witnesses, if any. Following~~;

(b) following direct testimony, any other Party may question such witness, in an order to be determined by the Arbitral Tribunal. The Party who initially presented the witness shall subsequently have the opportunity to ask additional questions on the matters raised in the other Parties' questioning~~. The~~;

(c) thereafter, the Claimant shall ordinarily first present the testimony of its Party-Appointed Experts, followed by the Respondent presenting the testimony of its Party-Appointed Experts. The Party who initially presented the Party-Appointed Expert shall subsequently have the opportunity to ask additional

questions on the matters raised in the
other Parties' questioning;

(d) the Arbitral Tribunal may question a
Tribunal- Appointed Expert, and he or
she may be questioned by the Parties or
by any Party- Appointed Expert, on
issues raised in the Tribunal-Appointed
Expert Report, in the Parties' submissions
or in the Expert Reports made by the
Party-Appointed Experts;

(e) if the arbitration is organised into
separate issues or phases (such as
jurisdiction, preliminary determinations,
liability and damages), the Parties may
agree or the Arbitral Tribunal may order
the scheduling of testimony separately for
each issue or phase;

(f) the Arbitral Tribunal, upon request of a
Party or on its own motion, may vary this
order of proceeding, including the
arrangement of testimony by particular
issues or in such a manner that witnesses
~~presented by different Parties~~ be
questioned at the same time and in
confrontation with each other. ~~The~~
(witness conferencing);

(g) the Arbitral Tribunal may ask questions
to a witness at any time.

4. ~~Any~~A witness of fact providing testimony
shall first affirm, in a manner determined
appropriate by the Arbitral Tribunal, that
he or she ~~is telling the truth~~commits to tell

the truth or, in the case of an expert
witness, his or her genuine belief in the
opinions to be expressed at the
Evidentiary Hearing. If the witness has
submitted a Witness Statement or an
Expert Report, the witness shall confirm it.
The Parties may agree or the Arbitral
Tribunal may order that the Witness
Statement or Expert Report shall serve as
that witness's direct testimony.

5. Subject to the provisions of Article 9.2, the
    Arbitral Tribunal may request any person
    to give oral or written evidence on any issue
    that the Arbitral Tribunal considers to be
    relevant to the case and material to its
    outcome. Any witness called and
    questioned by the Arbitral Tribunal may
    also be questioned by the Parties.

**Article 9 Admissibility and Assessment of
Evidence**

1. The Arbitral Tribunal shall determine
    the admissibility, relevance, materiality and
    weight of evidence.

2. The Arbitral Tribunal shall, at the request
    of a Party or on its own motion, exclude
    from evidence or production any
    ~~document~~Document, statement, oral

testimony or inspection for any of the
following reasons:

(a) lack of sufficient relevance to the case or
materiality to its outcome;

(b) legal impediment or privilege under the
legal or ethical rules determined by the
Arbitral Tribunal to be applicable;

(c) unreasonable burden to produce the
requested evidence;

(d) loss or destruction of the
~~document~~Document that has been
~~reasonably~~ shown with reasonable
likelihood to have occurred;

(e) grounds of commercial or technical
confidentiality that the Arbitral Tribunal
determines to be compelling;

(f) grounds of special political or
institutional sensitivity (including
evidence that has been classified as secret
by a government or a public international
institution) that the Arbitral Tribunal
determines to be compelling; or

(g) considerations of procedural economy,
proportionality, fairness or equality of the
Parties that the Arbitral Tribunal
determines to be compelling.

3. In considering issues of legal impediment
or privilege under Article 9.2(b), and
insofar as permitted by any mandatory
legal or ethical rules that are determined
by it to be applicable, the Arbitral
Tribunal may take into account:

(a) any need to protect the confidentiality of
     a Document created or statement or oral
     communication made in connection with
     and for the purpose of providing or
     obtaining legal advice;

(b) any need to protect the confidentiality of
     a Document created or statement or oral
     communication made in connection with
     and for the purpose of settlement
     negotiations;

(c) the expectations of the Parties and their
     advisors at the time the legal impediment
     or privilege is said to have arisen;

(d) any possible waiver of any applicable
     legal impediment or privilege by virtue of
     consent, earlier disclosure, affirmative
     use of the Document, statement, oral
     communication or advice contained
     therein, or other wise; and

(e) the need to maintain fairness and equality
     as between the Parties, particularly if they
     are subject to different legal or ethical
     rules.

4. The Arbitral Tribunal may, where
    appropriate, make necessary
    arrangements to permit evidence to be
    presented or considered subject to
    suitable confidentiality protection.

5. If a Party fails without satisfactory
    explanation to produce any
    documentDocument requested in a

Request to Produce to which it has not
objected in due time or fails to produce
any ~~document~~<ins>Document</ins> ordered to be
produced by the Arbitral Tribunal, the
Arbitral Tribunal may infer that such
document would be adverse to the
interests of that Party.

6. If a Party fails without satisfactory
    explanation to make available any other
    relevant evidence, including testimony,
    sought by one Party to which the Party to
    whom the request was addressed has not
    objected in due time or fails to make
    available any evidence, including
    testimony, ordered by the Arbitral Tribunal
    to be produced, the Arbitral Tribunal
    may infer that such evidence would be
    adverse to the interests of that Party.

7. <ins>If the Arbitral Tribunal determines that a
    Party has failed to conduct itself in good
    faith in the taking of evidence, the Arbitral
    Tribunal may, in addition to any other
    measures available under these Rules, take
    such failure into account in its assignment
    of the costs of the arbitration, including
    costs arising out of or in connection with
    the taking of evidence.</ins>

Annex 2:
ICC Techniques for Controlling Time and Costs in Arbitration

Table of Contents   Para.

Preface

One of the salient characteristics of arbitration as a dispute resolution mechanism is that the rules of arbitration themselves present a framework for arbitral proceedings but rarely set out detailed procedures for the conduct of the arbitration. For example, rules of arbitration do not generally specify whether there should be one, two or more exchanges of briefs. They do not contain any detailed provisions concerning document production. They do not specify how hearings should be conducted and how witnesses, if any, should be heard.

This important characteristic entails that the specific procedures can be tailor-made as appropriate for each dispute and adapted to the legal cultures of the parties and the arbitrators. In order to establish the appropriate procedures for a given arbitration, it is useful and efficient for the parties and the tribunal to make conscious decisions as early as possible on the procedures best suited to the dispute at hand. In making those decisions, it is possible to shape the arbitral proceedings so that the duration and cost of the arbitration are commensurate with what is at stake in the case and appropriate in light of the claims and issues presented.

With the above in mind, the Task Force on Reducing Time and Costs in Arbitration, set up by the ICC Commission on Arbitration and excellently co-chaired by Yves Derains and Christopher Newmark, has prepared the following document setting out a large number of techniques which can be used for organizing the arbitral proceedings and controlling their duration and cost. This document can provide valuable assistance to the parties and the tribunal in developing appropriate procedures for their arbitration. It is intended to encourage them to create a new dynamic at the outset of an arbitration, whereby the parties can review the suggested techniques and agree upon appropriate procedures and, if they fail to agree, the tribunal can decide upon such procedures. For example, an arbitral tribunal can send this document to the parties at the start of the proceedings, indicating that early in the proceedings they might seek to agree upon appropriate procedures in consultation with the tribunal. In that process, all may agree upon the use of certain techniques. If one party wishes to use a particular technique and the other party does not, the tribunal, after obtaining the views of each party on the matter, can decide whether or not to adopt that procedure. The use of this approach, coupled with the proactive involvement of the tribunal in the management of the proceedings, can result in meaningful savings of time and cost in the arbitration.

The techniques suggested in the document are not intended to be exhaustive. On the contrary, they are open-ended, and the parties and the tribunal are encouraged to think of this document as a basis from which to develop the procedures to be used. Indeed, it is the intention of the ICC Commission on Arbitration to revise and republish this document in the future, taking into account further suggestions which will emerge from the use of the document. As a corollary, it should be clear that parties and arbitrators are in no way obligated to follow any of the techniques. Moreover, the document is a product of the ICC Commission on Arbitration and not of the ICC International Court of Arbitration and thus it is not part of or interpretative of the ICC Rules of Arbitration or in any way binding upon the Court. Rather, it is a practical tool designed to stimulate the conscious choice of arbitral procedures with a view to organizing an arbitration which is efficient and appropriately tailor-made. Finally, while this document was conceived with the ICC Rules of Arbitration in mind, the vast majority of the techniques as well as the dynamics generated by the document can be used in all arbitrations.

It is the sincere hope of the Task Force that this document will be used and be of use in the crafting of efficient arbitration procedures in which time and cost will be proportionate to the needs of the dispute.

Peter M. Wolrich
Chairman, ICC Commission on Arbitration

Introduction

Statistics provided by the ICC International Court of Arbitration based on ICC cases that went to a final award in 2003 and 2004 show that the costs incurred by the parties in presenting their cases constituted the largest part of the total cost of ICC arbitration proceedings. On average, the costs in these ICC arbitration cases were spread as follows:

Costs borne by the parties to present their cases: 82%

(including, as the case may be, lawyers› fees and expenses, expenses related to witness and expert evidence, and other costs incurred by the parties for the arbitration other than those set forth below)

Arbitrators' fees and expenses: 16%

Administrative expenses of ICC: 2%

It follows that if the overall cost of the arbitral proceedings is to be minimized, special emphasis needs to be placed on steps aimed at reducing the costs connected with the parties' presentation of their cases. Such costs are often caused by unnecessarily long and complicated proceedings with unfocused requests for disclosure of documents and unnecessary witness and expert evidence. Costs can also be unnecessarily increased when counsel from different legal backgrounds use procedures familiar to them in a manner that leads to needless duplication.

The increasing and, on occasion, unnecessary complication of the proceedings seems to be the main explanation for the long duration and high cost of many international arbitrations. The longer the proceedings, the more expensive they will be.

These Techniques for Controlling Time and Costs in Arbitration are designed to assist arbitral tribunals, parties and their counsel in this regard.

Pursuant to Article 15 of the ICC Rules of Arbitration, the procedure in an ICC arbitration is governed firstly by the ICC Rules and, where they are silent, by any rules which the parties or, failing them, the arbitral tribunal may settle on. Many other arbitration rules provide for similar solutions. As a result, arbitrations may be conducted using different procedural traditions, depending on the origins of the parties, their counsel and the arbitrators.

These Techniques provide guidance to the parties and their counsel on certain procedures that they may be able to agree upon for the efficient management of their proceedings. The solutions proposed herein are not the only ones available and it is not suggested that they are appropriate to all kinds of arbitrations.

This document can be provided to the parties by the arbitral tribunal as soon as it has received the file, so that they can discuss and seek to reach agreement on procedures suitable for their case. If the parties cannot reach agreement, the Techniques may also assist the arbitral tribunal in adopting procedures that it considers appropriate, taking into account its obligation, under Article 20(1) of the ICC Rules, to establish the facts of the case within as short a time as possible, whilst ensuring that each party has a reasonable opportunity to present its case.

The Techniques are in no way prescriptive, nor should they be regarded as a code of best practice. Rather, they provide ideas that may assist in arriving at procedures that are efficient and will reduce both cost and time. Certain procedures will be appropriate for one arbitration, but inappropriate for another. There may be other procedures not mentioned here that are well suited to a particular case. In all instances, it is for the parties and the arbitral tribunal to select the procedures that are best suited for the case.

The table of contents to this document can serve as a checklist of points to consider.

The Techniques embody two underlying principles. First, wherever possible, the parties and the arbitral tribunal should make a conscious and deliberate choice early in the proceedings as to the specific procedures suitable for their case. Second, the arbitral tribunal should work proactively with the parties to manage the procedure from the outset of the case.

While the main focus of the Techniques is to provide guidance on the procedure during the arbitration, the first two sections give suggestions on the drafting of arbitration agreements and the initiation of arbitral proceedings.

Arbitration agreement

KEEPING CLAUSES SIMPLE

1   Simple, clearly drafted arbitration clauses will avoid uncertainty and disputes as to their meaning and effect. They will minimize the risk of time and costs being spent on disputes regarding, for example, the jurisdiction of the arbitral tribunal or the process of appointing arbitrators. In all cases, ensure that the arbitration clause conforms with any relevant applicable laws.

2   Use of the standard ICC arbitration clause, which can be found in the booklet containing the ICC Rules of Arbitration (ICC Publication 838), is recommended. Modifications to the standard clause can result in unintended and undesirable consequences. In addition to the standard clause, specify in separate sentences the place of the arbitration, the language of the arbitration and the rules of law governing the contract. Be cautious about adding further provisions to this clause relating to the procedure for the arbitration. However, multi-party and multi-contract transactions may require specific additional provisions.

SELECTION AND APPOINTMENT OF ARBITRATORS

3   High-value and complex contracts can give rise to small disputes for which a three-member tribunal may be too expensive. Although parties may desire the certainty of appointing either a one- or a three-person tribunal in their arbitration agreement, consideration should be given to staying with the standard ICC arbitration clause and providing for one or more arbitrators. This will enable ICC to appoint or the parties to agree

on a sole arbitrator where the specific nature of any subsequent dispute does not warrant a three-person tribunal (See ICC Rules, Article 8(2)).

4   If the parties wish ICC to select and appoint all members of the arbitral tribunal (see paragraph 13 below), then the following wording can be used: "All arbitrators shall be selected and appointed by the ICC International Court of Arbitration."

5   Adding special requirements as to the expertise and qualifications of arbitrators to be appointed will reduce the pool of available arbitrators and may increase the time taken to select a tribunal.

FAST-TRACK PROCEDURES

6   Consideration may be given to setting out fast-track procedures in the arbitration clause. Indeed Article 32(1) of the ICC Rules enables the parties to shorten time limits provided for in the Rules, while Article 32(2) enables the Court to extend those shortened time limits when necessary. Fast-track procedures are designed to enable an arbitration to proceed quickly, given the specific nature of the contract and disputes that are likely to arise. However, experience shows that in practice it is difficult at the time of drafting the clause to predict with a reasonable degree of certainty the nature of disputes and the procedures that will be suitable for those disputes. Also, disagreements can arise later as to the interpretation or application of fast-track clauses. Careful thought should therefore be given before such provisions are included in an arbitration agreement. Once a dispute has arisen, the parties could at that time agree upon a fast-track procedure, if appropriate.

TIME LIMITS FOR RENDERING THE AWARD

7   One commonly used provision that can give rise to significant difficulties is the requirement that an award be produced within a certain number of weeks or months from the commencement of the arbitration. Such specific time limits can create jurisdictional and enforcement problems if it turns out that the time limit specified is unrealistic or not clearly defined.

SUBMISSION TO ICC ARBITRATION

8   If the parties agree to submit a dispute to ICC arbitration after the dispute has arisen, they can consider specifying in some detail the procedure for the arbitration, taking into account the nature of the dispute in

question. This procedure may include some of the suggestions set out below to reduce time and costs.

Initiation of proceedings

Selection of counsel

COUNSEL WITH EXPERIENCE

9   Consider appointing counsel with the skills necessary for handling the arbitration at hand. Such counsel are more likely to be able to work with the arbitral tribunal and the other party›s counsel to devise an efficient procedure for the case.

COUNSEL WITH TIME

10 Ensure that the counsel you have selected has sufficient time to devote to the case.

Selection of arbitrators

USE OF SOLE ARBITRATOR

11 After a dispute has arisen, consider agreeing upon having a sole arbitrator, when appropriate. Generally speaking, a one-person tribunal will be able to act more quickly than a three-person tribunal, since discussions between tribunal members are not needed and diary clashes for hearings will be minimized. A one-person tribunal will obviously also be cheaper.

ARBITRATORS WITH TIME

12 Whether selecting a sole arbitrator or a three-person tribunal, it is advisable to make sufficient enquiries to ensure that the individuals selected have sufficient time to devote to the case in question. If there is particular need for speed, this must be made clear to ICC so that it can be taken into consideration when making any appointments.

SELECTION AND APPOINTMENT BY ICC

13 Consider allowing ICC to select and appoint the arbitral tribunal, whether it be a sole arbitrator or a three-person tribunal. This will generally be the quickest way to constitute the arbitral tribunal, if there is no

agreement between the parties on the identity of all arbitrators. It will also reduce the risk of challenges, facilitate the constitution of a tribunal with a variety of specialist skills and create a different dynamic within the arbitral tribunal. If the parties wish to have input into the selection of the tribunal by ICC at this stage, they can request that ICC disclose the names of possible arbitrators for selection by ICC in accordance with a procedure to be agreed upon by the parties in consultation with ICC.

AVOIDING OBJECTIONS

14 Objections to the appointment of an arbitrator, whether or not warranted, will delay the constitution of the arbitral tribunal. When selecting an arbitrator, give careful thought as to whether or not the appointment of that arbitrator might give rise to an objection.

SELECTING ARBITRATORS WITH STRONG CASE-MANAGEMENT SKILLS

15 A tribunal that is proactive and skilled in case management will be able to assist in managing the arbitration so as to make it as cost- and time-effective as possible, given the issues in dispute and the nature of the parties. This may be of particular value where the parties wish to use a fast-track procedure. Careful consideration should therefore be given to selecting tribunal members, especially the sole arbitrator or chairman.

Request for Arbitration and Answer

COMPLYING WITH THE ICC RULES

16 The Claimant should ensure that it includes all of the elements required by Article 4 of the ICC Rules in its Request for Arbitration. Failure to do so can result in the Secretariat needing to revert to the Claimant before the Request can be forwarded to the Respondent in accordance with Article 4(5). This causes delay. Similarly, when filing its Answer, the Respondent should include all elements required by Article 5 of the Rules.

17 The ICC Rules do not require a Request for Arbitration or an Answer to set out full particulars of either the claim or defence (or, where applicable, a counterclaim). Whether or not detailed particulars of the claim are given in the Request for Arbitration can have an impact on the efficient management of the arbitration. Where the Request does contain detailed particulars of the claim, and a similar approach is taken by the Respondent in the Answer, the parties and the arbitral tribunal will be in a position to hold a case-management conference to establish the pro-

cedure for the arbitration at a very early stage in the proceedings (see paragraphs 31–34 below).

Preliminary procedural issues

Language of the arbitration

DETERMINATION OF LANGUAGE BY THE ARBITRAL TRIBUNAL

18 If the parties have not agreed on the language of the arbitration, the arbitral tribunal should consider determining the language of the arbitration by means of a procedural order, pursuant to Article 16 of the ICC Rules, prior to establishing the Terms of Reference and after ascertaining the position of the parties.

PROCEEDINGS INVOLVING TWO OR MORE LANGUAGES

19 In general, the use of more than one language should be considered only when doing so would reduce rather than increase time and cost. If the parties have agreed or the arbitral tribunal has decided that the arbitration will be conducted in two or more languages, the parties and the arbitral tribunal should consider agreeing upon practical means to avoid duplication. In cases where the members of the arbitral tribunal are fluent in all applicable languages, it may not be necessary for documents to be translated. Consideration should also be given to avoiding having the Terms of Reference, procedural orders and awards in more than one language. If it is not possible to avoid preparing one or more of those documents in more than one language, the parties would be well advised to agree that only one version shall be binding.

Relationship among the Terms of Reference, the provisional timetable and the early case-management conference

20 Pursuant to Article 18 of the ICC Rules, the Terms of Reference must be drawn up as soon as the arbitral tribunal has received the file from the Secretariat (see paragraphs 24–30 below). Article 18(4) also requires the arbitral tribunal to establish a provisional timetable for the conduct of the arbitration either when drawing up the Terms of Reference, or as soon as possible thereafter.

21 While an early case-management conference (sometimes called a "procedural conference") is not required under the ICC Rules, such confer-

ences are commonly used in ICC arbitrations. Such a conference can play an important role in enabling the parties and the arbitral tribunal to discuss and agree on a procedure that is tailored to the specific case and enables the dispute to be resolved as efficiently as possible (see paragraphs 31–34 below).

22 Where the parties have set out their cases in sufficient detail in the Request for Arbitration and the Answer, it may be possible to hold a case-management conference during the meeting at which the Terms of Reference are finalized and immediately following their signature. In such circumstances, it may be possible for the provisional timetable required by Article 18(4) to include detailed provisions on procedure for the entire arbitration.

23 Where the case has not been set out in such detail at the time the Terms of Reference are finalized, it may be necessary to defer the case-management conference until after the parties have set out their cases in sufficient detail. In such circumstances, the provisional timetable required by Article 18(4) will need to describe the steps that the parties are to take in order promptly to set out their cases in sufficient detail prior to the case-management conference. At the case-management conference, a revised provisional timetable can be established and communicated to the parties and the International Court of Arbitration in accordance with Article 18(4).

Terms of Reference

SUMMARIES OF CLAIMS AND RELIEF SOUGHT

24 The arbitral tribunal should consider whether it is appropriate for it to draft the summary of claims and/or the relief sought or whether it would assist if each party provided a draft summary for inclusion in the Terms of Reference in accordance with Article 18(1)(c) of the ICC Rules. In the latter case, the arbitral tribunal should consider requesting that the parties limit their summaries to an appropriate fixed number of pages. Further guidance on preparing Terms of Reference can be found in the article of Serge Lazareff ("Terms of Reference", *ICC International Court of Arbitration Bulletin* Vol. 17/No.1-2006, pp. 21–32).

USE OF DISCRETION IN APPORTIONMENT OF COSTS

25 The arbitral tribunal should consider promptly informing the parties that any unreasonable failure to comply with procedures agreed or ordered in the arbitration or any other unreasonable conduct will be taken into

account by the arbitral tribunal in determining who shall bear what portion of the costs of the arbitration, pursuant to Article 31 of the ICC Rules (see further at paragraph 85 below under the heading ‹Costs›).

EMPOWERING CHAIRMAN ON PROCEDURAL ISSUES

26 Where there is a three person tribunal, it may not be necessary for all procedural issues to be decided upon by all three arbitrators. The parties should consider empowering the chairman to decide on certain procedural issues alone. In all events, consider authorizing the chairman to sign procedural orders alone.

ADMINISTRATIVE SECRETARY TO THE ARBITRAL TRIBUNAL

27 Consider whether or not an administrative secretary to the arbitral tribunal would assist in reducing time and cost. If it is decided to use such a secretary, the parties and the arbitral tribunal should take into account the Note from the Secretariat of the ICC Court concerning the Appointment of Administrative Secretaries by Arbitral Tribunals (published in the *ICC International Court of Arbitration Bulletin,* Vol. 6/No. 2-November 1995, pp. 77–78) which deals with the duties of the secretary, the secretary's independence, the tribunal's responsibility for the secretary's work, and the basis for payment of the secretary.

NEED FOR A PHYSICAL MEETING

28 Consider whether it is appropriate to agree upon and sign the Terms of Reference without a physical meeting, e.g. by way of a telephone or video conference, as appropriate. In making that decision, the advantages of having a physical meeting at the start of the proceedings should be weighed against the time and cost involved.

COUNTERPARTS

29 If there is no physical meeting for signing the Terms of Reference, the arbitral tribunal should consider having the Terms of Reference signed in counterparts.

COMPLIANCE WITH ARTICLE 18(3)

30 If a party refuses to take part in drawing up the Terms of Reference or refuses to sign them, the arbitral tribunal should make certain that the Terms of Reference to be submitted to the International Court of Arbi-

tration for approval pursuant to Article 18(3) of the ICC Rules do not contain any provisions that would require the parties' agreement or any decisions by the arbitral tribunal.

Early case-management conference

TIMING OF CASE-MANAGEMENT CONFERENCE

31 Consider holding a case-management conference (sometimes called a "procedural conference") as soon as the parties have set out their respective cases in sufficient detail for the arbitral tribunal and the parties to identify the issues in the case and the procedural steps that will be necessary to resolve the case. If the Request for Arbitration and the Answer do not set out the substance of the case in such detail, consideration should be given to holding the case-management conference as soon as this has been done (see paragraph 23 above).

PROACTIVE CASE MANAGEMENT

32 At the case-management conference, directions concerning the procedure for the arbitration will be agreed upon or ordered. The more information the arbitral tribunal has about the issues in the case prior to such conference, the better able it will be to assist the parties to devise a procedure that will deal with the dispute as efficiently as possible.

For example, a tribunal that has made itself familiar with the details of the case from the outset can be proactive and give appropriate, tailor-made suggestions as to the issues to be addressed in documentary and witness evidence, the areas on which it will be assisted by expert evidence, and the extent to which disclosure of documents by the parties is needed in order to address the issues in dispute. The techniques set out in this document can be used by the arbitral tribunal and the parties at the case-management conference to assist in arriving at the most appropriate procedures (see section entitled ‹Subsequent procedure for the arbitration› below). A provisional timetable with the shortest times that are realistic should be established.

33 The arbitral tribunal should consider informing the parties that it will proactively manage the procedure throughout the arbitration so as to assist the parties in resolving the dispute as efficiently as possible.

CLIENT ATTENDANCE

34 The parties should consider having a person from within the client›s organization attend the case-management conference. Client representatives and witnesses, including any experts, should be kept informed of the input that will be required from them in order to comply with each step in the provisional timetable. The arbitral tribunal may specifically request that client representatives attend this conference.

Timetable for the proceedings

COMPLIANCE WITH THE PROVISIONAL TIMETABLE

35 The arbitrators and the parties should make all reasonable efforts to comply with the provisional timetable. Extensions and revisions of the timetable should be made only when justified. Any revisions should be promptly communicated to the Court and the parties in accordance with Article 18(4) of the ICC Rules.

NEED FOR A HEARING

36 Consider whether or not it is necessary for there to be a hearing in order for the arbitral tribunal to decide the case. If it is possible for the arbitral tribunal to decide the case on documents alone, this will save significant costs and time.

FIXING THE HEARING DATE

37 If a hearing is necessary, then early in the proceedings (ideally at the early case-management conference) consider fixing the date for this hearing. This will reduce the likelihood that the arbitral proceedings will become drawn out and will enable the procedure leading up to the hearing to be adapted to the time available.

PRE-HEARING CONFERENCE

38 Consider organizing a conference with the arbitral tribunal, which may be by telephone, to discuss the arrangements for any hearing. At such a pre-hearing conference, held a suitable time before the hearing itself, the parties and the arbitral tribunal can discuss matters such as time allocation, use of transcripts, translation issues, order of witnesses and other practical arrangements that will facilitate the smooth conduct of the hearing. The arbitral tribunal may consider using the occasion of the

pre-hearing conference to indicate to the parties the issues on which it would like the parties to focus at the forthcoming hearing.

USE OF IT

39 The arbitral tribunal should consider discussing with the parties how IT systems can be used during the arbitration. The parties can be referred to the ICC publication *Using Technology to Resolve Business Disputes* (2004 Special Supplement of the *ICC International Court of Arbitration Bulletin*), which contains useful guidance on the use of IT in international arbitration proceedings. The parties can also be offered the use of the online ICC service NetCase, which enables correspondence and documents for the arbitration to be stored and exchanged within a secure online environment hosted by ICC. Consideration can also be given to the use of video and telephone conferences for procedural and other hearings where attendance in person is not essential.

SHORT AND REALISTIC TIME PERIODS

40 In deciding upon the length of the final hearing and the amount of time required for all procedural steps up until that hearing, choose the shortest times that are realistic. Unrealistically short time periods are likely to result in a longer rather than a shorter proceeding, should they need to be re-scheduled.

BIFURCATION AND PARTIAL AWARDS

41 The arbitral tribunal should consider bifurcating the proceedings or rendering a partial award when doing so may genuinely be expected to result in a more efficient resolution of the case.

BRIEFING EVERYONE INVOLVED IN THE CASE

42 As soon as the proceedings are started, parties should give thought to the input that will be needed in order to comply with each step in the anticipated timetable. Once the timetable is set, the parties should consider precisely what input is needed in order to meet the timetable. It will be useful for all relevant personnel to be briefed accordingly (e.g. management within the client organization, witnesses, internal and external lawyers, experts, etc.). This will greatly assist in enabling everyone to reserve the time they need to provide input at the relevant point in the procedure and will assist in enabling each party to adhere to deadlines set in the timetable.

Settlement

ARBITRAL TRIBUNAL'S ROLE IN PROMOTING SETTLEMENT

43 The arbitral tribunal should consider informing the parties that they are free to settle all or part of the dispute at any time during the course of the ongoing arbitration, either through direct negotiations or through any form of ADR proceedings. For example, ADR proceedings can be conducted under the ICC ADR Rules, further information on which can be found in the article of Peter Wolrich entitled "ICC ADR Rules: The Latest Addition to ICC's Dispute Resolution Services" (in *ADR-International Applications,* 2001 Special Supplement of the *ICC International Court of Arbitration Bulletin*). The parties may also request the arbitral tribunal to suspend the arbitration proceedings for a specific period of time while settlement discussions take place.

Subsequent procedure for the arbitration

Introduction

44 The paragraphs that follow give guidance on the points to be discussed by the parties and the arbitral tribunal when establishing procedural directions for the arbitration. They provide suggestions that may assist in reducing the cost and duration of the proceedings.

Written submissions

45 Written submissions come in different forms and are given different names. They include the Request for Arbitration and Answer, statements of case and defence, memorials or other written arguments, and opening and closing written submissions. These comments apply to written submissions generally.

SETTING OUT THE CASE IN FULL EARLY IN THE PROCEEDINGS

46 If the parties set out their cases in full early in the proceedings, this will enable the parties and the arbitral tribunal to understand the key issues at an early stage and adopt procedures to address them in its procedural orders (see paragraphs 17, 22–23 and 31 above). It will help ensure that the procedure used during the case is efficient and that time and costs are not spent on matters that turn out to be of no direct relevance to the issues that need to be determined.

AVOIDING REPETITION

47 Avoid unnecessary repetition of arguments. Once a party has set out its position in full, it should not be necessary to repeat the arguments at later stages (for example, in pre-hearing memorials, oral submissions and post-hearing memorials), and the arbitral tribunal may direct that there be no such repetition.

SEQUENTIAL OR SIMULTANEOUS DELIVERY

48 Consider whether it is more effective for written submissions to be sequential or simultaneous. Whilst simultaneous submissions enable both parties to inform each other of their cases at the same time (and this may make things quicker), it can also result in inefficiency if the parties raise different issues in their submissions and extensive reply submissions are required.

SPECIFYING FORM AND CONTENT

49 Consider specifying the form and content of written submissions. For example, clarify whether the first round of written submissions should or should not be accompanied by witness statements and/or expert reports.

LIMITING THE LENGTH OF SUBMISSIONS

50 Consider agreeing on limiting the length of specific submissions. This can help focus the parties on the key issues to be addressed and is likely to save time and cost.

LIMITING THE NUMBER OF SUBMISSIONS

51 Consider limiting the number of rounds of submissions. This may help to avoid repetition and encourage the parties to present all key issues in their first submissions.

Documentary evidence

ORGANIZATION OF DOCUMENTS

52 From the outset of the case the parties should consider using a coherent system for numbering or otherwise identifying documents produced in the case. This process can start with the Request for Arbitration and the Answer, and a system for the remainder of the arbitration can be es-

tablished with the arbitral tribunal at the time of the case-management conference.

PRODUCING DOCUMENTS ON WHICH THE PARTIES RELY

53 The parties will normally each produce the documents upon which they intend to rely. Each party should consider avoiding requests for production of documents from another party unless such production is relevant and material to the outcome of the case. When the parties have agreed upon non-controversial facts, no documentary evidence should be needed to prove those facts.

ESTABLISHING PROCEDURE FOR REQUESTS FOR PRODUCTION

54 When there are to be requests for the production of documents, the parties and the arbitral tribunal should consider establishing a clear and efficient procedure for the submission and exchange of documents. In that regard, they could consider referring to Article 3 of the IBA Rules on the Taking of Evidence in International Commercial Arbitration for guidance. In addition, the parties and the arbitral tribunal should consider establishing an appropriate time frame for the production of documents. In most situations, this is likely to be after the parties have set out their cases in full for the first time.

MANAGING REQUESTS FOR PRODUCTION EFFICIENTLY

55 Time and costs associated with requests for production of documents, if any, can further be reduced by agreeing upon one or more of the following:

- Limiting the number of requests;

- Limiting requests to the production of documents (whether in paper or electronic form) that are relevant and material to the outcome of the case;

- Establishing reasonable time limits for the production of documents;

- Using the Schedule of Document Production devised by Alan Redfern and often referred to as the Redfern Schedule, in the form of a chart containing the following four columns:

First Column: identification of the document(s) or categories of documents that have been requested;

Second Column: short description of the reasons for each request;

Third Column: summary of the objections by the other party to the production of the document(s) or categories of documents requested; and

Fourth Column: left blank for the decision of the arbitral tribunal on each request.

AVOIDING DUPLICATION

56 It is common for each of the parties to produce copies of the same documents appended to their statements of case, witness statements or other written submissions. Avoiding duplication where possible will save costs.

SELECTION OF DOCUMENTS TO BE PROVIDED TO THE ARBITRAL TRIBUNAL

57 It is wasteful to provide the arbitrators with documents that are not material to their determination of the case. In particular, it will not usually be appropriate to send to the arbitral tribunal all documents produced pursuant to production requests. This not only generates unnecessary costs, but also makes it harder for the arbitral tribunal to prepare efficiently.

MINIMIZING CREATION OF HARD COPIES

58 Consider minimizing the volume of hard copy paper that needs to be produced. Exchanging documents in electronic form can reduce costs (see the ICC publication *Using Technology to Resolve Business Disputes* referred to in paragraph 39 above (2004 Special Supplement of the *ICC International Court of Arbitration Bulletin*)).

TRANSLATIONS

59 Try to agree how translations of any documents are to be dealt with. Minimizing the need for certified translations will reduce costs. Such certified translations may only be required where translation issues emerge from unofficial translations.

AUTHENTICITY OF DOCUMENTS

60 Consider providing that documents produced by the parties are deemed to be authentic unless and until such authenticity is challenged by another party.

Correspondence

CORRESPONDENCE BETWEEN COUNSEL

61 Avoid unnecessary correspondence between counsel. The arbitral tribunal may consider informing the parties that the persistent use of such correspondence may be viewed as unreasonable conduct and be a factor taken into consideration by the arbitral tribunal in the exercise of its discretion on costs (see paragraph 85 below).

SENDING CORRESPONDENCE TO THE ARBITRAL TRIBUNAL

62 Avoid sending correspondence between counsel to the arbitral tribunal unless a decision of the arbitral tribunal is required. Any such correspondence that is addressed to the arbitral tribunal should be copied to the Secretariat in accordance with Article 3(1) of the ICC Rules.

Witness statements

LIMITING THE NUMBER OF WITNESSES

63 Every witness adds to the costs, both when a witness statement is prepared and considered and when the witness attends to give oral evidence. Costs can be saved by limiting the number of witnesses to those whose evidence is required on key issues. The arbitral tribunal may assist in identifying those issues on which witness evidence is required and focusing the evidence from witnesses on those issues. This whole process will be facilitated if the parties can reach agreement on non-controversial facts that do not need to be addressed by witness evidence.

MINIMIZING THE NUMBER OF ROUNDS OF WITNESS STATEMENTS

64 If there are to be witness statements, consider the timing for the exchange of such statements so as to minimize the number of rounds of statements that are required. For example, consider whether it is preferable for witness statements to be exchanged after all documents on which the parties wish to rely have been produced, so that the witnesses can comment on those documents in a single statement.

Expert evidence

PRESUMPTION THAT EXPERT EVIDENCE NOT REQUIRED

65 It is helpful to start with a presumption that expert evidence will not be required. Depart from this presumption only if expert evidence is needed in order to inform the arbitral tribunal on key issues in dispute.

ICC INTERNATIONAL CENTRE FOR EXPERTISE

66 If either the parties or the arbitral tribunal require assistance in identifying an expert witness, recourse can be had to the ICC International Centre for Expertise pursuant to the ICC Rules for Expertise. Where an ICC tribunal seeks a proposal from the Centre in respect of a tribunal-appointed expert, the services of the Centre are available at no cost. Further information regarding the operation of the ICC Rules for Expertise and the services of the Centre can be found in the "Guide to ICC Expertise", produced by the Task Force on Guidelines for ICC Expertise Proceedings, chaired by Hilmàr Raeschke-Kessler (published in the *ICC International Court of Arbitration Bulletin,* Vol. 16/No. 1-Spring 2005, pp. 19–31).

CLARITY REGARDING THE SUBJECT MATTER AND SCOPE OF REPORTS

67 It is essential for there to be clarity at an early stage (by agreement, if possible) over the subject matter and scope of any expert evidence to be produced. This will ensure that experts with the same subject-matter expertise are appointed by both parties and that they address the same issues.

NUMBER OF EXPERTS

68 Other than in exceptional circumstances, it should not be necessary for there to be more than one expert per party for any particular area of expertise.

NUMBER OF REPORTS

69 Consider agreeing on a limit to the number of rounds of expert reports and consider whether simultaneous or sequential exchange will be more efficient.

MEETINGS OF EXPERTS

70 Experts will often be able to narrow the issues in dispute if they can meet and discuss their views after they have exchanged reports. Consideration should therefore be given to providing that experts shall take steps to agree issues in advance of any hearing at which their evidence is to be presented. Time and cost can be saved if the experts draw up a list recording the issues on which they have agreed and those on which they disagree.

USE OF SINGLE EXPERT

71 Consider whether a single expert appointed either by the arbitral tribunal or jointly by the parties might be more efficient than experts appointed by each party. A single tribunal-appointed expert may be more efficient in some circumstances. An expert appointed by the arbitral tribunal or jointly by the parties should be given a clear brief and the expert's report should be required by a specified date consistent with the timetable for the arbitration.

Hearings

MINIMIZING THE LENGTH AND NUMBER OF HEARINGS

72 Hearings are expensive and time-consuming. If the length and number of hearings requiring the physical attendance of the arbitral tribunal and the parties are minimized, this will significantly reduce the time and cost of the proceedings.

CHOOSING THE BEST LOCATION FOR HEARINGS

73 Pursuant to Article 14(2) of the ICC Rules, hearings do not need to be held at the place of arbitration. The arbitral tribunal and the parties can select the most efficient place to hold hearings. In some cases, it may be more cost-effective to hold hearings at a location that, for example, is convenient to the majority of the witnesses due to give evidence at that hearing.

TELEPHONE AND VIDEO CONFERENCING

74 For procedural hearings in particular, consider the use of telephone and video conferencing, where appropriate. Also, consider whether certain witnesses can give evidence by video link, so as to avoid the need to travel to an evidentiary hearing.

PROVIDING SUBMISSIONS IN GOOD TIME

75 The arbitral tribunal should be provided with all necessary submissions (e.g. pre-hearing briefs, if any) sufficiently in advance of any hearing, so as to enable it to read, prepare and become fully informed as to the issues to be addressed.

CUT-OFF DATE FOR EVIDENCE

76 Consider fixing a cut-off date in advance of any evidentiary hearing, after which no new documentary evidence will be admitted unless a compelling reason is shown.

IDENTIFYING CORE DOCUMENTS

77 Consider providing the arbitral tribunal, in advance of any hearing, with a list of the documents it needs to read in preparation for the hearing. Where appropriate, this can be done by preparing and delivering to the arbitral tribunal a bundle of "core" documents on which the parties rely.

AGENDA AND TIMETABLE

78 Consider agreeing on an agenda and timetable for all hearings, with an equitable division of time for each party. Consider the use of a chess clock to monitor the fair allocation of time.

AVOIDING REPETITION

79 Consideration should be given to whether it is necessary to repeat pre-hearing written submissions in opening oral statements. This is some-times done because of concern that the arbitral tribunal will not have read or digested the written submissions. If the arbitral tribunal has been provided with the documents it needs to read in advance of the hearing and has prepared properly, this will not be necessary.

NEED FOR WITNESSES TO APPEAR

80 Prior to any hearing, consider whether all witnesses need to give oral evidence. This is a matter on which counsel for the parties can confer and seek to reach agreement.

USE OF WRITTEN STATEMENTS AS DIRECT EVIDENCE

81 Witness statements are commonly used as direct evidence at a hearing. Cost and time can be saved by limiting or avoiding direct examination of witnesses.

WITNESS CONFERENCING

82 Witness conferencing is a technique in which two or more fact or expert witnesses presented by one or more parties are questioned together on particular topics by the arbitral tribunal and possibly by counsel. Consider whether this technique is appropriate for the arbitration at hand.

LIMITING CROSS-EXAMINATION

83 If there is to be cross-examination of witnesses, the arbitral tribunal, after hearing the parties, should consider limiting the time available to each party for such cross-examination.

CLOSING SUBMISSIONS

84 Consider whether post-hearing submissions can be avoided in order to save time and cost. If post-hearing submissions are required, consider providing for either oral or written closing submissions. The use of both will result in additional time and cost. In order to give focus, the arbitral tribunal should consider providing counsel with a list of questions or issues to be addressed by the parties in the closing submissions. Any written submissions should be provided by an agreed date as soon as reasonable following the hearing.

Costs

USING ALLOCATION OF COSTS TO ENCOURAGE EFFICIENT CONDUCT OF THE PROCEEDINGS

85 The allocation of costs can provide a useful tool to encourage efficient behaviour and discourage unreasonable behaviour. The arbitral tribunal has discretion to award costs in such a manner as it considers appropriate. It may be helpful to specify at the outset of the proceedings that in exercising its discretion in allocating costs the arbitral tribunal will take into account any unreasonable behaviour by a party. Unreasonable behaviour could include: excessive document requests, excessive legal argument, excessive cross-examination, dilatory tactics, exaggerated claims, failure to comply with procedural orders, unjustified interim

applications, unjustified failure to comply with the procedural calendar, etc.

Deliberations and awards

86 Before closing the proceedings, the arbitral tribunal should ensure that time has been reserved in each of the arbitrators' diaries for prompt deliberation thereafter. The arbitral tribunal should promptly comply with Article 22(2) of the ICC Rules and indicate to the Secretariat an approximate date by which it will submit the draft award to the International Court of Arbitration. The arbitral tribunal shall use its best efforts to submit the draft award as quickly as possible. Further guidance on drafting awards can be found in the article "Drafting Awards in ICC Arbitrations" by Humphrey LLoyd, Marco Darmon, Jean-Pierre Ancel, Lord Dervaird, Christoph Liebscher and Herman Verbist (published in the *ICC International Court of Arbitration Bulletin,* Vol. 16/No. 2-2005, pp. 19–40).

Annex 3:
UNCITRAL Notes on Organizing
Arbitral Proceedings

Preface

The United Nations Commission on International Trade Law (UNCITRAL) finalized the Notes at its twenty-ninth session (New York, 28 May–14 June 1996). In addition to the 36 member States of the Commission, representatives of many other States and of a number of international organizations had participated in the deliberations. In preparing the draft materials, the Secretariat consulted with experts from various legal systems, national arbitration bodies, as well as international professional associations.

The Commission, after an initial discussion on the project in 1993,<1> considered in 1994 a draft entitled "Draft Guidelines for Preparatory Conferences in Arbitral Proceedings".<2> That draft was also discussed at several meetings of arbitration practitioners, including the XIIth International Arbitration Congress, held by the International Council for Commercial Arbitration (ICCA) at Vienna from 3 to 6 November 1994.<3> On the basis of those discussions in the Commission and elsewhere, the Secretariat prepared "draft Notes on Organizing Arbitral Proceedings".<4> The Commission considered the draft Notes in 1995,<5> and a revised draft in 1996,<6> when the Notes were finalized.<7>

<1> *Report of the United Nations Commission on International Trade Law on the work of its twenty-sixth session, Official Records of the General Assembly, Forty-eighth Session, Supplement No. 17 (A/48/17) (reproduced in UNCITRAL Yearbook, vol. XXIV: 1993, part one), paras. 291–296.*

<2> *The draft Guidelines have been published as document A/CN.9/396/ Add.1 (reproduced in UNCITRAL Yearbook, vol. XXV: 1994, part two, IV); the considerations of the Commission are reflected in the report of the United Nations Commission on International Trade Law on the work of its twenty-seventh session, Official Records of the General Assembly, Forty-ninth Session Supplement No. 17 (A/49/17) (reproduced in UNCITRAL Yearbook, Vol. XXV: 1994, part two, IV), paras. 111–195.*

<3> *The proceedings of the Congress are published in Planning Efficient Arbitration Proceedings/The Law Applicable in International Arbitration, ICCA Congress Series No. 7, Kluwer Law International, The Hague, 1996.*

<4> *The draft Notes have been published as document A/CN.9/410 (and will be reproduced in UNCITRAL Yearbook, vol. XXVI: 1995, part two, III).*

<5> *Report of the United Nations Commission on International Trade Law on the work of its twenty-eighth session, Official Records of the General Assembly, Fiftieth Session, Supplement No. 17 (A/50/17) (and will be reproduced in UNCITRAL Yearbook, vol. XXVI: 1995, part one), paras. 314–373.*

<6> *The revised draft Notes have been published as document A/CN.9/423 (and will be reproduced in UNCITRAL Yearbook, vol. XXVII: 1996, part two).*

<7> *Report of the United Nations Commission on International Trade Law on the work of its twenty-ninth session, Official Records of the General Assembly, Fifty-first Session, Supplement No. 17 (A/51/17) (and will be reproduced in UNCITRAL Yearbook, vol. XXVII: 1996, part one), paras. 11 to 54.*

UNCITRAL SECRETARIAT
VIENNA INTERNATIONAL CENTRE
P.O. BOX 500
A-1400 VIENNA
AUSTRIA

Telephone: (43-1) 26060-4060/61
Telefax: (43-1) 26060-5813
E-mail: uncitral@uncitral.org

CONTENTS

Preface

Introduction

List of matters for possible consideration in organizing arbitral proceedings

Annotations

INTRODUCTION

Purpose of the Notes

1. The purpose of the Notes is to assist arbitration practitioners by listing and briefly describing questions on which appropriately timed decisions on organizing arbitral proceedings may be useful. The text, prepared with a particular view to international arbitrations, may be used whether or not the arbitration is administered by an arbitral institution.

Non-binding character of the Notes

2. No legal requirement binding on the arbitrators or the parties is imposed by the Notes. The arbitral tribunal remains free to use the Notes as it sees fit and is not required to give reasons for disregarding them.

3. The Notes are not suitable to be used as arbitration rules, since they do not establish any obligation of the arbitral tribunal or the parties to act in a particular way. Accordingly, the use of the Notes cannot imply any modification of the arbitration rules that the parties may have agreed upon.

Discretion in conduct of proceedings and usefulness of timely decisions on organizing proceedings

4. Laws governing the arbitral procedure and arbitration rules that parties may agree upon typically allow the arbitral tribunal broad discretion and flexibility in the conduct of arbitral proceedings.<8> This is useful in that it enables the arbitral tribunal to take decisions on the organization of proceedings that take into account the circumstances of the case, the expectations of the parties and of the members of the arbitral tribunal, and the need for a just and cost-efficient resolution of the dispute.

<8> *A prominent example of such rules are the UNCITRAL Arbitration Rules, which provide in article 15(1)[article 17(1) of the 2010 UNCITRAL Arbitration Rules]: "Subject to these Rules, the arbitral tribunal may conduct the arbitration in such manner as it considers appropriate, provided that the parties are treated with equality and that at [an appropriate] stage of the proceedings each party is given a [reasonable] opportunity of presenting [its] case."*

5. Such discretion may make it desirable for the arbitral tribunal to give the parties a timely indication as to the organization of the proceedings and the manner in which the tribunal intends to proceed. This is particularly desirable in international arbitrations, where the participants may be accustomed to differing styles of conducting arbitrations. Without such guidance, a party may find aspects of the proceedings unpredictable and difficult to prepare for. That may lead to misunderstandings, delays and increased costs.

Multi-party arbitration

6. These Notes are intended for use not only in arbitrations with two parties but also in arbitrations with three or more parties. Use of the Notes in multi-party arbitration is referred to below in paragraphs 86–88 (item 18).

Process of making decisions on organizing arbitral proceedings

7. Decisions by the arbitral tribunal on organizing arbitral proceedings may be taken with or without previous consultations with the parties. The method chosen depends on whether, in view of the type of the question to be decided, the arbitral tribunal considers that consultations are not necessary or that hearing the views of the parties would be beneficial for increasing the predictability of the proceedings or improving the procedural atmosphere.

8. The consultations, whether they involve only the arbitrators or also the parties, can be held in one or more meetings, or can be carried out by correspondence or telecommunications such as telefax or conference telephone calls or other electronic means. Meetings may be held at the venue of arbitration or at some other appropriate location.

9. In some arbitrations a special meeting may be devoted exclusively to such procedural consultations; alternatively, the consultations may be held in conjunction with a hearing on the substance of the dispute. Practices differ as to whether such special meetings should be held and how they should be organized. Special procedural meetings of the arbitrators and the parties separate from hearings are in practice referred to by expressions such as "preliminary meeting", "pre-hearing conference", "preparatory conference", "pre-hearing review", or terms of similar meaning. The terms used partly depend on the stage of the proceedings at which the meeting is taking place.

List of matters for possible consideration in organizing arbitral proceedings

10. The Notes provide a list, followed by annotations, of matters on which the arbitral tribunal may wish to formulate decisions on organizing arbitral proceedings.

11. Given that procedural styles and practices in arbitration vary widely, that the purpose of the Notes is not to promote any practice as best practice, and that the Notes are designed for universal use, it is not attempted in the Notes to describe in detail different arbitral practices or express a preference for any of them.

12. The list, while not exhaustive, covers a broad range of situations that may arise in an arbitration. In many arbitrations, however, only a limited number of the matters mentioned in the list need to be considered. It also depends on the circumstances of the case at which stage or stages of the proceedings it would be useful to consider matters concerning the organization of the proceedings. Generally, in order not to create opportunities for unnecessary discussions and delay, it is advisable not to raise a matter prematurely, i.e. before it is clear that a decision is needed.

13. When the Notes are used, it should be borne in mind that the discretion of the arbitral tribunal in organizing the proceedings may be limited by arbitration rules, by other provisions agreed to by the parties and by the law applicable to the arbitral procedure. When an arbitration is administered by an arbitral institution, various matters discussed in the Notes may be covered by the rules and practices of that institution.

LIST OF MATTERS FOR POSSIBLE CONSIDERATION IN ORGANIZING ARBITRAL PROCEEDINGS

1. Set of arbitration rules: paras. 14–16

   If the parties have not agreed on a set of arbitration rules, would they wish to do so: paras. 14–16

2. Language of proceedings 17–20

   (a) Possible need for translation of documents, in full or in part 18

   (b) Possible need for interpretation of oral presentations 19

   (c) Cost of translation and interpretation 20

ANNOTATIONS

1.   Set of arbitration rules

If the parties have not agreed on a set of arbitration rules, would they wish to do so

14. Sometimes parties who have not included in their arbitration agreement a stipulation that a set of arbitration rules will govern their arbitral proceedings might wish to do so after the arbitration has begun. If that occurs, the UNCITRAL Arbitration Rules may be used either without modification or with such modifications as the parties might wish to agree upon. In the alternative, the parties might wish to adopt the rules of an arbitral insti-

tution; in that case, it may be necessary to secure the agreement of that institution and to stipulate the terms under which the arbitration could be carried out in accordance with the rules of that institution.

15. However, caution is advised as consideration of a set of arbitration rules might delay the proceedings or give rise to unnecessary controversy.

16. It should be noted that agreement on arbitration rules is not a necessity and that, if the parties do not agree on a set of arbitration rules, the arbitral tribunal has the power to continue the proceedings and determine how the case will be conducted.

2. Language of proceedings

17. Many rules and laws on arbitral procedure empower the arbitral tribunal to determine the language or languages to be used in the proceedings, if the parties have not reached an agreement thereon.

(a) Possible need for translation of documents, in full or in part

18. Some documents annexed to the statements of claim and defence or submitted later may not be in the language of the proceedings. Bearing in mind the needs of the proceedings and economy, it may be considered whether the arbitral tribunal should order that any of those documents or parts thereof should be accompanied by a translation into the language of the proceedings.

(b) Possible need for interpretation of oral presentations

19. If interpretation will be necessary during oral hearings, it is advisable to consider whether the interpretation will be simultaneous or consecutive and whether the arrangements should be the responsibility of a party or the arbitral tribunal. In an arbitration administered by an institution, interpretation as well as translation services are often arranged by the arbitral institution.

(c) Cost of translation and interpretation

20. In taking decisions about translation or interpretation, it is advisable to decide whether any or all of the costs are to be paid directly by a party or whether they will be paid out of the deposits and apportioned between the parties along with the other arbitration costs.

3.   Place of arbitration

(a)   Determination of the place of arbitration, if not already agreed upon by the parties

21. Arbitration rules usually allow the parties to agree on the place of arbitration, subject to the requirement of some arbitral institutions that arbitrations under their rules be conducted at a particular place, usually the location of the institution. If the place has not been so agreed upon, the rules governing the arbitration typically provide that it is in the power of the arbitral tribunal or the institution administering the arbitration to determine the place. If the arbitral tribunal is to make that determination, it may wish to hear the views of the parties before doing so.

22. Various factual and legal factors influence the choice of the place of arbitration, and their relative importance varies from case to case. Among the more prominent factors are: (a) suitability of the law on arbitral procedure of the place of arbitration; (b) whether there is a multilateral or bilateral treaty on enforcement of arbitral awards between the State where the arbitration takes place and the State or States where the award may have to be enforced; (c) convenience of the parties and the arbitrators, including the travel distances; (d) availability and cost of support services needed; and (e) location of the subject-matter in dispute and proximity of evidence.

(b)   Possibility of meetings outside the place of arbitration

23. Many sets of arbitration rules and laws on arbitral procedure expressly allow the arbitral tribunal to hold meetings elsewhere than at the place of arbitration. For example, under the UNCITRAL Model Law on International Commercial Arbitration "the arbitral tribunal may, unless otherwise agreed by the parties, meet at any place it considers appropriate for consultation among its members, for hearing witnesses, experts or the parties, or for inspection of goods, other property or documents" (article 20(2)). The purpose of this discretion is to permit arbitral proceedings to be carried out in a manner that is most efficient and economical.

4.   Administrative services that may be needed for the arbitral tribunal to carry out its functions

24. Various administrative services (e.g. hearing rooms or secretarial services) may need to be procured for the arbitral tribunal to be able to carry

out its functions. When the arbitration is administered by an arbitral institution, the institution will usually provide all or a good part of the required
administrative support to the arbitral tribunal. When an arbitration administered by an arbitral institution takes place away from the seat of the institution, the institution may be able to arrange for administrative services to
be obtained from another source, often an arbitral institution; some arbitral
institutions have entered into cooperation agreements with a view to providing mutual assistance in servicing arbitral proceedings.

25. When the case is not administered by an institution, or the involvement
of the institution does not include providing administrative support, usually the administrative arrangements for the proceedings will be made by
the arbitral tribunal or the presiding arbitrator; it may also be acceptable to
leave some of the arrangements to the parties, or to one of the parties subject to agreement of the other party or parties. Even in such cases, a convenient source of administrative support might be found in arbitral institutions, which often offer their facilities to arbitrations not governed by the
rules of the institution. Otherwise, some services could be procured from
entities such as chambers of commerce, hotels or specialized firms providing secretarial or other support services.

26. Administrative services might be secured by engaging a secretary of
the arbitral tribunal (also referred to as registrar, clerk, administrator or
rapporteur), who carries out the tasks under the direction of the arbitral tribunal. Some arbitral institutions routinely assign such persons to the cases
administered by them. In arbitrations not administered by an institution or
where the arbitral institution does not appoint a secretary, some arbitrators
frequently engage such persons, at least in certain types of cases, whereas
many others normally conduct the proceedings without them.

27. To the extent the tasks of the secretary are purely organizational (e.g.
obtaining meeting rooms and providing or coordinating secretarial services), this is usually not controversial. Differences in views, however, may
arise if the tasks include legal research and other professional assistance
to the arbitral tribunal (e.g. collecting case law or published commentaries
on legal issues defined by the arbitral tribunal, preparing summaries from
case law and publications, and sometimes also preparing drafts of procedural decisions or drafts of certain parts of the award, in particular those
concerning the facts of the case). Views or expectations may differ especially where a task of the secretary is similar to professional functions of the
arbitrators. Such a role of the secretary is in the view of some commentators inappropriate or is appropriate only under certain conditions, such as
that the parties agree thereto. However, it is typically recognized that it is

important to ensure that the secretary does not perform any decision-making function of the arbitral tribunal.

5. Deposits in respect of costs

(a) Amount to be deposited

28. In an arbitration administered by an institution, the institution often sets, on the basis of an estimate of the costs of the proceedings, the amount to be deposited as an advance for the costs of the arbitration. In other cases it is customary for the arbitral tribunal to make such an estimate and request a deposit. The estimate typically includes travel and other expenses by the arbitrators, expenditures for administrative assistance required by the arbitral tribunal, costs of any expert advice required by the arbitral tribunal, and the fees for the arbitrators. Many arbitration rules have provisions on this matter, including on whether the deposit should be made by the two parties (or all parties in a multi-party case) or only by the claimant.

(b) Management of deposits

29. When the arbitration is administered by an institution, the institution's services may include managing and accounting for the deposited money. Where that is not the case, it might be useful to clarify matters such as the type and location of the account in which the money will be kept and how the deposits will be managed.

(c) Supplementary deposits

30. If during the course of proceedings it emerges that the costs will be higher than anticipated, supplementary deposits may be required (e.g. because the arbitral tribunal decides pursuant to the arbitration rules to appoint an expert).

6. Confidentiality of information relating to the arbitration; possible agreement thereon

31. It is widely viewed that confidentiality is one of the advantageous and helpful features of arbitration. Nevertheless, there is no uniform answer in national laws as to the extent to which the participants in an arbitration are under the duty to observe the confidentiality of information relating to the case. Moreover, parties that have agreed on arbitration rules or other

provisions that do not expressly address the issue of confidentiality cannot assume that all jurisdictions would recognize an implied commitment to confidentiality. Furthermore, the participants in an arbitration might not have the same understanding as regards the extent of confidentiality that is expected. Therefore, the arbitral tribunal might wish to discuss that with the parties and, if considered appropriate, record any agreed principles on the duty of confidentiality.

32. An agreement on confidentiality might cover, for example, one or more of the following matters: the material or information that is to be kept confidential (e.g. pieces of evidence, written and oral arguments, the fact that the arbitration is taking place, identity of the arbitrators, content of the award); measures for maintaining confidentiality of such information and hearings; whether any special procedures should be employed for maintaining the confidentiality of information transmitted by electronic means (e.g. because communication equipment is shared by several users, or because electronic mail over public networks is considered not sufficiently protected against unauthorized access); circumstances in which confidential information may be disclosed in part or in whole (e.g. in the context of disclosures of information in the public domain, or if required by law or a regulatory body).

7. Routing of written communications among the parties and the arbitrators

33. To the extent the question how documents and other written communications should be routed among the parties and the arbitrators is not settled by the agreed rules, or, if an institution administers the case, by the practices of the institution, it is useful for the arbitral tribunal to clarify the question suitably early so as to avoid misunderstandings and delays.

34. Among various possible patterns of routing, one example is that a party transmits the appropriate number of copies to the arbitral tribunal, or to the arbitral institution, if one is involved, which then forwards them as appropriate. Another example is that a party is to send copies simultaneously to the arbitrators and the other party or parties. Documents and other written communications directed by the arbitral tribunal or the presiding arbitrator to one or more parties may also follow a determined pattern, such as through the arbitral institution or by direct transmission. For some communications, in particular those on organizational matters (e.g. dates for hearings), more direct routes of communication may be agreed, even if, for example, the arbitral institution acts as an intermediary for doc-

uments such as the statements of claim and defence, evidence or written arguments.

8. Telefax and other electronic means of sending documents

(a) Telefax

35. Telefax, which offers many advantages over traditional means of communication, is widely used in arbitral proceedings. Nevertheless, should it be thought that, because of the characteristics of the equipment used, it would be preferable not to rely only on a telefacsimile of a document, special arrangements may be considered, such as that a particular piece of written evidence should be mailed or otherwise physically delivered, or that certain telefax messages should be confirmed by mailing or otherwise delivering documents whose facsimile were transmitted by electronic means. When a document should not be sent by telefax, it may, however, be appropriate, in order to avoid an unnecessarily rigid procedure, for the arbitral tribunal to retain discretion to accept an advance copy of a document by telefax for the purposes of meeting a deadline, provided that the document itself is received within a reasonable time thereafter.

(b) Other electronic means (e.g. electronic mail and magnetic or optical disk)

36. It might be agreed that documents, or some of them, will be exchanged not only in paper-based form, but in addition also in an electronic form other than telefax (e.g. as electronic mail, or on a magnetic or optical disk), or only in electronic form. Since the use of electronic means depends on the aptitude of the persons involved and the availability of equipment and computer programs, agreement is necessary for such means to be used. If both paper-based and electronic means are to be used, it is advisable to decide which one is controlling and, if there is a time-limit for submitting a document, which act constitutes submission.

37. When the exchange of documents in electronic form is planned, it is useful, in order to avoid technical difficulties, to agree on matters such as: data carriers (e.g. electronic mail or computer disks) and their technical characteristics; computer programs to be used in preparing the electronic records; instructions for transforming the electronic records into human-readable form; keeping of logs and back-up records of communications sent

and received; information in human-readable form that should accompany the disks (e.g. the names of the originator and recipient, computer program, titles of the electronic files and the back-up methods used); procedures when a message is lost or the communication system otherwise fails; and identification of persons who can be contacted if a problem occurs.

9.   Arrangements for the exchange of written submissions

38. After the parties have initially stated their claims and defences, they may wish, or the arbitral tribunal might request them, to present further written submissions so as to prepare for the hearings or to provide the basis for a decision without hearings. In such submissions, the parties, for example, present or comment on allegations and evidence, cite or explain law, or make or react to proposals. In practice such submissions are referred to variously as, for example, statement, memorial, counter-memorial, brief, counter-brief, reply, réplique, duplique, rebuttal or rejoinder; the terminology is a matter of linguistic usage and the scope or sequence of the submission.

(a)   Scheduling of written submissions

39. It is advisable that the arbitral tribunal set time-limits for written submissions. In enforcing the time-limits, the arbitral tribunal may wish, on the one hand, to make sure that the case is not unduly protracted and, on the other hand, to reserve a degree of discretion and allow late submissions if appropriate under the circumstances. In some cases the arbitral tribunal might prefer not to plan the written submissions in advance, thus leaving such matters, including time-limits, to be decided in light of the developments in the proceedings. In other cases, the arbitral tribunal may wish to determine, when scheduling the first written submissions, the number of subsequent submissions.

40. Practices differ as to whether, after the hearings have been held, written submissions are still acceptable. While some arbitral tribunals consider post-hearing submissions unacceptable, others might request or allow them on a particular issue. Some arbitral tribunals follow the procedure according to which the parties are not requested to present written evidence and legal arguments to the arbitral tribunal before the hearings; in such a case, the arbitral tribunal may regard it as appropriate that written submissions be made after the hearings.

(b)   Consecutive or simultaneous submissions

41. Written submissions on an issue may be made consecutively, i.e. the party who receives a submission is given a period of time to react with its counter-submission. Another possibility is to request each party to make the submission within the same time period to the arbitral tribunal or the institution administering the case; the received submissions are then forwarded simultaneously to the respective other party or parties. The approach used may depend on the type of issues to be commented upon and the time in which the views should be clarified. With consecutive submissions, it may take longer than with simultaneous ones to obtain views of the parties on a given issue. Consecutive submissions, however, allow the reacting party to comment on all points raised by the other party or parties, which simultaneous submissions do not; thus, simultaneous submissions might possibly necessitate further submissions.

10. Practical details concerning written submissions and evidence (e.g. method of submission, copies, numbering, references)

42. Depending on the volume and kind of documents to be handled, it might be considered whether practical arrangements on details such as the following would be helpful:

- Whether the submissions will be made as paper documents or by electronic means, or both (see paragraphs 35–37);

- The number of copies in which each document is to be submitted;

- A system for numbering documents and items of evidence, and a method for marking them, including by tabs;

- The form of references to documents (e.g. by the heading and the number assigned to the document or its date);

- Paragraph numbering in written submissions, in order to facilitate precise references to parts of a text;

- When translations are to be submitted as paper documents, whether the translations are to be contained in the same volume as the original texts or included in separate volumes.

11. Defining points at issue; order of deciding issues; defining relief or remedy sought

(a)   Should a list of points at issue be prepared

43. In considering the parties' allegations and arguments, the arbitral tribunal may come to the conclusion that it would be useful for it or for the parties to prepare, for analytical purposes and for ease of discussion, a list of the points at issue, as opposed to those that are undisputed. If the arbitral tribunal determines that the advantages of working on the basis of such a list outweigh the disadvantages, it chooses the appropriate stage of the proceedings for preparing a list, bearing in mind also that subsequent developments in the proceedings may require a revision of the points at issue. Such an identification of points at issue might help to concentrate on the essential matters, to reduce the number of points at issue by agreement of the parties, and to select the best and most economical process for resolving the dispute. However, possible disadvantages of preparing such a list include delay, adverse effect on the flexibility of the proceedings, or unnecessary disagreements about whether the arbitral tribunal has decided all issues submitted to it or whether the award contains decisions on matters beyond the scope of the submission to arbitration. The terms of reference required under some arbitration rules, or in agreements of parties, may serve the same purpose as the above-described list of points at issue.

(b)   In which order should the points at issue be decided

44. While it is often appropriate to deal with all the points at issue collectively, the arbitral tribunal might decide to take them up during the proceedings in a particular order. The order may be due to a point being preliminary relative to another (e.g. a decision on the jurisdiction of the arbitral tribunal is preliminary to consideration of substantive issues, or the issue of responsibility for a breach of contract is preliminary to the issue of the resulting damages). A particular order may be decided also when the breach of various contracts is in dispute or when damages arising from various events are claimed.

45. If the arbitral tribunal has adopted a particular order of deciding points at issue, it might consider it appropriate to issue a decision on one of the points earlier than on the other ones. This might be done, for example, when a discrete part of a claim is ready for decision while the other parts still require extensive consideration, or when it is expected that after deciding certain issues the parties might be more inclined to settle the remaining ones. Such earlier decisions are referred to by expressions such as "partial",

"interlocutory" or "interim" awards or decisions, depending on the type of issue dealt with and on whether the decision is final with respect to the issue it resolves. Questions that might be the subject of such decisions are, for example, jurisdiction of the arbitral tribunal, interim measures of protection, or the liability of a party.

(c)   Is there a need to define more precisely the relief or remedy sought

46. If the arbitral tribunal considers that the relief or remedy sought is insufficiently definite, it may wish to explain to the parties the degree of definiteness with which their claims should be formulated. Such an explanation may be useful since criteria are not uniform as to how specific the claimant must be in formulating a relief or remedy.

12. Possible settlement negotiations and their effect on scheduling proceedings

47. Attitudes differ as to whether it is appropriate for the arbitral tribunal to bring up the possibility of settlement. Given the divergence of practices in this regard, the arbitral tribunal should only suggest settlement negotiations with caution. However, it may be opportune for the arbitral tribunal to schedule the proceedings in a way that might facilitate the continuation or initiation of settlement negotiations.

13. Documentary evidence

(a)   Time-limits for submission of documentary evidence intended to be submitted by the parties; consequences of late submission

48. Often the written submissions of the parties contain sufficient information for the arbitral tribunal to fix the time-limit for submitting evidence. Otherwise, in order to set realistic time periods, the arbitral tribunal may wish to consult with the parties about the time that they would reasonably need.

49. The arbitral tribunal may wish to clarify that evidence submitted late will as a rule not be accepted. It may wish not to preclude itself from accepting a late submission of evidence if the party shows sufficient cause for the delay.

(b) Whether the arbitral tribunal intends to require a party to produce documentary evidence

50. Procedures and practices differ widely as to the conditions under which the arbitral tribunal may require a party to produce documents. Therefore, the arbitral tribunal might consider it useful, when the agreed arbitration rules do not provide specific conditions, to clarify to the parties the manner in which it intends to proceed.

51. The arbitral tribunal may wish to establish time-limits for the production of documents. The parties might be reminded that, if the requested party duly invited to produce documentary evidence fails to do so within the established period of time, without showing sufficient cause for such failure, the arbitral tribunal is free to draw its conclusions from the failure and may make the award on the evidence before it.

(c) Should assertions about the origin and receipt of documents and about the correctness of photocopies be assumed as accurate

52. It may be helpful for the arbitral tribunal to inform the parties that it intends to conduct the proceedings on the basis that, unless a party raises an objection to any of the following conclusions within a specified period of time: (a) a document is accepted as having originated from the source indicated in the document; (b) a copy of a dispatched communication (e.g. letter, telex, telefax or other electronic message) is accepted without further proof as having been received by the addressee; and (c) a copy is accepted as correct. A statement by the arbitral tribunal to that effect can simplify the introduction of documentary evidence and discourage unfounded and dilatory objections, at a late stage of the proceedings, to the probative value of documents. It is advisable to provide that the time-limit for objections will not be enforced if the arbitral tribunal considers the delay justified.

(d) Are the parties willing to submit jointly a single set of documentary evidence

53. The parties may consider submitting jointly a single set of documentary evidence whose authenticity is not disputed. The purpose would be to avoid duplicate submissions and unnecessary discussions concerning the authenticity of documents, without prejudicing the position of the parties concerning the content of the documents. Additional documents may be inserted later if the parties agree. When a single set of documents would be too voluminous to be easily manageable, it might be practical to select a

number of frequently used documents and establish a set of "working" documents. A convenient arrangement of documents in the set may be according to chronological order or subject-matter. It is useful to keep a table of contents of the documents, for example, by their short headings and dates, and to provide that the parties will refer to documents by those headings and dates.

(e) Should voluminous and complicated documentary evidence be presented through summaries, tabulations, charts, extracts or samples

54. When documentary evidence is voluminous and complicated, it may save time and costs if such evidence is presented by a report of a person competent in the relevant field (e.g. public accountant or consulting engineer). The report may present the information in the form of summaries, tabulations, charts, extracts or samples. Such presentation of evidence should be combined with arrangements that give the interested party the opportunity to review the underlying data and the methodology of preparing the report.

14. Physical evidence other than documents

55. In some arbitrations the arbitral tribunal is called upon to assess physical evidence other than documents, for example, by inspecting samples of goods, viewing a video recording or observing the functioning of a machine.

(a) What arrangements should be made if physical evidence will be submitted

56. If physical evidence will be submitted, the arbitral tribunal may wish to fix the time schedule for presenting the evidence, make arrangements for the other party or parties to have a suitable opportunity to prepare itself for the presentation of the evidence, and possibly take measures for safe-keeping the items of evidence.

(b) What arrangements should be made if an on-site inspection is necessary

57. If an on-site inspection of property or goods will take place, the arbitral tribunal may consider matters such as timing, meeting places, other arrangements to provide the opportunity for all parties to be present, and

the need to avoid communications between arbitrators and a party about points at issue without the presence of the other party or parties.

58. The site to be inspected is often under the control of one of the parties, which typically means that employees or representatives of that party will be present to give guidance and explanations. It should be borne in mind that statements of those representatives or employees made during an on-site inspection, as contrasted with statements those persons might make as witnesses in a hearing, should not be treated as evidence in the proceedings.

15. Witnesses

59. While laws and rules on arbitral procedure typically leave broad freedom concerning the manner of taking evidence of witnesses, practices on procedural points are varied. In order to facilitate the preparations of the parties for the hearings, the arbitral tribunal may consider it appropriate to clarify, in advance of the hearings, some or all of the following issues.

(a)   Advance notice about a witness whom a party intends to present; written witnesses' statements

60. To the extent the applicable arbitration rules do not deal with the matter, the arbitral tribunal may wish to require that each party give advance notice to the arbitral tribunal and the other party or parties of any witness it intends to present. As to the content of the notice, the following is an example of what might be required, in addition to the names and addresses of the witnesses: (a) the subject upon which the witnesses will testify; (b) the language in which the witnesses will testify; and (c) the nature of the relationship with any of the parties, qualifications and experience of the witnesses if and to the extent these are relevant to the dispute or the testimony, and how the witnesses learned about the facts on which they will testify. However, it may not be necessary to require such a notice, in particular if the thrust of the testimony can be clearly ascertained from the party's allegations.

61. Some practitioners favour the procedure according to which the party presenting witness evidence submits a signed witness's statement containing testimony itself. It should be noted, however, that such practice, which implies interviewing the witness by the party presenting the testimony, is not known in all parts of the world and, moreover, that some practitioners disapprove of it on the ground that such contacts between the party

and the witness may compromise the credibility of the testimony and are therefore improper (see paragraph 67). Notwithstanding these reservations, signed witness's testimony has advantages in that it may expedite the proceedings by making it easier for the other party or parties to prepare for the hearings or for the parties to identify uncontested matters. However, those advantages might be outweighed by the time and expense involved in obtaining the written testimony.

62. If a signed witness's statement should be made under oath or similar affirmation of truthfulness, it may be necessary to clarify by whom the oath or affirmation should be administered and whether any formal authentication will be required by the arbitral tribunal.

(b)   Manner of taking oral evidence of witnesses

(i)   Order in which questions will be asked and the manner in which the hearing of witnesses will be conducted

63. To the extent that the applicable rules do not provide an answer, it may be useful for the arbitral tribunal to clarify how witnesses will be heard. One of the various possibilities is that a witness is first questioned by the arbitral tribunal, whereupon questions are asked by the parties, first by the party who called the witness. Another possibility is for the witness to be questioned by the party presenting the witness and then by the other party or parties, while the arbitral tribunal might pose questions during the questioning or after the parties on points that in the tribunal's view have not been sufficiently clarified. Differences exist also as to the degree of control the arbitral tribunal exercises over the hearing of witnesses. For example, some arbitrators prefer to permit the parties to pose questions freely and directly to the witness, but may disallow a question if a party objects; other arbitrators tend to exercise more control and may disallow a question on their initiative or even require that questions from the parties be asked through the arbitral tribunal.

(ii)   Whether oral testimony will be given under oath or affirmation and, if so, in what form an oath or affirmation should be made

64. Practices and laws differ as to whether or not oral testimony is to be given under oath or affirmation. In some legal systems, the arbitrators are empowered to put witnesses on oath, but it is usually in their discretion whether they want to do so. In other systems, oral testimony under oath

is either unknown or may even be considered improper as only an official such as a judge or notary may have the authority to administer oaths.

(iii) May witnesses be in the hearing room when they are not testifying

65. Some arbitrators favour the procedure that, except if the circumstances suggest otherwise, the presence of a witness in the hearing room is limited to the time the witness is testifying; the purpose is to prevent the witness from being influenced by what is said in the hearing room, or to prevent that the presence of the witness would influence another witness. Other arbitrators consider that the presence of a witness during the testimony of other witnesses may be beneficial in that possible contradictions may be readily clarified or that their presence may act as a deterrent against untrue statements. Other possible approaches may be that witnesses are not present in the hearing room before their testimony, but stay in the room after they have testified, or that the arbitral tribunal decides the question for each witness individually depending on what the arbitral tribunal considers most appropriate. The arbitral tribunal may leave the procedure to be decided during the hearings, or may give guidance on the question in advance of the hearings.

(c) The order in which the witnesses will be called

66. When several witnesses are to be heard and longer testimony is expected, it is likely to reduce costs if the order in which they will be called is known in advance and their presence can be scheduled accordingly. Each party might be invited to suggest the order in which it intends to present the witnesses, while it would be up to the arbitral tribunal to approve the scheduling and to make departures from it.

(d) Interviewing witnesses prior to their appearance at a hearing

67. In some legal systems, parties or their representatives are permitted to interview witnesses, prior to their appearance at the hearing, as to such matters as their recollection of the relevant events, their experience, qualifications or relation with a participant in the proceedings. In those legal systems such contacts are usually not permitted once the witness's oral testimony has begun. In other systems such contacts with witnesses are considered improper. In order to avoid misunderstandings, the arbitral tribunal may consider it useful to clarify what kind of contacts a party is permitted to have with a witness in the preparations for the hearings.

(e)   Hearing representatives of a party

68. According to some legal systems, certain persons affiliated with a party may only be heard as representatives of the party but not as witnesses. In such a case, it may be necessary to consider ground rules for determining which persons may not testify as witnesses (e.g. certain executives, employees or agents) and for hearing statements of those persons and for questioning them.

16. Experts and expert witnesses

69. Many arbitration rules and laws on arbitral procedure address the participation of experts in arbitral proceedings. A frequent solution is that the arbitral tribunal has the power to appoint an expert to report on issues determined by the tribunal; in addition, the parties may be permitted to present expert witnesses on points at issue. In other cases, it is for the parties to present expert testimony, and it is not expected that the arbitral tribunal will appoint an expert.

(a)   Expert appointed by the arbitral tribunal

70. If the arbitral tribunal is empowered to appoint an expert, one possible approach is for the tribunal to proceed directly to selecting the expert. Another possibility is to consult the parties as to who should be the expert; this may be done, for example, without mentioning a candidate, by presenting to the parties a list of candidates, soliciting proposals from the parties, or by discussing with the parties the "profile" of the expert the arbitral tribunal intends to appoint, i.e. the qualifications, experience and abilities of the expert.

(i)   The expert's terms of reference

71. The purpose of the expert's terms of reference is to indicate the questions on which the expert is to provide clarification, to avoid opinions on points that are not for the expert to assess and to commit the expert to a time schedule. While the discretion to appoint an expert normally includes the determination of the expert's terms of reference, the arbitral tribunal may decide to consult the parties before finalizing the terms. It might also be useful to determine details about how the expert will receive from the parties any relevant information or have access to any relevant documents, goods or other property, so as to enable the expert to prepare the report. In order to facilitate the evaluation of the expert's report, it is advisable to

require the expert to include in the report information on the method used in arriving at the conclusions and the evidence and information used in preparing the report.

(ii)   The opportunity of the parties to comment on the expert's report, including by presenting expert testimony

72. Arbitration rules that contain provisions on experts usually also have provisions on the right of a party to comment on the report of the expert appointed by the arbitral tribunal. If no such provisions apply or more specific procedures than those prescribed are deemed necessary, the arbitral tribunal may, in light of those provisions, consider it opportune to determine, for example, the time period for presenting written comments of the parties, or, if hearings are to be held for the purpose of hearing the expert, the procedures for interrogating the expert by the parties or for the participation of any expert witnesses presented by the parties.

(b)   Expert opinion presented by a party (expert witness)

73. If a party presents an expert opinion, the arbitral tribunal might consider requiring, for example, that the opinion be in writing, that the expert should be available to answer questions at hearings, and that, if a party will present an expert witness at a hearing, advance notice must be given or that the written opinion must be presented in advance, as in the case of other witnesses (see paragraphs 60–62).

17. Hearings

(a)   Decision whether to hold hearings

74. Laws on arbitral procedure and arbitration rules often have provisions as to the cases in which oral hearings must be held and as to when the arbitral tribunal has discretion to decide whether to hold hearings.

75. If it is up to the arbitral tribunal to decide whether to hold hearings, the decision is likely to be influenced by factors such as, on the one hand, that it is usually quicker and easier to clarify points at issue pursuant to a direct confrontation of arguments than on the basis of correspondence and, on the other hand, the travel and other cost of holding hearings, and that the need of finding acceptable dates for the hearings might delay the proceedings. The arbitral tribunal may wish to consult the parties on this matter.

(b) Whether one period of hearings should be held or separate periods of hearings

76. Attitudes vary as to whether hearings should be held in a single period of hearings or in separate periods, especially when more than a few days are needed to complete the hearings. According to some arbitrators, the entire hearings should normally be held in a single period, even if the hearings are to last for more than a week. Other arbitrators in such cases tend to schedule separate periods of hearings. In some cases issues to be decided are separated, and separate hearings set for those issues, with the aim that oral presentation on those issues will be completed within the allotted time. Among the advantages of one period of hearings are that it involves less travel costs, memory will not fade, and it is unlikely that people representing a party will change. On the other hand, the longer the hearings, the more difficult it may be to find early dates acceptable to all participants. Furthermore, separate periods of hearings may be easier to schedule, the subsequent hearings may be tailored to the development of the case, and the period between the hearings leaves time for analysing the records and negotiations between the parties aimed at narrowing the points at issue by agreement.

(c) Setting dates for hearings

77. Typically, firm dates will be fixed for hearings. Exceptionally, the arbitral tribunal may initially wish to set only "target dates" as opposed to definitive dates. This may be done at a stage of the proceedings when not all information necessary to schedule hearings is yet available, with the understanding that the target dates will either be confirmed or rescheduled within a reasonably short period. Such provisional planning can be useful to participants who are generally not available on short notice.

(d) Whether there should be a limit on the aggregate amount of time each party will have for oral arguments and questioning witnesses

78. Some arbitrators consider it useful to limit the aggregate amount of time each party has for any of the following: (a) making oral statements; (b) questioning its witnesses; and (c) questioning the witnesses of the other party or parties. In general, the same aggregate amount of time is considered appropriate for each party, unless the arbitral tribunal considers that a different allocation is justified. Before deciding, the arbitral tribunal may wish to consult the parties as to how much time they think they will need.

79. Such planning of time, provided it is realistic, fair and subject to judiciously firm control by the arbitral tribunal, will make it easier for the parties to plan the presentation of the various items of evidence and arguments, reduce the likelihood of running out of time towards the end of the hearings and avoid that one party would unfairly use up a disproportionate amount of time.

(e)   The order in which the parties will present their arguments and evidence

80. Arbitration rules typically give broad latitude to the arbitral tribunal to determine the order of presentations at the hearings. Within that latitude, practices differ, for example, as to whether opening or closing statements are heard and their level of detail; the sequence in which the claimant and the respondent present their opening statements, arguments, witnesses and other evidence; and whether the respondent or the claimant has the last word. In view of such differences, or when no arbitration rules apply, it may foster efficiency of the proceedings if the arbitral tribunal clarifies to the parties, in advance of the hearings, the manner in which it will conduct the hearings, at least in broad lines.

(f)   Length of hearings

81. The length of a hearing primarily depends on the complexity of the issues to be argued and the amount of witness evidence to be presented. The length also depends on the procedural style used in the arbitration. Some practitioners prefer to have written evidence and written arguments presented before the hearings, which thus can focus on the issues that have not been sufficiently clarified. Those practitioners generally tend to plan shorter hearings than those practitioners who prefer that most if not all evidence and arguments are presented to the arbitral tribunal orally and in full detail. In order to facilitate the parties' preparations and avoid misunderstandings, the arbitral tribunal may wish to clarify to the parties, in advance of the hearings, the intended use of time and style of work at the hearings.

(g)   Arrangements for a record of the hearings

82. The arbitral tribunal should decide, possibly after consulting with the parties, on the method of preparing a record of oral statements and testimony during hearings. Among different possibilities, one method is that the members of the arbitral tribunal take personal notes. Another is that the presiding arbitrator during the hearing dictates to a typist a summary of

oral statements and testimony. A further method, possible when a secretary of the arbitral tribunal has been appointed, may be to leave to that person the preparation of a summary record. A useful, though costly, method is for professional stenographers to prepare verbatim transcripts, often within the next day or a similarly short time period. A written record may be combined with tape-recording, so as to enable reference to the tape in case of a disagreement over the written record.

83. If transcripts are to be produced, it may be considered how the persons who made the statements will be given an opportunity to check the transcripts. For example, it may be determined that the changes to the record would be approved by the parties or, failing their agreement, would be referred for decision to the arbitral tribunal.

(h)   Whether and when the parties are permitted to submit notes summarizing their oral arguments

84. Some legal counsel are accustomed to giving notes summarizing their oral arguments to the arbitral tribunal and to the other party or parties. If such notes are presented, this is usually done during the hearings or shortly thereafter; in some cases, the notes are sent before the hearing. In order to avoid surprise, foster equal treatment of the parties and facilitate preparations for the hearings, advance clarification is advisable as to whether submitting such notes is acceptable and the time for doing so.

85. In closing the hearings, the arbitral tribunal will normally assume that no further proof is to be offered or submission to be made. Therefore, if notes are to be presented to be read after the closure of the hearings, the arbitral tribunal may find it worthwhile to stress that the notes should be limited to summarizing what was said orally and in particular should not refer to new evidence or new argument.

18. Multi-party arbitration

86. When a single arbitration involves more than two parties (multi-party arbitration), considerations regarding the need to organize arbitral proceedings, and matters that may be considered in that connection, are generally not different from two-party arbitrations. A possible difference may be that, because of the need to deal with more than two parties, multi-party proceedings can be more complicated to manage than bilateral proceedings. The Notes, notwithstanding a possible greater complexity of multi-party arbitration, can be used in multi-party as well as in two-party proceedings.

87. The areas of possibly increased complexity in multi-party arbitration are, for example, the flow of communications among the parties and the arbitral tribunal (see paragraphs 33, 34 and 38–41); if points at issue are to be decided at different points in time, the order of deciding them (paragraphs 44–45); the manner in which the parties will participate in hearing witnesses (paragraph 63); the appointment of experts and the participation of the parties in considering their reports (paragraphs 70–72); the scheduling of hearings (paragraph 76); the order in which the parties will present their arguments and evidence at hearings (paragraph 80).

88. The Notes, which are limited to pointing out matters that may be considered in organizing arbitral proceedings in general, do not cover the drafting of the arbitration agreement or the constitution of the arbitral tribunal, both issues that give rise to special questions in multi-party arbitration as compared to two-party arbitration.

19. Possible requirements concerning filing or delivering the award

89. Some national laws require that arbitral awards be filed or registered with a court or similar authority, or that they be delivered in a particular manner or through a particular authority. Those laws differ with respect to, for example, the type of award to which the requirement applies (e.g. to all awards or only to awards not rendered under the auspices of an arbitral institution); time periods for filing, registering or delivering the award (in some cases those time periods may be rather short); or consequences for failing to comply with the requirement (which might be, for example, invalidity of the award or inability to enforce it in a particular manner).

Who should take steps to fulfil any requirement

90. If such a requirement exists, it is useful, some time before the award is to be issued, to plan who should take the necessary steps to meet the requirement and how the costs are to be borne.

Index

Index references refer to
[Article No. (or Preamble or Definitions)]: [annotation no.]